YOUR SECRET TO SPIRITUAL SUCCESS

CROSSWAY BOOKS BY JAMES A. SCUDDER

Beyond Failure
Your Secret to Spiritual Success

YOUR
SECRET TO
SPIRITUAL
SUCCESS

James A. Scudder

CROSSWAY BOOKS

A DIVISION OF
GOOD NEWS PUBLISHERS
WHEATON, ILLINOIS

Cover design: Cowley and Associates

First printing 2002

Printed in the United States of America

Scripture is taken from the King James Version of the Bible.

Library of Congress Cataloging-in-Publication Data
Scudder, James A., 1946-
    Your secret to spiritual success / James A. Scudder.
      p. cm.
    ISBN 1-58134-381-7 (tbk. : alk. paper)
    1. Spiritual life—Christianity. I. Title.
BV4501.3 .S38   2002
248.4—dc21   2002002482
                                      CIP

15	14	13	12	11	10	09	08	07	06	05	04	03	02
15	14	13	12	11	10	9	8	7	6	5	4	3	2	1

CONTENTS

ACKNOWLEDGMENTS

My sincere thanks to those at Crossway Books who have given of themselves for this book: Vice-President Marvin Padgett, Editorial Administrator Jill Carter, and Editor Lila Bishop. Also many thanks to the team at Quentin Road Ministries.

Thirty-one Parable Principles That Could Change Your Life

PARABLE PRINCIPLE #17—If you love the world, you do not love Christ.

PARABLE PRINCIPLE #18—Possess your possessions.

PARABLE PRINCIPLE #19—Don't compare your spiritual growth to that of other believers.

PARABLE PRINCIPLE #20—Fellowship with people who share your desire for spiritual growth.

PARABLE PRINCIPLE #21—Develop the habit of prayer.

PARABLE PRINCIPLE #22—It is a privilege to share the light of the Gospel with others.

PARABLE PRINCIPLE #23—How you live affects your witness for Christ.

PARABLE PRINCIPLE #24—You will be judged for deeds done for Christ.

PARABLE PRINCIPLE #25—You will be judged by how much of the Word you use.

PARABLE PRINCIPLE #26—The more you hear, the more you gain.

PARABLE PRINCIPLE #27—God will correct you when you don't obey Him.

PARABLE PRINCIPLE #28—Be faithful; God will bring the harvest.

PARABLE PRINCIPLE #29—God's way starts small and grows slowly.

PARABLE PRINCIPLE #30—God does a lot with mustard-seed faith.

PARABLE PRINCIPLE #31—Don't worry about how much faith you have. Look to the object of your faith, the Lord Jesus Christ.

1

THE SPIRITUAL LIFE

I longed to be a flame of fire continually glowing in the divine service and building up of Christ's kingdom to my last and dying breath.
—DAVID BRAINERD

THE SUN BEAT DOWN MERCILESSLY. The boat was dead in the water. Jim and Dave shifted uncomfortably in their miniature life-jackets. I stared at the back of my friend's head as he got sick over the side of the boat. I knew it for sure once again: The Christian life is never boring.

Persuaded to take a fishing trip on Lake Michigan, I boarded a boat owned by Jim, who works for our ministry. Also on board were Dave, a West Point graduate who serves in our Bible college, and my son Jim. We looked forward to catching some salmon and grilling it for dinner.

We motored about a mile from shore, and just as everyone got their gear together to start fishing, the lower unit of the motor stopped working. After fiddling with the motor for a while, Jim decided he'd better call the coast guard. Dave started to get seasick, and as we sat waiting for help, I could tell that the rocking of the boat wasn't helping him at all. In fact, he ran to the side a few times to "bait fish."

While we waited, I couldn't resist having some fun with Jim. "I think the fines are huge for this kind of thing," I said. "I heard of another guy who had to be towed back to the dock and ended up paying about $5,000 before it was all over."

Jim tried to ignore me, but I could tell he was a little worried. He scrambled into the hold to get lifejackets because he knew that was the first thing the coast guard would check. He pulled what seemed like ten children's lifejackets out of the hold. When I say children, I mean, three- to six-year-olds. These were tiny! At the very bottom of the pile lay two adult lifejackets. The problem? There were four of us.

My son Jim and I quickly commandeered the adult ones just as the coast guard boat approached. Over the loudspeaker we heard the words, "Make sure your lifejackets are on." Jim and Dave had no choice. They grabbed two of the children's lifejackets. The sight of those big men in lifejackets that barely reached their armpits brought fresh humor to the situation, though Jim and Dave couldn't appreciate it. The coastguardsmen seemed to be holding back laughter. One of them winked at me, and I knew we were going to have some fun with Jim. But Jim didn't see the wink and worried all the way to shore.

Jim was fortunate. He didn't get fined for the lack of adequate lifejackets. He didn't even have to pay for the coast guard tow. What seemed at first like a string of unfortunate circumstances fit together to bring fresh awareness of the enjoyment we can have together in the Christian life.

Perhaps you are a seasoned spiritual sailor who wants new inspiration for your journey, or you may feel that your boat is "dead in the water." It could be that you haven't been a Christian for very long. You are excited about having found eternal life, and possibly you just need some pointers from the Word of God to keep you headed in the right direction. Whatever the case, the coast guard is on the way! There is help and hope for your walk with the Lord. You will experience spiritual sailing at its best when you use the Thirty-one Parable Principles as tools for your Christian journey.

YOUR TOOLS

A skilled gardener doesn't just keep tools on a few random hooks in the garage. Often the capable gardener has a shed where everything is in neat order. Various tools make it much easier for the gardener to work. Imagine trying to dig without a shovel or snipping branches without pruning shears! Each tool has a specific purpose, and each tool makes the gardener's job a lot easier.

It is the same in the Christian life. God has not only saved you from eternal punishment in hell forever, but He has also given you every tool needed to lead an effective Christian life. The first key is to know which tools exist for your use; the second is to learn the specific function of each tool; the third is to actually use the tools.

If your tools are in proper working order, with each essential spiritual tool at your disposal, then you will experience Christian growth.

THE PARABLE PRINCIPLES

As I studied the parables in Mark 4, I found thirty-one dynamic principles for living the Christian life. Whether you are in the workplace and concerned with making an impact on your associates' lives, a young person in school, or a senior citizen ready to really do something for Christ, you will find in these parables some keys to make your spiritual life grow by leaps and bounds. The hard-working mother will find her spiritual life deeper than ever before. The teenager ready to go to the next level for the Lord will find great help as well. Jesus spoke of those who produce much fruit in their Christian lives. He said the seed of the Word settled into good ground and then produced fabulous results. Do you want results in your own life? Of course you do. We all want to experience spiritual victory on a daily basis.

It's possible to experience a joy-filled, growing spiritual walk with the Lord. We can learn to exercise our faith and tell others about Christ. And we can grow daily through His Word and prayer. The Thirty-one Parable Principles will help us do all these things.

A CHRISTIAN INDEED

Please bear with me for a short time because the next section might seem too basic. Yet this necessary foundation can give you assurance of your salvation, practical assistance when you witness to others, and understanding of the difference between salvation and service, an important distinction if you wish to grow spiritually.

Not long ago my wife, Linda, and I traveled to another state where I spoke at several churches. When it was time to come home, we boarded our plane and waited while the crew secured it for takeoff. Just as we started to taxi down the runway, we heard an announcement on the loudspeaker: "There are two extra passengers on this flight."

Suddenly I remembered something. When we first sat down, a man behind us said quietly to his companion, "Don't say anything. Just be quiet so no one notices us."

I wondered if the people in back of me were going to stand up.

Another announcement came: "We are going to call off all the seats of the paying passengers. We suggest that those extra passengers come to the front of the plane."

Just when I thought the people behind me weren't going to get up, they both stood and walked toward the front. After a little while the plane took off without its two extra passengers!

I imagined then a plane with the destination of heaven, loaded with unsaved people. If a similar scenario occurred, the flight attendant might say, "If you have trusted Jesus Christ as your Savior, then you are on the right plane. Happy traveling. If you are trusting in anything else for your salvation, please deplane immediately."

Bewilderment, shock, or disbelief would register on some faces. I imagine some nice person saying, "What do you mean, I have to trust in Jesus Christ? I thought when I attended church faithfully that God would see me as the kind of person who deserves heaven."

God's Word says something quite different from what most people believe about heaven. It says that no one deserves heaven. We all have to pay for our sin, and the only way to do that is to spend eternity in a place called hell. The trip to heaven can't be purchased like an airline ticket. Arrival there is only possible through the shed blood of Christ on the cross. Your belief in His payment for your sin gives you eternal life in heaven.

So to grow in Christ, you have to first be on the Christian plane. This book will be of no consequence to you if you don't know for sure you are going to heaven when you die.

THE RIGHT PLANE

Are you on the right plane? Ephesians 2:8-9 states, "For by grace are ye saved through faith; and that not of yourselves: it is the gift of God: not of works, lest any man should boast."

Grace is undeserved mercy. We don't pay to get on God's plane. Instead, we accept the gift that has already been given us. It is not our own good works that make us acceptable in God's eyes.

Suppose a couple is invited to a close friend's home for dinner. Ted and Nancy are served a lovely seven-course meal of the very finest foods. They visit after the meal, and when they stand to go, Ted reaches for his wallet. "I'd like to pay for that delicious meal," he says.

Nancy stares at Ted in horror. "Ted," she says in a loud whisper, "you aren't supposed to offer to pay. You're insulting our friends!"

The same principle holds with eternal life. No matter how hard we try, we could never pay for heaven by our own good works. All of us are sinners; we have all done wrong things. Romans 3:23 explains, "For all have sinned, and come short of the glory of God." To sin means to miss the mark of God's perfection. Author C. S. Lewis said, "We must not suppose that if we succeeded in making everyone nice, we should have saved their souls. A world of nice people content in their own niceness, looking no further, turned away from God, would be just as desperately in need of salvation as a miserable world."[1]

We might believe ourselves to be good people, better than our neighbors. Yet we fail miserably. No one can attain perfection because we have all missed God's mark.

My grandson Jamie enjoys archery very much. One day Neal, my son-in-law, took him to an archery range. Though Jamie did manage to hit the target, he missed the bull's-eye. We have the same problem in our spiritual lives.

But the good news is just around the corner! Our gracious heavenly Father has made a way for imperfect people to go to heaven. He sent His Son, Jesus Christ, to die on the cross for our sins. First John 4:14 says, "And we have seen and do testify that the Father sent the Son to be the Saviour of the world." When Jesus died on the cross, He paid the penalty for our sin.

In 1992 a Los Angeles County parking control officer came upon a brown El Dorado Cadillac illegally parked next to the curb on street-sweeping day. Ignoring the man seated at the wheel, the officer reached inside the open car window and placed a thirty-dollar citation on the dashboard.

The driver of the car made no excuses. No argument ensued—and with good reason. He had been shot in the head ten to twelve hours before but was sitting up, stiff as a board, slumped slightly forward, with blood on his face. He was dead. The officer, preoccupied with ticket-writing, was unaware of anything out of the ordinary. He got back in his car and drove away.[2]

We are spiritually in the same condition before we trust Christ as our Savior. Some people might tell us we need a citation or that we need to try harder. The reality is that we are spiritually dead. Just as the dead man could not drive to his destination, there is nothing we can do to earn our own way to heaven.

Accept the payment Christ made for you on the cross if you haven't already done so. Say something like this: "God, I know I'm a sinner, and I know I can't do anything to save myself. The best I know how, I'm accepting the payment of your shed blood for my sins. I believe You died, were buried, and rose again to pay for my sin. I thank You for giving me eternal life."

Now that you know Christ as your Savior, you might pray something like this, "Lord, please give me the will to live for You. I am so grateful for what You have done for me. Now I want to do what You want me to do. I don't want to live to please myself anymore."

First John 5:13 explains, "These things have I written unto you that believe on the name of the Son of God; that ye may know that ye have eternal life, and that ye may believe on the name of the Son of God."

You can know for sure that you are going to heaven! You don't have to hope or think, *Maybe I'll go to heaven.* Going to heaven is a know-so business! I hope that if you have never trusted Christ as your Savior before, you have done so right now. After you've trusted Christ, you are ready to learn about the tools God has given to help you grow.

SAVED AND SERVING

You might be thinking, *If I don't have to do anything to get to heaven, why are you encouraging me to do things for Christ?* No question about it—salvation *is* a free gift to any person who trusts Christ as his or her Savior. Yet salvation and service are two different things. Our service to Christ comes from a grateful heart for all that He has done for us. Our good works after salvation are not done because we are trying to earn Christ's favor, for He has already bestowed His favor on us. We serve Christ for God's glory, and in the process others may see our changed lives and then come to know the Lord.

There are many churches and preachers today who don't separate this idea of salvation and service. If you hear them give the Gospel of Jesus Christ, you might be confused and wonder if you had to "commit" your life to be saved or "stop sinning" before you can trust Christ. The truth is, before we are saved, we are dead in trespasses and sins. Ephesians 2:4-5 says, "But God . . . even when we were dead in sins, hath quickened us together with Christ (by grace ye are saved)."

There is no way that before you knew Christ as your Savior you could do anything to earn His grace. Salvation is a free gift. You came to Christ with your sins, apart from any works—with only the empty hands of faith.

After we are saved, we are encouraged in the Bible to perform good works. In Matthew 5.16 Jesus Himself says, "Let your light so shine before men, that they may see your good works, and glorify your Father which is in heaven." Once you are a Christian, your good works bring glory to the Father.

Ephesians 2:10 says, "For we are his workmanship, created in Christ Jesus unto good works, which God hath before ordained that we should walk in them." Notice the word *should* in this verse. We are encouraged to do good works in order to grow in Christ—not *for* salvation but *because of* salvation. This distinction is vital if you really want to grow in Christ. It is important to understand that our good works are to glorify the Father, not to continue to earn His favor. It puts a different perspective on your service and will make you all the more eager to serve Him.

Have you lived with some misconceptions about your salvation? I encourage you right now to put away your mistaken beliefs about Christian growth. Realize that salvation is a free gift, given to you the moment you accepted Christ as your Savior. Now because you are saved, you should desire to serve God every day. You should yearn to take the necessary steps in order to grow as a Christian.

Why don't you stop right now and evaluate the reasons you serve Christ? Have you thought that doing more good works would somehow make God happier with you? Remember that while we were yet sinners, Christ died for us. He died for us before we did one thing for Him. When we realize the truth of God's unconditional love in sending His Son to die for us, it takes the burden out of our service. For our service is simply an outpouring of love and gratitude for what has already happened inside of us. If you are abiding in God's love, you will find that service is no longer a burden but a delight, an expression of adoration and gratefulness to your Lord.

YOUR HELP AND DEFENSE

Louis Lesce was on the eighty-sixth floor of the World Trade Center's north tower when a hijacked airplane slammed into the building on September 11, 2001. CNN's Natalie Allen interviewed Lesce just two days after the catastrophe. Lesce said that when the building was first hit, he and five others fled to a conference room. Most of them assumed from the shaking of the building that it was an earthquake. They felt reasonably sure that the structure could withstand an earthquake. When they opened the door of the conference room, black smoke filled the hallway. After a little while, they knew they had to try to make it down the stairwell. As Lesce started down, he could see the light of flashlights and could hear screaming and sirens. There was lots of water coming out of the walls, with about three inches of water on the steps.

As Lesce and hundreds of others walked down, he noticed unbelievingly that firemen were going up. He said, "Just as we were trying to escape, they were going to it."

Nobody knew what had happened, but people comforted each other. Someone said to Lesce, "You know, you look kind of tired, buddy. Let me hold your jacket." And he did. "Someone else asked to hold my briefcase," Lesce related.

Somehow Lesce reached the mall level. He heard a huge whooshing sound and turned around and noticed that everything around him was collapsing. He fell down and hugged the ground as debris buried him. A man walking by uncovered Lesce and picked him up, and both of them walked out. They both joined a group of about five who were making their way out of the building. But as they continued, people turned different directions, and suddenly he was with only one other man. The man told him, "I'm going to go through that door." It wasn't a door. It was really broken glass. He didn't see the man again. When Lesce stepped out into the plaza, he saw nobody.

"I felt like the last man on earth," Lesce said. He walked about a hundred yards and started to go up a nearby street to call his wife when he heard another loud sound. He turned around to see another part of the building collapse. He threw himself on the ground and waited a second time for the darkness to end. Then he noticed a tiny pinpoint of light and heard someone's voice asking him to stand up. Rescued once again, Lesce found emergency help.

In this tragedy that is beyond imagining, we see one man's struggle to get out of a collapsing building. Not knowing what to do or where to go, he continued to put one foot in front of the other. In the darkness he could only keep moving. Other people showed concern for him, people that he didn't even know. When he was buried under the first pile of ash, someone helped him get up and keep moving. When he could see nothing in the darkness, another helping hand kept him going in the right direction. Lesce experienced continued help and comfort from those he would probably never see again. In the face of the most cowardly and appalling event in American history, Lesce experienced the powerful touch of human comfort.

Dear friend, do you know that you can experience the same comfort in your spiritual walk? There are times when you are not going to know what to do or where to go. There are going to be trials and hardships, for the Christian life is a spiritual battlefield—make no mistake about that. But there is hope from God's Word. There is help from Christian friends. There is comfort from God's own Holy Spirit, given to you at the moment of salvation. Go ahead and take the helping hand offered you. You can make it!

Over 2,000 years ago Jesus Christ walked among men. He taught His disciples, His followers, and the crowds in parables they could apply to their lives. Hidden in these parables are tools that will help you in many specific areas. When you study all thirty-one parable principles, you will see how they fit together into a harmonious whole. You will be knowledgeable about the different aspects of the Christian life and will see how best to please God. Are you ready for your first tool? Here's Parable Principle #1!

PARABLE PRINCIPLE #1—Jesus taught in parables so that Christians could apply truth to their lives in practical ways.

First, realize the reason Jesus taught in parables in the first place. Why did He choose this method of teaching when the Pharisees and Sadducees, the religious teachers of the day, taught differently?

You need to understand one thing about Jesus. He wasn't concerned about protocol or tradition. He was not concerned with learning just to learn or with teaching just to teach. Jesus taught so that those listening could understand. Therein lies the difference in teaching methods. And therein lies one of the reasons why the religious leaders opposed Him in the first place. His methods frightened them. His teaching was so different from their own perfunctory readings of the law in the temple. They weren't familiar with this easygoing, interesting style that attracted the masses and began to change them one by one.

To be honest, not many teachers paid much attention to me as I was growing up. Oh, they stood in front of me and taught basic facts. I might or might not have listened. If they bored me, I immediately switched gears to more interesting topics such as fishing with my friend Sam or building a go-cart with my dad.

One teacher was different. It wasn't that she was particularly dynamic in her educational style. She wasn't a gifted communicator, but there was a difference. I felt it the instant I entered her classroom. She cared about me, and I could sense it. She looked me straight in the eye when I entered the room, smiling and speaking my name. She called on me in class and seemed to actually enjoy what I had to say. Since most of my teachers never seemed to notice me, I was surprised by her kindness. I found myself wanting to do well for her sake.

One day the class was going to vote on the best voice to read a certain part for an end-of-the-year performance. The usual show-offs sauntered to the front of the room and read the part effortlessly. Other kids were clearly nervous, and yet I knew that each one of them would do a far better job than I could. Knots started to form in my stomach as I waited. I wasn't a praying boy, but I found myself starting to pray that the bell would ring before my time to perform. My prayer wasn't answered, at least not in the way I asked. When my turn came, I felt like I was crawling toward the front. I looked at the class and then at the copy I was to read. Then I looked at my teacher. Her smile was enough. I shuffled my way through the reading.

The class voted on who had the best voice. When the votes were tallied, one of the most popular kids in the entire school won. I knew why. His performance was, in my opinion, flawless. Then the teacher said something that shocked the whole class, especially me.

"I think James Scudder has the best voice. You voted for the wrong person."

It was probably the closest I've ever come to fainting. My eyes widened in surprise, and I remember that when I walked home that day, my feet hardly seemed to touch the road. My teacher thought I had a decent voice. It was about the first good thing I remember a teacher saying about me. Suddenly it didn't matter what anyone else thought. She cared. She saw something good in me that no one else saw. Her simple statement gave me the courage to try out for debate the next year. And even now I can hear her hearty encouragement echoing through me when I am faced with a particularly daunting task, even one that doesn't involve speaking in public.

Jesus was that kind of encourager. He didn't come to minister to effortless performers. Instead He ministered to the downtrodden, the ordinary, the everyday common nobodies.

Jesus used parables so that people could understand great truths about the Christian life. He didn't stand in front of the crowds and exhort them to obey ancient laws and little-known philosophy; instead He spoke in the everyday vernacular, using illustrations from life that would bring great fulfillment to those who listened.

YOUR TRUTH PICTURE

The Greek word for parable, *parabole*, means a "similitude." A parable uses activities from everyday life to teach spiritual truths. Parables are fictitious, but they convey truths. Jesus used parables to teach God's exalted truths in common language.

For example, Jesus told the Parable of the Sower, and the next time one of His hearers worked in the field, the person might think of what Jesus had said. A daughter in a farm family saw her father and mother plant the fields. The girl witnessed the truth of the parable when she ate a slice of bread for dinner. So Jesus' unique parable principles had a way of penetrating not just immediately, but also later as the listeners did these activities themselves.

The story of a woman named Carol illustrates the way parables work. She hadn't been to church much throughout her life, but one Christmas when she was eleven, she was invited to a Christmas pageant. The lights, the actors playing Mary and Joseph, even a live donkey—all of this made a deep impression on her. During most family Christmas celebrations, her grandfather dressed up as Santa Claus and distributed gifts to the children. No one mentioned the greatest gift of all—Jesus Christ. She vowed in childish earnestness that when she married and had children, she would seek to show them the true meaning of Christmas.

The first year she held her son Josh in her arms, she sought a church at Christmastime. It was a beautiful service, and Carol sat in the back with the baby on her lap. Tears ran down her cheeks as she realized for the first time that Jesus Christ was born, lived, and died *for her*. She trusted Him as her Savior during that service.

Carol never forgot the Christmas story she saw acted out as a child. And that simple service was a reminder to her throughout the years to go back to church when she became an adult.

Jesus used parables for much the same reason: To make sure people understood what He was saying and to make such an impression on them that they never forgot His message. Parables were not given to confuse but to confirm. They established the important principles Christ conveyed. They confirmed Jesus' teaching in a personal, practical way so that His followers and disciples could apply the truths to their lives.

Can you think back on an experience, perhaps from your childhood or teen years, that made a spiritual truth easier to understand? My son Jim told me that when his daughter Amy learned to swim, she didn't want to let go of her daddy's arms. As he encouraged her to trust him and assured her that he wouldn't let her drown, she finally let go and swam a few feet on her own. Jim thought about how God must feel when He wants His children to trust Him completely, and yet they won't let go of their prideful independence. This example from his life confirmed in his mind a truth about trusting the Lord.

I encourage you to think about some instance in your own life that has made you understand something about God's truth. In this way you can take the tools of the parable principles and use them to experience new levels of spiritual growth.

BACKGROUND CHECK

When we look at Mark 3:5, we see another reason why Jesus used parables as a teaching tool: "And when he had looked round about on them with anger, being grieved for the hardness of their hearts . . ." Jesus knew that His teaching was causing a stir among the religious rulers. He understood why and was willing to change His method for a while in order that His precious truths could continue to impact those who wanted to follow Him.

The Pharisees recognized that He taught truths diametrically opposed to their own teaching. Since they were also in many ways the ruling class, the entire political climate was growing increasingly antagonistic toward Christ.

Why were the Pharisees so angry with Jesus? His claim to forgive sin put them on edge. They realized that no one could forgive sin but God; so if Jesus could do that, then He must be God. Bottom line— they didn't accept Him as God. The same problem often occurs today. The real reason some people are so opposed to Christians is that if they accept Christian teaching, they have to acknowledge Christ as God.

Jesus showed them up too. The Pharisees enjoyed a show of religiosity. They loved to dress in their gaudiest robes and stand in the midst of the temple, praying loudly so that others would think they were intensely spiritual. Yet here was a man radically different from anyone they had ever encountered, a man who didn't care about Himself, whose every thought was for others. When Jesus spent time with the publicans (the hated tax collectors of the day) and sinners (Matthew 9:10-11), it showed up the Pharisees' religious facade and revealed their indifference toward others.

The religious leaders also refused to see His love and care for all mankind and said that Jesus did His miracles only by the power of the devil (John 10:20). Count on the world to take the only perfect man and compare Him to the worst thing they know! We see this happening more and more in today's culture. Those who stand for righteousness are seen as the narrow religious right, while liberals are praised no matter what they do. If this sort of thing happened during the time of Christ, then why should we be surprised that it happens today? So looking at the context of Jesus' day, the political and religious climate, helps us gain a clearer picture of what He taught.

NOW I SEE!

Our children need pictures and illustrations to help them learn, and so do we. It is a foolish teacher who believes that people learn in only one way. A dull teacher fails to make learning interesting to students.

My four-year-old granddaughter Amanda had trouble learning her letters. Her teacher went over each letter, showing her an animal that began with that letter. Now Amanda knows her letters and enjoys writing them too.

God's Word is full of truth pictures. We can use these pictures to gain a deeper understanding of what Christ has done for us. One of the ordinances that Jesus wanted Christians to observe is called the Lord's Supper. This ceremony is a picture of truth. Jesus had a special time with His disciples just before He went to the cross. He spoke immortal words as the disciples ate and drank with Him. These words went deep into each soul, and when He died and then rose again, the believers continued to have this time of fellowship together. The Lord's Supper is like a parable in this way. This observance is a means by which we physically remember something essential to the reason we became Christians in the first place, the broken body and shed blood of our Lord Jesus.

In 1 Corinthians 11:23-25, Paul explains about the Lord's Supper, "For I have received of the Lord that which also I delivered unto you, That the Lord Jesus the same night in which he was betrayed took bread: And when he had given thanks, he brake it, and said, Take, eat: this is my body, which is broken for you: this do in remembrance of me. After the same manner also he took the cup, when he had supped, saying, This cup is the new testament in my blood: this do ye, as oft as ye drink it, in remembrance of me."

I remember the first time I took Communion after I was saved. I silently prayed as I confessed my sin. I ate the cracker and remembered the broken body of our Lord. Tears came to my eyes as I thought of His body bruised and battered for me. Then when I drank the small cup of grape juice, I remembered His blood shed for me. The experience was so emotionally moving that it was almost more than I could bear. Every time I lead my own congregation in Communion, I feel the same way. It takes me back to the day of my salvation and keeps me at the foot of the cross.

I challenge you to take part in a Communion service as often as you can. You need this picture of the Lord's death to remind you of the price paid for your salvation. This remembrance will help you grow in your walk with the Lord.

YOUR HEART'S CRY

Let's not miss one essential truth right now. The Pharisees' hearts were like stone, regardless of the teaching method Jesus used. Imagine what would happen if you tried to plant a seed in a stone. It just wouldn't grow! While there were many Pharisees who believed in Christ (Nicodemus, for example, John 3:1), there were many others who didn't listen. Many chose to let their spiritual eyes stay blind and their hearts become more resistant to truth. Their own pride kept them from seeing Christ for who He was.

Sometimes an incident that seems like no big deal can pack down and harden the "soil" of our lives. A man named Larry found this happening in his own life. A concerned dad, he visited church only because he had full custody of his four-year-old daughter Shelly. It had been a nasty divorce. The parents had argued in the presence of their little girl before their separation. After the divorce, Larry determined that life would be better for his child, and so he took her to Sunday school.

When he went to pick her up, he found that she loved Sunday school and wanted to attend the church service immediately following. Mainly because he didn't have anything else to do, he went. Sitting in that service, he heard things from the Bible he had never heard before. He realized that he hadn't read a page of the Bible since his grandmother had told him Bible stories when he was younger than his own daughter. Shelly's dark head lay against his shoulder, and his heart began to heal. When the pastor gave the Gospel, Larry trusted Christ.

This was the beginning of many church services for Larry and Shelly. One day the pastor approached Larry and asked him if he would mind doing some maintenance on the church grounds during the weekends. The janitor had a broken leg and couldn't work for a while.

Larry didn't let it show, but he was angered by the request. Didn't the pastor realize that he didn't have enough free time as it was? Larry felt his heart harden with pride. He was about to refuse until he looked at the huge smile on Shelly's face.

"Daddy," Shelly exclaimed, "we can do it together! Remember when you showed me how to pull weeds from the flowerbeds? I could do that around the churchyard while you mow the grass."

Larry agreed to the pastor's request. Later he realized that his pride had almost messed up not only his own spiritual growth but also his daughter's. He vowed not to let that happen again. When Larry became active in ministry, he found himself growing closer to his daughter and strengthened in his Christian life.

Our hearts can become hardened so quickly because of pride. God wants us to have hearts that are moldable like clay, not hard like a rock. Perhaps pride has kept you from becoming the person God wants you to be. One wise man said, "Pride is like a beard. It just keeps growing. The solution? Shave it every day." Pray right now that God will help you cultivate a willing spirit, a spirit that isn't filled with pride. When our pride is dealt with properly, spiritual growth can take place.

Jesus said in Matthew 13:16, "But blessed are your eyes, for they see: and your ears, for they hear." In the realm of the spiritual, what are you doing with your eyes and ears? Are you using your eyes to read Scripture? Are you using your ears to hear the Word of God as it is preached? Do you apply those principles to your life? When your senses are keenly in tune with the things of God, then you will avoid the hardness of heart Jesus was talking about. Your heart will be softened and ready, like good soil, to receive the great truths God would have you learn. Our first parable principle brings to light Jesus' desire for us to apply His truth to our lives. Won't you open your heart right now to His Word?

Spiritual growth is exhilarating when you have the right tools. These tools are the means by which God's will is performed in your life. Are you ready for the exciting journey ahead, *your* life of growth?

2

ENDURING SUPPORT

All the good from the Savior of the world is communicated through this book; but for the book, we could not know right from wrong. All the things desirable to man are contained in it.

—ABRAHAM LINCOLN

PAVEMENT. YELLOW PAINT. Automobiles. Then a riot of color in a two-foot space between Amy Michelson's parking space and a fence. A tiny garden of flowers flourishes there, giving the rest of the owners of the Village Green Condominiums beauty and inspiration. Orange and yellow day lilies, blue bachelor buttons, pink hollyhocks, and blue and purple morning glories overflow from the sidewalks and wooden fences that encircle an otherwise drab landscape. Other owners were inspired by Amy's handiwork and so have created their own miniature gardens. Amy's sister, who works as a seed farmer in North Carolina, supplies her with seeds for her various gardening projects.

As with her other gardens (she has cultivated one in front of her home and another in her small backyard), the courtyard project has been the result of experimenting. If a certain type of plant doesn't flourish or complement its surroundings, she moves it to another spot.

"Gardening is a work in progress," she says. "It's an obsession of mine."[1]

Christians are a work in progress also. We need to make sure the seed of the Word has a chance to get planted in our lives. God's Word is available to us twenty-four hours a day, seven days a week, in the pages of a book that is divinely inspired and preserved. Let's look at this inestimable seed, this Bible, and study key strategies for utilizing its full potential.

A SEED CALLED STUDY

Do you place yourself in situations where the seed of the Word of God can be sown in your life? Do you read the Bible daily so that you can glean eternal truth? Our second parable principle comes from Mark 4:2-3, which states, "And he taught them many things by parables, and said unto them in his doctrine, Hearken; Behold, there went out a sower to sow." What did the sower sow? The precious Word of God.

Vicky grew up in a Christian home and trusted Christ at a young age. Yet something always seemed to be lacking in her Christian life. She couldn't quite put her finger on it until she heard a sermon about having daily devotions. She realized that she didn't know what it was to devote time each day to her spiritual development.

Now she spends fifteen minutes to half an hour each morning reading a passage of the Bible before she goes to work. She started with the Gospels and then read through the book of Philippians. When problems occur during her day, she remembers the verses she read that morning. It is easier for her to handle hardships, and she feels she has found the missing component to her spiritual growth.

Perhaps you are like Vicky and haven't considered reading the Bible on a daily basis. It might seem tricky to schedule in a quiet time at first. Know that Satan will be waiting with a thousand distractions to keep you from doing it. But when you systematically take time to study Scripture, you will grow in your Christian life. You will give the seed of the Word of God the ability to penetrate deeply into your heart.

PARABLE PRINCIPLE #2—Devote time every day to Bible reading.

After having read the Bible through one hundred times, George Mueller made this statement:

> I look upon it as a lost day when I have not had a good time over the Word of God. Friends often say, "I have so much to do, so many people to see, I cannot find time for Scripture study."

Perhaps there are not many who have more to do than I. For more than half a century, I have never known one day when I had not more business than I could get through. For four years, I have had annually about 30,000 letters, and most of these have passed through my own hands.

Then, as pastor of a church with 1,200 believers, great has been my care. Besides, I have had charge of five immense orphanages; also, at my publishing depot, the printing and circulating of millions of tracts, books, and Bibles; but I have always made it a rule never to begin work until I have had a good season with God and His Word. The blessing I have received has been wonderful. (Source unknown.)

Mueller understood a vital secret of the Christian life. He knew that it was his responsibility to study the Bible, and he took that responsibility seriously. There is no doubt in my mind that one of the reasons Mueller accomplished so much for Christ was that he studied the Word daily.

Jude 20-21 explains, "But ye, beloved, building up yourselves on your most holy faith, praying in the Holy Ghost, keep yourselves in the love of God, looking for the mercy of our Lord Jesus Christ unto eternal life."

How do you build yourself up in your holy faith? First, by prayer. In a few more chapters, we will cover this topic in detail. Another commandment in the Jude passage is to keep yourself in the love of God.

I know God loves me. I know that my status in God's eyes doesn't change whether I do works for Him or not. His love rescued me and put my sin upon His spotless Son. Yet I know that studying the Word helps me to reflect on God's love. I am reminded of His mercy. I remember His ever-present help in times of trial. He builds my faith. He strengthens my determination to live a strong, fruitful Christian life.

Throughout the many building programs our church has undertaken, one truth always remains clear. A structure must be built correctly in order for it to stand. Not long ago a decision was made to build a horse barn on our property. We wanted to give our school kids a chance to take riding lessons on our two horses, Sunny and Bo. A staff member told a woman who owned a large barn with many horses about our plans for a barn. When the barn owner learned the dimensions of the barn we wanted to build, she inquired how long we thought it would take to build it.

"About a month," the staff member said.

The woman laughed. "You can't build a horse barn in a month."

She couldn't have known that we have built all of our own buildings through the years, mammoth structures involving steel beams and miles of concrete. Constructing a simple horse barn would almost seem like child's play.

Less than a month later, Sunny and Bo moved to their new quarters. They both seemed to like their clean stalls and particularly the mountain of hay by the door.

Just as the barn had to be built correctly, so must the Christian life. But it takes a lot longer than a month to build a strong believer! Jude's command to build faith includes regular Bible study. Such a practice sustains our spiritual usefulness. Psalm 126:5-6 states, "They that sow in tears shall reap in joy. He that goeth forth and weepeth, bearing precious seed, shall doubtless come again with rejoicing, bringing his sheaves with him."

When you apply Parable Principle #2 to your life, you will be balanced. Building the study of His Word into the framework of your life will make you aware of the Lord's leading during the events of your day. Are you building correctly on your faith? Commit yourself to making Bible study an essential component of each day.

LAWNMOWER LONGEVITY

Not long ago I ate lunch with a businessman. He said that part of his business dealt with a certain lawnmower company. I recognized the brand as one of my personal favorites through the years.

"Our church used to own a camp in northern Minnesota," I told him. "The acres of grass needed a lot of mowing. We bought that brand of lawnmower because it cost only ninety dollars, but it lasted a year. The secret was to change the oil every other time we mowed the grass. What a bargain."

My friend laughed. "That particular lawnmower you're describing is a loss leader. The big chains buy them for ninety-five dollars and sell them for ninety dollars to attract people to their stores. They definitely lost money on you!"

I thought about those lawnmowers and all the use we got from them. I know that I want to be that kind of person, used by the Lord over the long haul. We can liken daily Bible reading to an oil change for the lawnmower. The fresh oil kept the lawnmower operating long past the time it should have quit, and so it is with us. When we study the Word, we add usefulness and longevity to our Christian service.

WHICH GROUP ARE YOU?

The Barna Research Group indicates that almost every household in America (92 percent) owns at least one copy of the Bible. This includes most homes in which the adults are not practicing Christians, as well as the homes of hundreds of thousands of atheists.[2] The Bible promises comfort, strength, hope, wisdom, knowledge, joy, power, and purpose. However, just because you have a Bible doesn't mean you're going to benefit from it.[3] You must read it for it to help you.

There are four basic groups of Bible-reading Christians. The first group subscribes to Vicky's former philosophy. The whole thought of reading the Bible each day overwhelms them. They don't think they know enough about it to understand how to do it effectively. This is understandable. No one likes to try something new without some basic knowledge first.

The first day of a new job often causes the same trepidation. There is no way to know ahead of time all that is expected of you. And those little nagging unknowns can get in the way, at least initially, of learning your new duties.

Don't forget. You have the Holy Spirit as your constant guide. He will help you to understand what you are reading *right where you are.* Don't let a lack of knowledge keep you from opening and drinking from this well of strength.

Perhaps you belong to the second group of Bible-readers. You read the Bible most days. The problem? You aren't getting much out of it. You will find many helps for benefiting from your time in the Word throughout this chapter. Bible reading is much more than an empty ritual or a boring chore.

If you are reading the Word regularly and find yourself learning what God has for you, then you belong to the third group. Congratulations! I appreciate the effort you're making in becoming more like Christ.

Perhaps everyone belongs to the fourth group, the group who wants to make their daily Bible reading even more dynamic than it already is. You desire to see God's hand working in your life, and you know that the more you study and learn, the more you will understand what He wants you to do.

RECEIVING THE WORD

James 1:21 states, "Wherefore lay apart all filthiness and superfluity of naughtiness, and receive with meekness the engrafted word, which is able to save your souls." How do we receive the Word? This verse states that we must lay aside all filthiness. We already understand that this command is impossible to carry out on our own. Jesus Christ paid the price for our sin on the cross. When we trusted Him as our Savior, He paid for our sins—past, present, and future. Yet we need a daily cleansing—not for salvation but for fellowship.

We find another aspect of receiving the Word in John 15:26: "But when the Comforter is come, whom I will send unto you from the Father, even the Spirit of truth, which proceedeth from the Father, he shall testify of me." The Holy Spirit who dwells inside of us will help us discern the truth of Scripture.

Ephesians 4:30 urges, "And grieve not the holy Spirit of God, whereby ye are sealed unto the day of redemption." How do you grieve the Holy Spirit? When you sin, you hinder His work in your life. You will be unable to absorb the truth of God's Word the way you can when your fellowship with the Lord is unbroken.

Before you begin reading your Bible, confess your sins to the Lord. He will hear you, and, better yet, He promises to forgive! With no known sins blocking your fellowship with God, you are now prepared to get the most out of your Bible.

Hebrews 2:1 tells us, "Therefore we ought to give the more earnest heed to the things which we have heard, lest at any time we should let them slip." When you read the Word, you must give earnest heed to it. Give it your full attention.

Remember Joshua 1:8: "This book of the law shall not depart out of thy mouth; but thou shalt meditate therein day and night, that thou mayest observe to do according to all that is written therein: for then thou shalt make thy way prosperous, and then thou shalt have good success." When we meditate on the Word of God, we are promised a successful and joy-filled spiritual journey.

I Need Energy

By law manufacturers have to list nutrition information about their food products in a readable way on the label. On some sports drinks, instead of listing 210 *calories*, the label says 210 grams of *energy*. The manufacturer wants the customer to associate the product with the energy it is supposed to give. In this case, the words *energy* and *calorie* are interchangeable. Do you want spiritual energy? Discover Parable Principle #2. It will bring new vigor to your daily walk.

On one trip to Israel Linda and I traveled to Elot with the famous Zvi from Friends of Israel. Zvi is known throughout the world for his love for Christ. We traveled with our dear friends, Pastor Bob and Ruth Gray. One day Zvi's son brought Ruth and me some fresh orange juice, saying, "This is the freshest orange juice in all of Israel."

I sampled a mouthful, but I had to try hard to keep from spitting it out. Somehow I forced it down. I glanced over at Ruth and noticed that she had the same problem.

"He said it was the freshest orange juice in all of Israel," I said. We shrugged and drank it.

Suddenly Zvi's son ran toward us. "Don't drink it! It's spoiled. I didn't know." Ruth and I looked at our empty glasses. We wondered how much time on this earth we had left! But God was good, and neither one of us got sick.

However, the vigor daily Bible reading gives your spiritual walk is unsurpassed. You can always trust that the energy you receive from it is fresh, vibrant, and straight from God Himself.

BIBLE STUDY SECRETS OF FAMOUS CHRISTIANS

Martin Luther said, "I study my Bible like I gather apples. First, I shake the whole tree that the ripest may fall. Then I shake each limb, and when I have shaken each limb, I shake each branch and every twig. Then I look under every leaf. I search the Bible as a whole, like I shook the whole tree. Then I shake every limb—study book after book. Then I shake every branch, giving attention to the chapters. Then I shake every twig, or a careful study of the paragraphs and sentences and words and their meanings."

John Newton, author of my favorite song "Amazing Grace," wrote a letter to a woman interested in reading Scripture. This letter has some helpful pointers for anyone's quest to study the Bible.

> I know not a better rule of reading the Scripture than to read it through from beginning to end, and when we have finished to begin it once again. We shall meet with many passages which we can make little improvement of, but not so many in the second reading as in the first, and fewer in the third than in the second: provided we pray to him who has the keys to open our understanding, and to anoint our eyes with his spiritual ointment. The course of reading today will prepare some light for what we shall read tomorrow, and throw a farther light upon what we read yesterday. Experience only can prove the advantage of this method, if steadily persevered in. To make a few efforts and then give over is like making a few steps and then standing still, which would do little toward completing a long journey. But, though a person walked slowly, and but a little way in a day, if he walked every day, and with his face always in the same direction, year after year, he might in time encompass the globe. By thus traveling patiently and steadily through Scripture, and repeating our progress, we should increase in knowledge to the end of life.[4]

Great preacher and teacher Charles Spurgeon once said:

> I suggest the question as to whether you do read your Bibles or not? I am afraid that this is a magazine reading age, a newspaper reading age, a periodical reading age, but not so much a Bible reading age as it ought to be. In the old Puritanical times men used to have a

scant supply of other literature, but they found a library enough in the one Book, the Bible. And how they did read the Bible! How little of Scripture there is in modern sermons compared with the sermons of those masters of theology, the Puritanical divines! Almost every sentence of theirs seems to cast side lights upon a text of Scripture; not only the one they are preaching about, but many others as well are set in a new light as the discourse proceeds. They introduce blended lights from other passages which are parallel or semi-parallel thereunto, and thus they educate their readers to compare spiritual things with spiritual.

Spurgeon also thought that we should meditate on the meaning of the Scripture we read. He said:

> We must try to make out, as far as our finite mind can grasp it, what God means by this and what he means by that; otherwise we may kiss the book and have no love to its contents; we may reverence the letter and yet really have no devotion toward the Lord who speaks to us in these words. Beloved, you will never get comfort to your soul out of what you do not understand, nor find guidance for your life out of what you do not comprehend; nor can any practical bearing upon your character come out of that which is not understood by you.[5]

Spurgeon gave additional helps for Scripture reading that will assist you to make this practice a daily habit.

1. *Read the Bible with an earnest desire to understand it.* Don't be content just to read the words of Scripture. Seek to grasp the message they contain.

2. *Read the Scriptures with a simple, childlike faith and humility.* Believe what God reveals. Reason must bow to God's revelation.

3. *Read the Word with a spirit of obedience and self-application.* Apply what God says to yourself and obey His will in all things.

4. *Read the holy Scriptures every day.* We quickly lose the nourishment and strength of yesterday's bread. We must feed our souls daily upon the manna God has given us.

5. *Read the whole Bible and read it in an orderly way.* "All scripture is given by inspiration of God, and is profitable for doctrine, for reproof,

for correction, for instruction in righteousness" (2 Timothy 3:16). I know of no better way to read the Bible than to start at the beginning and read straight through to the end, a portion every day, comparing Scripture with Scripture.

6. *Read the Word of God fairly and honestly.* As a general rule, any passage of Scripture means what it appears to mean. Interpret every passage in this simple manner, in its context.

7. *Read the Bible with Christ in view.* The whole book is about Him. Look for Him on every page. He is there. If you fail to see Him there, you need to read that page again.

George Mueller gave some valuable insights into reading the Word:

> It is a common temptation of Satan to make us give up the reading of the Word and prayer when our enjoyment is gone; as if it were of no use to read the Scriptures when we do not enjoy them, and as if it were no use to pray when we have no spirit of prayer. The truth is that in order to enjoy the Word, we ought to continue to read it, and the way to obtain a spirit of prayer is to continue praying. The less we read the Word of God, the less we desire to read it, and the less we pray, the less we desire to pray.[6]

R. A. Torrey said:

> A verse must be read often, and re-read and read again before the wondrous message of love and power that God has put into it begins to appear. Words must be turned over and over in the mind before their full force and beauty take possession of us. One must look a long time at the great masterpieces of art to appreciate their beauty and understand their meaning, and so one must look a long time at the great verses of the Bible to appreciate their beauty and understand their meaning.[7]

WHAT DOES THE WORD MEAN TO YOU?

Psalm 119 shows us how we should perceive the Bible. In this psalm we see the intense longings and love of the psalmist for the Scriptures.

If we consider what the Word really is to us in our Christian lives, I would think that we could scarcely be kept from it!

Direct Path

Psalm 119:1 states, "Blessed are the undefiled in the way, who walk in the law of the LORD." The law of the Lord keeps us on track for Him. It helps us to focus our eyes on the finish line and run steadily toward that goal. It will help us persevere and not get sidetracked.[8]

Cleansing Water

Psalm 119:9 asks, "Wherewithal shall a young man cleanse his way? by taking heed thereto according to thy word." When we heed the Word as we read it, we are encouraged to continue confessing our sins. This helps us to stay in fellowship with the Lord.

Encouraging Song

Psalm 119:54 states, "Thy statutes have been my songs in the house of my pilgrimage." When you read the Word, the Lord fills your mind with His truth. I wasn't gifted musically, and yet the Word does make me sing for joy.

Solid Gold

Psalm 119:72 says, "The law of thy mouth is better unto me than thousands of gold and silver." Don't worry if your earthly bank account doesn't hold much money. Know that when you study the Word, you are making yourself spiritually rich.

Wholesome Food

Psalm 119:103 tells us, "How sweet are thy words unto my taste! yea, sweeter than honey to my mouth!" When you study the Bible, its words will be sweet to you. You will find yourself craving it and wanting more.

Guiding Light

Psalm 119:105 says, "Thy word is a lamp unto my feet, and a light unto my path." When you study the Word, you will know the next step to take. You will have light in the darkness of the world.

Amazing Heritage

Psalm 119:111 states, "Thy testimonies have I taken as an heritage for ever: for they are the rejoicing of my heart." The Bible offers a heritage for the believer. Reading about those who have gone on before will inspire you to pass on your own legacy of faith.

FOUR HELPS FOR YOUR DAILY READ

When Julie and Jim were young, we enjoyed downhill skiing. I remember scouting out garage sales for equipment and loading up our two-door diesel Volkswagen Rabbit for a trip. Linda fried some chicken and squeezed the picnic lunch into the hatchback. We had a great time on those trips.

But imagine a person trying to ski without warm clothing, skis, or proper boots. The skier must have the right equipment in order to enjoy the sport to its maximum. In the same way, we must take some basic steps to ensure that our time in the Word will be spent "smoothly gliding down the hill rather than bumpily grinding to a halt." If you are already reading your Bible daily and understand what I cover next, you may be interested in the online resources I have listed at the end of the chapter.

The Right Equipment

Invest in a Bible. You may count it one of your wisest investments, for what else will profit you like a Bible? Consider getting a study Bible and benefit from the helpful notes. Here are some to try.

Thompson Chain-Reference Bible
Daily Walk Bible
Scofield Bible

I suggest that you begin by reading these books of the Bible in this order:

Matthew	Galatians	Esther
Mark	Ephesians	Psalms
Luke	Philippians	Proverbs
John	Colossians	Jonah
Acts	Genesis	

Make a daily appointment to read the Bible. Stick to your commitment. Early morning tends to work best, but do it any time as long as you are consistent. My daughter Julie tells me that one of her earliest memories is walking downstairs in the mornings and seeing me reading the Bible in my favorite chair.

How much do you read? You can read as much of the Bible as time permits. However, don't read so much that it means nothing to you. If you have fifteen minutes, then spend the entire time on the chapter you've chosen. Try to minimize interruptions. If you slow down a bit from your normally rushed lifestyle, Scripture will mean a lot more to you.

The Proper Technique

As I mentioned earlier, first ask for forgiveness for your sins. Then ask the Holy Spirit to be your teacher. You could pray this verse: "Blessed art thou, O LORD: teach me thy statutes" (Psalm 119:12). Ask God for understanding. Psalm 119:73 says, "Thy hands have made me and fashioned me: give me understanding, that I may learn thy commandments."

Pray that the Lord will change your life by the Scripture you read. Don't just read for trivial knowledge. Ask yourself these questions: How does this passage apply to my life? To what aspects of my life does this passage speak?

Be quick to re-read and to ask questions. When Rembrandt's famous painting *The Night Watch* was restored and returned to Amsterdam's Rijksmuseum, the curators performed a simple and yet remarkable experiment. They asked visitors to submit questions about the painting. The curators then prepared answers to over fifty questions, ranking the questions according to popularity.

Some of these questions focused on issues that curators usually don't like to include: How much does the painting cost? Has this painting ever been forged? Are there mistakes in the painting? Other questions focused on traditional artistic issues: Why did Rembrandt paint the subject? Who were the people in the painting? What techniques did Rembrandt pioneer in the particular work?

In a room next to the gallery that held the painting, the curators papered the walls with these questions (and answers). Visitors had to pass through this room before entering the gallery. The curious outcome was that the average length of time people spent viewing the painting increased from six minutes to over half an hour. Visitors alternated between reading questions and answers and examining the painting. They said that the questions encouraged them to look longer, to look closer, and to remember more. The questions created for them a richer experience of the painting and helped them see it in new ways.[9]

Ask yourself questions about what you are reading, and you will discover a key in understanding Scripture. God's Word can be compared to a masterful painting where the meaning grows clearer when we probe and ask questions.

Staying Power

Perhaps you enjoy reading the Word but find yourself neglecting it after a while. You benefit from Bible-reading and understand how important it is to study it each day, and yet the demands of life get in the way of continuing this discipline over the long term.

Rethink the time you read your Bible. Would doing it earlier ensure that you do it every day? Think about having a quiet time in the evening after the children are asleep or perhaps even during part of your lunch hour. Whatever you decide, if the time is convenient, it will be easier for you to be faithful.

Understand that on some days you will get more out of your Bible reading than on others. This should come as no surprise. Your own tiredness level, the situations you are facing—all these factors affect your daily Bible time.

Make more out of your time in the Word. Start each day's reading with a psalm or a proverb, and then go to the Bible passage you are working your way through. Write down your thoughts about the passage and tell how you could apply it to your life. Ask the Lord to help you keep the passage in mind throughout the day.[10] I enjoy reading the Word aloud. It adds a new dimension.

Read specific Scriptures. When you are facing a difficult situation, it is wise to read the Psalms. There is no book that better communicates the intense feelings that people have when enduring trials. If you have a chain-reference Bible and you encounter a specific subject you would like to learn more about, say angels or prophecy, follow the number under the verse to its matching place on the page. Look up the other references suggested until you've done a specific study on that doctrine.

Here are God's emergency numbers:

When in sorrow—call John 14.

When you are lonely or fearful—call Psalm 23.

When you want to be fruitful—call John 15.

When you have sinned—call Psalm 51.

When you grow bitter and critical—call 1 Corinthians 13.

When you worry—call Matthew 6:19-34.

When you feel down and out—call Romans 8:31-39.

When you are in danger—call Psalm 91.

When your faith needs stirring—call Hebrews 11.

When God seems far away—call Psalm 139.

When others fail you—call Psalm 27.

When you leave home to labor or travel—call Psalm 121.

When you want assurance—call Romans 8:1-30.

For Paul's secret of happiness—call Colossians 3:12-17.

When the world seems bigger than God—call Psalm 70 and Jeremiah 33:3.[11]

Write on a 3x5 card specific Scriptures that helped you during your quiet time.

Post a particular verse you read in your quiet time in your home or office. It will serve as a constant reminder. Imagine you were about to make a sarcastic comment to your spouse. Just before you say it, your eyes light on a verse such as Proverbs 15:1: "A soft answer turneth away wrath: but grievous words stir up anger." This just might help you bite your tongue. If your supervisor doesn't like you putting up verses in your workplace, tape them inside a book or a drawer.

Incorporate systematic Bible memory into your daily time in the Word. Awana Clubs International does a great job of helping children memorize Scripture. Many people have told me that as adults, they still remember the Scriptures memorized when they were children. Why don't you systematically memorize the Bible as you study it in your quiet time? What a wonderful way to carry its meaning with you all day long. Start with one verse a month and work yourself up to one verse or more a week.

Noted Bible teacher E. Schuyler English told of Michael Billester, a Bible distributor who visited a small hamlet in Poland shortly before World War II. Billester gave a Bible to a villager, who was converted by reading it. The new believer then passed the book on to others. The cycle of conversions and sharing continued until two hundred people had become believers through that one Bible. When Billester returned in 1940, this group of Christians met together for a worship service in which he was to preach the Word. He normally asked for testimonies, but this time he suggested that several in the audience recite verses of Scripture. One man stood and asked, "Perhaps we have misunderstood. Did you mean verses or chapters?"

These villagers had not memorized a few select verses of the Bible but whole chapters and books. Thirteen people knew Matthew, Luke, and half of Genesis. Another person had committed to memory the Psalms. That single copy of the Bible given by Billester had done its work. Transformed lives bore witness to the power of the Word. So your transformed life will bear witness of this daily habit of Bible reading.

BIBLE SOFTWARE

Do you want the challenge of in-depth study along with the ease of looking up passages on your personal computer? Bible study software is for you. I have listed the websites, but you can also purchase these products at your local Christian bookstore.

Wordsearch by iExalt Publishing, *www.wordsearchbible.com*. The most popular Bible study software program. An easy-to-use search program, Wordsearch has a vast number of materials that can be added onto the program for an additional cost.

QuickVerse by Parsons Technology, *www.quickverse.com*. Another Bible study software program that includes many add-ons to be purchased at additional cost.

The Online Bible, *onlinebible.com*. This is a free download of a Bible search program. It is not as easy to use as Wordsearch or QuickVerse.

ONLINE BIBLE STUDY HELPS

Devotionals

Daily Reflections with Dr. James Scudder, *www.dailyreflections.org*. This is the online edition of my daily reflections that appear every month in the four-color magazine published by Quentin Road Ministries.

My Utmost for His Highest by Oswald Chambers, *www.gospelcom.net/devotionals/*

Our Daily Bread, *www.gospelcom.net/rbc/odb/*

Back to the Bible, *www.backtothebible.org*. A collection of devotionals including some by Elisabeth Elliot and some from Charles Spurgeon's classic *Morning and Evening*.

Bible Study

The Bible Gateway, *www.biblegateway.com*. Look up any Bible passage in any translation and in seventeen different languages.

Crosswalk Bible Study Tools, *bible.crosswalk.com*. The most complete collection of commentaries and study tools on the Web. Bible Study Tools features a searchable Bible in any version. It has helpful links to commentaries, encyclopedias, and dictionaries. Bible Study Tools also features parallel and interlinear Bibles, Greek and Hebrew Lexicons, illustrations databases, and historical works, including *Foxe's Book of Martyrs*.

The Blue Letter Bible, *www.blueletterbible.org*. Includes a searchable Bible along with a limited selection of maps and commentaries.

Audio Scripture and Hymns

The Audio Bible, *www.audiobible.com*. Listen to the entire Bible read by Alexander Scourby. You can select verses, whole chapters, or whole books.

The Cyber Hymnal, *www.cyberhymnal.org*. Look up and listen to your favorite hymns and the corresponding passages of Scripture.

The Bible on Your Handheld

Olive Tree Software, *www.olivetree.com*. The King James Version download is free for the Palm OS, Windows CE, and Pocket PC formats.

Back to the Bible Devotions, *www.backtothebible.org/devotions* Download Spurgeon's *Morning and Evening*, Elisabeth Elliot's devotional thoughts, and other classic devotionals to your handheld.

Parable Principle #2 is so important. Sow the precious seed of the Word in your soul every day. For Scripture to take hold and give enduring support, it must be read daily. Whether you regularly read the Bible or are struggling to begin a daily quiet time, I challenge you to take some of the suggestions given in this chapter about reading Scripture. God's words convict of sin and are sharper than any two-edged sword. They bring comfort and peace in the midst of your greatest confusion. They inspire and offer encouragement, faith, and assistance for your spiritual journey. Why don't you start right now?

3

A SEED CALLED PREACHING

*The church is so constituted that every member matters, and matters
in a very vital sense.*

—DR. M. LLOYD-JONES

WE WERE FEELING LANDLOCKED in our church and schools,
unable to grow. At the end of the recession in the early eighties, we
located forty acres of land eight miles north on the same road,
Quentin Road. We had no reason to believe we needed that much
space. Ten acres would have been more than sufficient at the time. Yet
we had faith that God was going to do a great work. My conviction
grew stronger when I brought the matter up to the congregation, and
they unanimously gave their approval.

Since our second building in 1975, our people always worked to
build our own facilities with no outside contractors. I had undertaken
the job of making sure the concrete was poured, since the building
was to be built on a slab. The structure was to be 24,000 square feet,
which seemed to us as immense as the Sears Tower.

The pressure to build increased as we settled into the third week
of June. Our Christian schools needed to start in September. I
decided to order concrete for the upcoming Saturday. The foreman
informed me of Saturday's weather forecast—heavy rain. Since no
other orders had come in for that day, he would have to charge me
for any concrete ordered, even if his trucks couldn't pour. He pushed
me to order the concrete another day. But I remained firm. I knew
we had to pour. We had no choice. "We will take the concrete," I said.

The next morning I listened to the forecast on the radio—100
percent chance of rain. My faith began to falter. As I arrived at the

property, I noticed that clouds as dark and deep as the Rocky Mountains surrounded the area. Now I knew it for sure—we were going to pay big for concrete we couldn't use. Furthermore, if the trucks did happen to pour, and it rained as they poured, our men would have to chip it out and try to find somewhere to dump it. I tried to imagine how we would pay for nine truckloads of concrete from our already thin coffers. The prospects of completing this building at all grew dimmer with each passing minute.

All around our property, it started to rain heavily. We looked at each other, grimly shaking our heads, waiting for the curtain of clouds to advance a few feet and begin dumping their water big-time. But they never did. The first truck pulled onto our property. The driver jumped out of his truck and ran toward us. "You won't believe it!" he said. "The rain is so bad that the rest of the trucks are stopped by the side of the road right now. But as soon as I turned onto this property, the rain stopped!"

The next driver was just as excited. "This would make a believer out of an atheist," he said. And so it continued. All nine trucks poured their concrete. Not a drop of rain fell on our property. Just as the foundation needed some water to finish it, God brought in a few clouds for a light sprinkling.

This story sounds so unbelievable that I would never tell it if I did not have more than a hundred people as witnesses. And understand this as well—God is not at my beck and call. A month or two earlier, I had prayed that it wouldn't rain for a church picnic, but it still did. God gave us a miracle when no agent on earth could come to our aid. He knew that we needed to build His church, and if we didn't get the foundation poured that day, it would never have been finished on time.

When September arrived, the schools started on time. There were many other trials as we finished the building and many other times when God helped us. But that particular day stands out in my mind—the day God demonstrated His power over nature so we could build His church. God will build His church, and the gates of hell will not prevail against it. God will always come through for you when you are faced with trials. Your miracle may be as significant as the miracle of the rain, or it may be just as astounding but not as public. Whatever the case, you can count on one thing: In your deepest need, God is there. He has not forgotten you, and He has not forgotten His church.

God wants us to understand how important His church is. He knows we need a church, a place to meet in, a place to fellowship, a place to grow spiritually, a place to bring others, a place to learn about the Bible, and a place to be used by the body of Christ.

This idea of Christians needing other Christians contradicts the self-sufficiency of our culture. We admire the cowboy, the pioneer, the man who doesn't need anyone or anything but who possesses within himself all the resources. This philosophy causes many professing followers of Jesus to make their faith a private affair. They think they can manage without becoming members of a local church. I have yet to meet a Christian who has successfully led a vibrant spiritual life apart from local church involvement. Yet I meet many who try.

One preacher said, "Millions of Christians today are unchurched Christians, trying to live lives devoted to Jesus Christ . . . alone. They are like a kidney surgically removed from a body and placed in a jar, all alone, cut off, unable to receive nourishment or provide sustenance for the rest of the body."[1]

His point is important, for it shows the view many believers take of the church. Instead of understanding that their participation in a local church contributes to the good of the body of Christ, they choose to go it alone. When Jesus told the Parable of the Sower, He gave us many helps in living the Christian life. He shared how essential the seed is, His precious Word. Without the seed, no growth can take place. In the last chapter we saw that consistent Bible reading gives the believer enduring support in Christian growth. Now Parable Principle #3 gives us another important truth about our walk as believers.

PARABLE PRINCIPLE #3—Make it a habit to attend a Bible-believing, Bible-teaching church.

A woman volunteer at a telephone hotline for shut-ins regularly checked on people who needed a little extra care because of financial or health problems. One of her "regulars" was an elderly woman living on a fixed income. Through their conversations, she learned that this woman desperately needed a new overcoat but could not afford one. Wanting to help, the volunteer withdrew $200 from her bank account and sent it to the woman with an anonymous note reading: "For a new coat."

The next time she called, the woman had some good news. "Someone sent me money for a new overcoat!" she said. "I don't know who it was, but they sent $200."

"Did you get a coat?" asked the volunteer.

"Yes," replied the woman, "but I found one for $150. You've been so nice to me, I'm sending you the extra $50 so the hotline center can help others."[2]

This woman doesn't realize it, but she is giving us a picture of the church in action. She was quick to donate the rest of the money she could have used on herself. First Corinthians 12:25-26 says, "That there should be no schism in the body; but that the members should have the same care one for another. And whether one member suffer, all the members suffer with it; or one member be honoured, all the members rejoice with it."

When you become part of a local body of believers, your own spiritual needs are met, and at the same time you are able to reach out and help others spiritually. It is a dynamic, living circle of joy.

A SEED CALLED PREACHING

With a light spiritual diet and diminishing personal discipline, many Christians have decided that attending church is not important. *U.S. News and World Report* says that eight of every ten Americans today believe that it's possible to be a good Christian without attending a church. Increasing numbers of people are either staying away from church or identifying with church at arm's length. With larger congregations today, it's easy to say you attend such and such a church while remaining anonymous. Perhaps no one there even knows you personally.[3]

Yet the importance of regularly attending a Bible-believing

church can hardly be emphasized enough! There is a tremendous difference in spiritual growth between those Christians who attend church and those who don't! How could there not be? When a person exposes himself to as much of the Word of God as he possibly can, the chance for growth increases exponentially.

Some of my church members now tell me that before they came out to church, their spiritual life was in a slump. There would be times when they would feel convicted to do something about their spiritual direction, and yet they lacked accountability and the instruction to change. Now that they attend regularly, they are able to grow systematically. When I preach on issues that they are facing in the office, they feel encouraged to keep plugging along. When I explain difficult Bible verses to them, they can use that explanation to help others.

One couple attended our Sunday morning service for over ten years before they came to any other services. It took time for them to understand the importance of getting as much of the Word of God as they could. Now that they see how much their lives have changed, they try not to miss a service.

Bible teacher and commentator J. C. Ryle said, "The church is where the work of Christ is done upon the earth. Its members are a little flock, and few in numbers, compared with the children of the world; one or two here, and two or three there—a few in this place and a few in that. But these are they who shake the universe; these are they who change the fortunes of kingdoms by their prayers. . . ."[4]

The church is the visible, physical presence of Jesus Christ in the world. We are not merely His representatives; we are not just His ambassadors. Through the Holy Spirit, Christ lives in us, both individually as believers and corporately as the church. In order to have spiritual life and power, you must abide in Christ. However, the church is God's presence in the world today. In order to be in fellowship with Christ, you have to be in fellowship with the church. A person who tries to be a solo Christian is cutting himself or herself off from the God-appointed means of spiritual vitality and strength. Many Christians have missed church and thereby missed many chances for the Lord to work in their lives.

Perhaps you might say, "I had to miss church because of my job." Maybe you've said, "I neglected church because company was coming," "I failed to attend church because I had an appointment," "I skipped church because I was just too tired."

What is actually happening when you miss church? You are missing an opportunity to be in God's presence. Of course, He is omnipresent, or present everywhere. However, you will experience the presence of God at church like nowhere else. So when you decide to work at your job instead of going to church, you are choosing to avoid His special presence. When you schedule company for the same time as church, you are choosing company over His special blessing. At that appointment scheduled with no thought for church, you are choosing to dwell on something else rather than God's presence. When you are absent from church because you are just too tired, you are forgetting that church would probably energize you!

Hebrews 10:25 doesn't give us many excuses for missing church. It says, "Not forsaking the assembling of ourselves together, as the manner of some is; but exhorting one another: and so much the more, as ye see the day approaching."

EIGHT REASONS TO WORSHIP

I've had a few people say throughout the years, "I can worship God on the golf course just as well as I can in church" or "I think about the Lord when I'm fishing; so I'm worshiping Him then." There are plenty of excuses when it comes to skipping church. I don't know if I've heard them all, but I've heard a lot!

Since we live in the Chicagoland area, fall is a lovely time of year, and it brings out all of the tree-watchers (or if you live in New England, the trendy term is leaf peepers). For some reason it seems that many tree-watchers feel that this activity is a Sunday event, thereby ruling out church. I'm convinced that the same tree-watchers turn into weather-watchers, not wanting to go outside when it is snowing or raining. The weather-watchers turn into event-watchers, not wanting to miss any spring events scheduled on Sundays. The event-watchers turn into the vacation-watchers in the summer, making sure to take a vacation every Sunday of the year.

These believers shouldn't be surprised when they find their spiritual pulse weakening. They shouldn't be surprised that they're not excited about the Lord anymore. How could they stay excited about the Lord so far away from His body? The Bible is clear that we need to worship, and while we can worship God in other places besides the church, we can't experience His presence and blessing in the same way anywhere else. Here are eight reasons to worship God in church.

1. *Church worship celebrates God's presence.* Worship is a personal encounter with God in which one expresses love for God, concentrates on His attributes, and brings the focus back to Him. His presence is something to celebrate because in His presence is fullness of joy. Psalm 16:11 says, "Thou wilt show me the path of life: in thy presence is fulness of joy; at thy right hand there are pleasures for evermore."

2. *Worship gives you an opportunity to talk with God.* While you can talk with God anywhere, there is nothing like church to get your mind focused on what He wants for your life. Also you can share your concerns with your pastor and other believers in the church, and they can pray with you.

3. *Worship makes spiritual things real.* When you listen to the Word of God preached week after week, spiritual things will become more real to you. In other words, you will begin to see how the principles you are learning apply to specific situations you might face. Strengthen your knowledge of the faith by listening to biblical preaching.

4. *Regular church attendance will keep you out of harmful places.* There are many places that a Christian should stay away from. A regular pattern of church attendance leaves less time and offers fewer opportunities for one to be tempted to do things he or she shouldn't do. Remember the replacement principle in the Christian life. Don't just eliminate a particular habit and fail to replace it with something of value. Church attendance is a good habit to develop.

5. *Church attendance keeps you focused on eternity.* When you hear the Word taught, you will be reminded of God's power and strength. Such reminders will help you remain thankful for what He has done for you by giving you eternal life, the Holy Spirit, and many other

beautiful gifts. The Word will keep you focused on heavenly things, and you will then view life the way God wants you to see it. Colossians 3:2 says, "Set your affection on things above, not on things on the earth."

6. *Volunteering to help out at church makes your life fruitful.* To make you really productive in your spiritual life, there is no substitute for the local church. Perhaps you will have an opportunity to witness to young children (volunteering in your church's youth program), minister to others by an act of service (cleaning or keeping up the landscaping around the church), build up others in the faith (teaching a Bible class), or a myriad of other possibilities. Don't miss out on a chance to live a fruitful Christian life by failing to get involved with a local body of believers! Talk·to your pastor or your church leaders about areas of ministry where you might fit. Don't be afraid to do what they suggest. Give God a chance to work in your life by trying something you've never tried before. You just might be surprised at how your life changes. Galatians 6:10 says, "As we have therefore opportunity, let us do good unto all men, especially unto them who are of the household of faith."

7. *Worshiping with other believers brings heaven to earth.* There is no greater joy in my life than leading Quentin Road Bible Baptist Church. The congregation loves me, and they love each other. I often think when I preach and look at their dear faces, *This is heaven on earth—the fellowship that we share, the trials we've experienced together, the prayers we've seen answered.* We have been blessed to see God's hand through the years. When we celebrate Communion together, that is also a very special time. I know the people feel especially close to the Lord and to each other when they partake of the Lord's Supper.

8. *Church attendance keeps you accountable.* Do you ever feel that you really want to grow and that you need accountability? You want to last over the long term; yet you understand your own tendency to slide toward carnality. When you attend church regularly, you will have fellow believers to keep you accountable. You can go to godly men and women there for counsel and help and strength when you face diffi-

cult decisions. Proverbs 11:14 says, "Where no counsel is, the people fall: but in the multitude of counsellors there is safety."

GOD'S SNAPSHOT OF THE CHURCH

Bradley showed his mother his latest Lego creation. "Wow, Bradley," his mother said. "What is it?"

"It's a church. I had to make it all different colors because I didn't have enough of one color. Do you think God will mind?" Bradley asked.

Rowena assured him that God wouldn't mind, and then Bradley scampered out the front door.

"What are you doing?" Rowena asked.

"I'm going outside to get a rock. I learned in Sunday school that Jesus will build His church upon a rock."

As Bradley headed out the door, Rowena smiled. Bradley's interpretation was a bit off, but he was cute.

The first mention of the church in the New Testament is in Matthew 16:18: "And I say also unto thee, That thou art Peter, and upon this rock I will build my church; and the gates of hell shall not prevail against it."

Peter had just confessed Jesus as the Christ, the Messiah. Jesus then shares a truth about the church. Peter's name meant "rock," but this doesn't mean that Peter was the first pope, with all authority over the church. The rock that Christ is referring to is Himself. But Peter would be the one who officially "opened" the first church, and his position as a disciple would give him the authority necessary to do this. Ephesians 2:19-22 states, "Now therefore ye are no more strangers and foreigners, but fellowcitizens with the saints, and of the household of God; and are built upon the foundation of the apostles and prophets, Jesus Christ himself being the chief corner stone; in whom all the building fitly framed together groweth unto an holy temple in the Lord: In whom ye also are builded together for an habitation of God through the Spirit."

The word *build* doesn't mean constructing a church building. A church does not have to have a physical structure to be a church. In America we often picture the traditional white building with a steeple and automatically label it "church." But a church is unlike any other organization.

The word *church* means "a called-out assembly." No physical building of any type is mentioned in this definition. There are churches in India, China, Vietnam, and many other places around the world that don't have a place in which to meet. Inclement weather means a lot more to these believers than it would to you and me, cozily sitting in our padded pews. But these churches are composed of believers who assemble together to build God's church.

THE BODY OF CHRIST

God's universal church is composed of all people who have trusted Christ, the head of this church. Believers around the world make up this church, called the body of Christ. This church is bigger than ourselves, because it is being built by God Himself. Sometimes as Americans, we get tunnel vision. We forget that there are many other peoples who are followers of Jesus Christ, who pledge allegiance to His name. Many of these people assemble despite persecution. They understand how important it is to be a part of God's church. So the church is a body, a living organism composed of all believers working together to accomplish His will. Romans 12:4-5 says, "For as we have many members in one body, and all members have not the same office: So we, being many, are one body in Christ, and every one members one of another."

Do you realize how vitally important you are to this body, this universal church? Whatever job you are supposed to do in the body of Christ is just as important as the job a physical member of your own body does. Perhaps you could still function without an arm or a leg, but it is surely easier when every member does its job. In your local church, you have a chance to live out your faith. Each of us should be contributing to this local body, this living organism.

A living body is a balance between the whole and the parts, as each part contributes to the whole but with each part also receiving its nourishment from the whole. The key word for a living system like a human body is *interdependence*. Each part is both dependent on the whole and independent from the whole. Each part both gives and takes in proper proportion to sustain life. Having a body part that only gives or that only takes is a sign of sickness. In order for the entire system to function in a healthy way, each body part has to do its part for the whole. Colossians 2:19 says, "And not holding the Head, from which all the body by joints and bands having nourishment ministered, and knit together, increaseth with the increase of God."

If you have sometimes thought, *I'm not very important to God's kingdom*, then perhaps these words have brought conviction to your heart. Now you understand that you are a vital member of this universal body and that your function is essential to keeping every other part running as smoothly as possible. This conviction should change the way you view your position in God's church and should fill you with excitement as you consider the future assignments that come your way.

HERE COMES THE BRIDE

My granddaughters Amy and Erica like to play dress-up, and of course they enjoy dressing as brides. They march down the middle of their room while one of them sings, "Here comes the bride!" Sometimes I will tease them and say, "Who are you going to marry?"

"Papa," they say, "we don't want to get married. We just like pretending to be a bride!"

From marriage emerges a beautiful picture that Christ uses to describe His church. Ephesians 5:25-30 states:

> *Husbands, love your wives, even as Christ also loved the church, and gave himself for it; That he might sanctify and cleanse it with the washing of water by the word, That he might present it to himself a glorious church, not having spot, or wrinkle, or any such thing; but that it should be holy and without blemish. So ought men to love their wives as their own bodies. He that loveth his wife loveth himself. For no man ever yet hated his own flesh; but nourisheth and cherisheth it, even as the Lord the church: For we are members of his body, of his flesh, and of his bones.*

The focus of this chapter isn't the husband-wife relationship; rather it is the picture this relationship gives of the church. The image of the church as the bride of Christ is a common one in the New Testament. When a man and woman got engaged, they were legally bound to each other even though they weren't married yet. If they wanted to break off the engagement, they had to file for divorce, like Joseph almost did when he found out Mary was pregnant (Matthew 1:18). The picture the Bible presents is that of an engagement between Christ and the church, legally bound though not yet fully married, with the marriage supper for Christ and His church coming at the end of the age (Revelation 19:6-9).

Ephesians tells us that Jesus gave everything for the church, that He sacrificially loves the church and is preparing it for the marriage. What does this image of a bride tell us about the church? Since the church is precious to Jesus, since He loves her much more than any man could ever love his bride, we need to treat the church with love too.

Perhaps we have gotten into the habit of criticizing the church. We say that the pastor preaches too loudly, or the music is too soft. We complain about Sister Smith and Brother Jack's gossiping tongues. And in a lot of ways, the church today does need to change and become more like Jesus Christ. One preacher shared, though, that one time he was criticizing his church when an image of a bride and groom popped into his mind. In that mental image he walked up to the groom and said to him, "Your bride sure is ugly." The pastor realized that he would never do that because no matter what the bride looks like, she is still beautiful to the groom. The Lord spoke to his heart: "Every time you criticize My church, you're telling Me that My bride is ugly." That moment the pastor changed the way he viewed the church. He realized he needed to love the church in spite of its imperfections and failures.[5]

THE PURPOSE OF THE CHURCH

Evangelism

One of the purposes of the church is to spread the good news of the Gospel through evangelism. The pastor is to proclaim the message of salvation so that all who enter the doors of the church have an opportunity to hear the Word. The people are edified and prepared to spread the Gospel to their own communities and workplaces. When the Gospel is given to the unsaved and they trust Christ, they will desire to grow in Christ. Of course, what better place to do that than in the local church.

Fellowship

Fellowship with like-minded believers is necessary for growth and development in the Christian life. This fellowship is an essential element of a healthy local church. I remember the story of a family who agreed to meet downstairs in the social hall for a quick ice cream cone after the evening service. The little boy said, "A *quick* ice cream cone? But that's not fellowship!"

Fellowship is more than hastily eaten ice cream. It is enjoying the company of other believers. It is being accountable to the body of Christ. It is helping each other in times of need. Acts 2:46-47 says, "And they, continuing daily with one accord in the temple, and breaking bread from house to house, did eat their meat with gladness and singleness of heart, praising God, and having favour with all the people. And the Lord added to the church daily such as should be saved."

Discipleship

One of the church's jobs is to bring those who trust Christ to a more complete knowledge of the Word of God. Paul says in Hebrews 5:12-14, "For when for the time ye ought to be teachers, ye have need that one teach you again which be the first principles of the oracles of God; and are become such as have need of milk, and not of strong meat. For every one that useth milk is unskilful in the word of righteousness: for he is a babe. But strong meat belongeth to them that are of full age, even those who by reason of use have their senses exercised to discern both good and evil."

When we attend church regularly, we receive first the "milk," or the easier parts of the Word, and then we receive the "meat," or the hard parts of the Word. Then we become disciples or followers of Christ, ready to help others in their own spiritual quest.

THE CHURCH: YOUR PRIORITY?

How important is the church in your life? Do you realize what you are teaching your children when you miss church? Do you understand that if you don't make church a priority, they never will? Don't be a parent who just drops the children off at Sunday school and drives away. There is probably no greater harm you could do to your children than to tell them it is important for them to go to church and yet never go yourself. Does this seem like a radical position to you—placing so much importance on church attendance? While it might appear extreme in today's "comfortable" Christian culture, it is actually what the Bible teaches; so it isn't extreme at all. Don't take church lightly. You will make much more progress in your spiritual life if you give high priority to your church life.

WHAT TO LOOK FOR IN A CHURCH

A mother set a plate in front of her six-year-old son Jacob.

"Cool, Mom," Jacob said. "This is the best dinner you ever made!"

No wonder. On the plate sat a pile of gummy worms, a Twinkie, four Oreos, and six jelly beans. While the aforementioned "dinner" might appeal to children, parents know that more wholesome food is better suited to growing bodies.

The church offers a different kind of nourishment, a spiritual sustenance essential to Christian growth. This food is called the preaching of the Word, and no Christian can grow in grace and in the knowledge of the Lord Jesus Christ without it.

How do you avoid a "junk food" church? The church needs to teach sound doctrine. One man wrote, "Warning: Do not attend a church which prefers science to Scripture, reason to revelation, theories to truth, culture to conversion, benevolence to Blood, goodness to grace, sociability to spirituality, play to praise, programs to power, reformation to regeneration, speculation to salvation, jubilation to justification, feelings to faith, politics to precepts."[6]

When you attend a church, ask for a copy of their doctrinal statement. In this you will learn what the church believes right away and will avoid much trouble later. The statement of faith should contain these doctrines:

1. The Bible, in its original documents, is the inspired Word of God, the written record of His supernatural revelation of Himself to people, absolute in its authority, complete in its revelation, final in its content, and without any errors in its statements. (Psalm 89:34; John 10:35; 2 Timothy 3:16; Hebrews 6:18; 2 Peter 3:16)

2. There is one God, eternally existent, creator of heaven and earth. He is manifested in three persons—Father, Son, and Holy Spirit. (Genesis 1:2; Isaiah 7:14; 9:6; John 14:9; 1 Timothy 3:16; 1 John 4:7)

3. The Lord Jesus Christ is fully God, who took on flesh and dwelt on earth. He was sinlessly perfect and gave Himself as a substitutionary sacrifice by shedding his blood and dying on the cross. He then came back from the dead. This was to pay for all sins (past, present, and future) for all who believe. (Acts 13:38-41; 2 Corinthians 5:21; Hebrews 9:2-28; 1 Peter 2:24; 1 John 3:5)

4. To go to heaven, a person must understand that he cannot trust in his good works. He must believe that the shed blood of the Lord Jesus Christ makes the atoning payment for his sin. (John 3:16; Ephesians 2:8-9; Romans 5:8)

5. There will be a resurrection of the saved and of the lost—the saved unto eternal life and the lost unto eternal conscious punishment. These two resurrections are separated by at least 1,000 years. (Daniel 12:2; Matthew 25:41; 1 Thessalonians 4:13-18; Revelation 20:1-5)

6. Satan is a real person, the author of sin, and he and his angels shall be eternally punished. (Isaiah 14:12-15; Ezekiel 28:15, 17; Matthew 25:41; Revelation 20:10)

If you find that the church you wish to attend holds to these doctrines, then you are on the right track! You should understand what the church believes before you join. Then you can be reassured, knowing that what they will teach from the pulpit coincides with Scripture. It is a good idea to bring your Bible with you to church so that you can check what is said against the Scriptures.

YOUR PASTOR'S ROLE

I was the pastor of one Methodist church while I attended the University of Kentucky. Later on I was the pastor of five churches at one time in another part of the state. I preached at four on Sunday and then at another on Wednesday. Every week I preached at each church at least once.

In one of the churches in Columbus, Kentucky, the congregation told me a story about one of their former preachers. One Sunday the people had assembled, waiting for the service to begin. After about twenty minutes, they began to wonder what had happened to the pastor. Several members went to the parsonage and knocked on the door. To their surprise, the pastor answered it! He had overslept and was horrified. He ran back inside, got dressed, didn't shave, and walked out the door and into the pulpit to preach.

I know that has always been one of my own worst fears. I can't imagine how terrible it would be to oversleep, especially now that we broadcast on television and radio. However, the role of a pastor is public. He can't get away from that; nor should he want to. He realizes that from the moment God called him into the ministry, he was called into the public arena.

A pastor's job is important. I think sometimes believers today downplay the role of the pastor in the church. First Peter 5:2 says, "Feed the flock of God which is among you, taking the oversight thereof, not by constraint, but willingly; not for filthy lucre, but of a ready mind." The word for "feed" in the Greek is the same as the word for "shepherd." This verse could read, "Shepherd the flock of God." The word suggests instruction, protection, provision, supervision, and direction. This pretty well defines the pastor's role in the church. The shepherd is to feed, protect, and guide the flock.

The Holy Spirit has placed the pastor as the head of a church. This doesn't mean that the pastor is to be a dictator; there ought to be checks and balances in the church. Yet it is important to remember that the pastor should lead the church. The pastor is more than a caretaker. He is a humble servant called by God to lead the local body of believers.

Second Timothy 4:2 states, "Preach the word; be instant in season, out of season; reprove, rebuke, exhort with all longsuffering and doctrine." In the midst of my sometimes crazy schedule, my favorite job is to preach. I enjoy teaching the Word more than anything else. I want to be instant in season and out of season, continuing to give the Gospel and admonishing believers everywhere to grow in Christ. Have you perhaps not realized how essential your pastor's role is in leading your church? It could be that you have never seen from Scripture the importance of his ministry. Maybe you haven't supported your pastor in prayer or in other ways. It could be that at times you've even gossiped about him. Now you recognize and appreciate his position. You are now in the perfect position to really help your pastor.

HELPING YOUR PASTOR

Your pastor needs your help! The Bible is clear about how we should treat pastors. First Thessalonians 5:12 states, "And we beseech you, brethren, to know them which labour among you, and are over you in the Lord, and admonish you." You should respect your pastor. This doesn't mean you should worship him. Worship belongs only to the Lord Jesus. First Timothy 5:17 says, "Let the elders that rule well be counted worthy of double honour, especially they who labour in the word and doctrine." Also let's look at Hebrews 13:17: "Obey them that have the rule over you, and submit yourselves: for they watch for your souls, as they that must give account, that they may do it with joy, and not with grief: for that is unprofitable for you."

While this might sound like a doctrine pastors invented, the Bible is clear that those who labor in the Word are to be treated with respect. Too many times people take their pastor for granted. They fail to treat him in a biblical way and hurt the church, the body of Christ, by their careless attitude. As a result another preacher wants to give up, too discouraged to continue.

Do you have a picture of the ideal preacher in your mind? Does he need to deliver his sermon in a certain way, or does he need a pleasant personality for you to approve of him? The ideal that people have in their minds is too often far from what the Bible says is ideal. A pastor wrote the following: "The ideal preacher preaches only twenty minutes but thoroughly expounds the Word. He condemns sin but never hurts anyone's feelings. He works from 8 A.M. to 10 P.M. doing every type of work. He makes a hundred dollars a week, wears good clothes, buys good books regularly, has a nice family, drives a nice car, and gives fifty dollars a week back to the church. He stands ready to give to any good cause. He is twenty-six years old and has been preaching for thirty years. He has a burning desire to work with teenagers and to spend all his time on the old people. He makes fifteen calls a day on church members, spends all his time evangelizing the unchurched, and is never out of the office when you need him."

Don't be hard on your pastor. Keep in mind that as long as he meets biblical criteria, you should support him 100 percent. He needs your prayers. He needs your help. He needs your encouragement. He needs your respect. When you respond to him according to the Bible's admonition, you are not only going to be blessed by God, but you are setting a great example for those around you.

GETTING THE MOST OUT OF A SERMON

Not only is it important that we pray for our pastor, but it is very important that we are prepared to hear the Word taught from the pulpit. It is your responsibility, not just your pastor's, to make sure the seed comes into good soil. Here are some helps for getting the most out of a sermon.

1. *Don't plan any big events on Saturday night.* Instead plan for church the next day. If you have children, lay out their clothes and decide what you are going to wear. If you have to iron a shirt, do it then—not five minutes before you walk out the door on Sunday morning! Here's a great tradition to start. Buy something easy for breakfast on Sunday. Maybe a special coffee cake or doughnuts would simplify the morning rush because everyone could get their own breakfast.

2. *Give yourself plenty of time to get to church.* Get up early enough so that everyone isn't in a bad mood as they rush out the door.

3. *Bring your Bible, a notebook, and a pen to church.* Not only will this help you get more out of the sermon, but taking notes during the preaching can give you a reference that will help you throughout the week.

4. *During the opening hymns, pray that God will prepare your own heart to receive the Word*.

5. *Use the sermon throughout the week*. Don't just absorb all that knowledge without giving some of it away to others! Use the opportunities God gives you to apply what you have learned.

Ten years ago in the county I live in, there were many fields. Farmers planted corn and soybeans. But housing developments have replaced most of those fields. And now, of course, the farmers no longer drive their tractors and plant their crops. There is now no need for seed. Urban development is natural, but when our own lives no longer have a need for the seed of the Word, watch out! Our own hearts can be quickly turned into a development of worldliness, tangles of selfish weeds, and fields of wasted years.

To grow in our spiritual life, we must regularly receive the seed of the Word. Reading the Bible daily is an excellent start, but the local church is also important. There we will have the opportunity to hear the Word preached. There we will find other like-minded believers. There we will find strength and encouragement. There we will have opportunities to minister to others, and there we will have a chance to really grow.

If you haven't yet found a Bible-believing, Bible-teaching church, I encourage you to do so today. Attend a church for a few weeks before you draw a conclusion about it. At Quentin Road Bible Baptist Church, we ask people to take the Quentin Road Challenge—which is, try us for five weeks before you make a decision about our church. I've had many people tell me that attending for five weeks really gave them an understanding of our church and helped them make their decision to join.

If you aren't as involved as you should be in a good church, then decide right now to be more faithful. You will find the weekly strengthening invaluable in your spiritual journey.

4

READY, SET, PREPARE

The enjoyment of God is the only happiness with which our souls can be satisfied.

—JONATHAN EDWARDS

I SETTLED BACK IN THE narrow plane seat, trying to imagine that I was comfortable. As I gazed out the window at the clouds, I reflected on our exciting trip. A friend, Pastor Bob Vanden Bosch, and I, along with our wives, had traveled to Israel to set up a future trip for our churches. We stayed two days in Paris on our return, and now I was anxious to get home, see my children, then sixteen and seventeen years old, and of course, to see the people at Quentin Road.

Plane hours feel a lot longer than regular hours! I remember studying for an upcoming sermon for a while, but then I realized I was starting to feel sick. I glanced at my wife, Linda, and noticed that she wasn't her normal perky self.

"Are you okay, honey?" I asked.

"No," she said. "I don't know what's wrong, but I feel terrible."

Pastor Vanden Bosch and Barb sat in the row ahead of us. He turned around. "We both feel sick too. Do you think it's something we ate in Paris?" he asked.

None of us knew for sure. Later we learned that we should have stuck to bottled water during our stay, but no one had told us that while we were there. Now I am careful about the water I drink in other countries, and I have never become that sick again (thank the Lord!). When we landed, we grabbed our luggage and made it home.

I greeted the kids, and they reminded us that the next day was the beginning of spring break. They had planned a rather unusual trip. They were driving to Kentucky to visit the places I had lived as a boy. They also planned to visit Jo and Bill Norris, the dear couple whose prayers helped lead me into the ministry. They were excited about their nostalgic tour. Linda and I hugged them good-bye.

I wasn't prepared for Julie's phone call the next day at about three in the afternoon. "Jim fell a short distance, and his foot twisted under him. I think his ankle is broken in several places." They had already traveled to a local hospital where it was determined that the hospital simply didn't have the resources to fix the ankle. Now at another hospital, Jim lay on a gurney, awaiting surgery.

An hour passed as Linda and I, still sick from our trip, rallied to pack. Julie called me again. She said that Jim was in terrible pain, still waiting in the hallway of the hospital. I asked her why he wasn't in surgery, and she said she'd just learned of a nursing home fire in the area. All the residents had been rushed to the hospital, causing near panic as nurses and doctors tried to get everyone situated.

I asked Julie to get a nurse on the phone. I remember feeling helpless—not knowing the extent of Jim's injury. The nurse assured me that they would get him into surgery as soon as possible, and in about ten minutes Julie called us back to say that Jim had been wheeled into the operating room. Miraculously, one of the top orthopedic doctors in the country happened to be in that hospital, and he operated on the ankle. In spite of three pins and steel holding his ankle together, Jim played basketball for his high school team the next school year!

I have often found that the hardship of crisis isn't the crisis itself. Rather it is waiting for the Lord's help. While I trusted the Lord and knew He would take care of Jim, I still was concerned as I waited to hear that he was okay. I felt in limbo. There was nothing I could do to help my own son.

Do you sometimes feel that your own Christian life is in limbo? That somehow you are waiting for God to show you what to do or where to go? Perhaps your friends and family don't understand why it is so important for you to serve the Lord. Maybe you feel misunderstood . . . and, yes, helpless, even lonely.

H. H. Staton in his book *A Guide to the Parables of Jesus* tells about a time when he was on an ocean liner headed to the Middle East:

> Nine hundred miles out to sea a sail was sighted on the horizon. As the liner drew closer, the passengers saw that the boat—a small sloop flying a Turkish flag—had run up a distress signal and other flags asking for its position at sea. Through a faulty chronometer the small vessel was lost. For nearly an hour the liner circled the little boat, giving its crew the correct latitude and longitude. Naturally, there was a great deal of interest in all the proceedings among the passengers on the liner. A boy of about twelve stood on the deck and watched all that was taking place. He remarked aloud to himself, "It's a big ocean to be lost in."

This world is a big place to feel lost in, and even believers can feel lost in a world of confused theology and skewed doctrine. Yet when we apply ourselves to the study of the Word of God, we don't have to be "lost" at all. Instead, spiritual success is right around the corner, just a sextant shot away. The observance of Jesus' helpful parable principles will take us out of limbo and move us into action!

PARABLE PRINCIPLE #4—Doctrine is essential to Christian growth.

Let's examine Mark 4:2: "And he taught them many things by parables, and said unto them in his doctrine . . ." I have heard some Christians remark that Jesus is not interested in doctrine. They feel that this aspect of Christianity is unimportant. Instead, we should fellowship with anyone who names the name of Jesus. It is dangerous to disregard doctrine, for it is upon doctrine that our Christian lives rest. I remember hearing Jim Bakker before his prison term say that doctrine doesn't matter, and he wasn't going to listen to it. I believe he has since changed his mind.

Don't be afraid of the word *doctrine*. It simply means instruction. If we are not concerned about doctrine, we are rejecting teaching. If there is anything worth fighting for, it is the teachings of Christ. Everything He uttered was for our good and instruction (Romans 15:4).

For every believer there are passages in Scripture that are difficult to understand. However, we have God's promise to enlighten our minds if we diligently search the meaning out. Every day that you walk with God, He will show you more and more things about Himself. You will learn more doctrine, and as you learn it, you will grow in your relationship with Christ. Simply put, doctrine solidifies your faith.

I remember marking imaginary X's on the walls of the churches I attended as a child. My Methodist preacher father served churches all over Kentucky as I was growing up, usually staying in any one town about four years. Each Sunday I mentally marked off another X, thinking that when the wall filled up with X's, I would never have to go to church again.

I grew up around Asbury College, at the time considered one of the most fundamental Methodist colleges. I saw people who read their Bibles, and I always wondered, "How can they read that stuff? It seems so boring to me."

Yet when I trusted Christ, one of my first desires was to study the Bible! The verses made sense to me! I wanted to learn more! Whereas I had considered the Bible a dull book without meaning, now I saw it as a living book full of truths I wanted to learn.

Even now there are passages of Scripture that bring fresh joy. I have been a pastor for thirty years, preaching over six thousand different sermons. The tapes of these sermons provide assistance to our researchers and print ministry even now. However, the more I learn, the more I desire to study. God's Word creates a hunger for more spiritual food.

And so it can be for you. No matter where you are in your Christian walk, there are always exciting truths in Scripture waiting to be unearthed, the way treasure hunters discover lost treasure. When you study the Bible, doctrine will become part of your very lifeblood.

Proverbs 2:3-5 tells us, "Yea, if thou criest after knowledge, and liftest up thy voice for understanding; if thou seekest her as silver, and searchest for her as for hid treasures; then shalt thou understand the fear of the LORD, and find the knowledge of God."

Perhaps your children have participated in a treasure hunt at a birthday party or other event. Someone writes down clues that lead to a treasure. Each hint brings the children one step closer to their prize. It is the same way with the Word of God. Each time we read a portion of it, we are brought a stride closer in our relationship with the Lord. Therefore, we need to continue to make the study of His Word a priority in our daily schedule. We must learn doctrine for a rich and deep spiritual life.

PUZZLE SOLVER

The moment you trusted Christ as your Savior, God gave you His very own Scripture discerner, the puzzle solver who will help you understand Scripture. You might be surprised to hear that you already possess the tools to understand the Bible. Why did Scripture suddenly make more sense to me once I was saved? I had the ultimate Puzzle Solver, the Holy Spirit. So it is for you. Now that you know Christ as your Savior, the Holy Spirit promises to guide you into all truth (John 16:13). We will study more about the Holy Spirit in future chapters, but I want you to understand now that the Holy Spirit will help you to understand the Bible. Better than any Scripture CD-ROM, the Holy Spirit will guide you in your study of doctrine and the parable principles—if you let Him.

Do you feel a bit stagnant right now? Then commit yourself to learning doctrine! Resolve to understand the truths of God's Word. When you are at your workplace, take a few minutes during your break to study the Bible. Listen to the Bible on tape while driving to work. Listen to great preaching. Attend a Bible-believing and Bible-teaching church every time the doors are open. When you learn doctrine, your excitement will be renewed, and you'll find yourself bursting to share with others what you're learning.

PARABLE PRINCIPLE #5—Other people may not value your desire to grow in Christ.

When I was thirteen years old, I enjoyed working at my brother-in-law's farm in Oklahoma. I remember those hot summers as some of the best times in my life. I felt privileged to drive a tractor and make a dollar an hour (top money in those days!). I drove the tractor the first twelve hours of the day, and my brother-in-law drove it the other twelve hours. We never shut it off. We fueled the tractor in the field so we would never have to stop harvesting. I felt lonely out there at times, but knowing that my brother-in-law trusted me to do such an important job kept me going.

In the Parable of the Sower, Jesus entrusted His disciples with great truths about the Christian life. Just as I felt privileged to participate in farm work, so the disciples felt privileged that Jesus had entrusted them with this knowledge of spiritual growth.

"Hearken; Behold, there went out a sower to sow" (Mark 4:3). This verse doesn't say, "Many sowers went out to sow." Rather only one sower is mentioned. I can picture him standing in his field, doing relentless physical toil all day every day without any thought of an immediate reward. He knew his family would enjoy his labor at the end of the harvest, but I'm sure there were times when he wondered why he continued to sow seeds.

Have you also found out that the Christian life can sometimes be lonely? You may feel alone as I did all those days on that tractor in Oklahoma. Why is the path toward spiritual development at times lonely? The Bible says that broad is the way that leads to destruction and narrow is the way that leads to eternal life (Matthew 7:13-14). This verse doesn't mean that the path toward heaven is narrow because it is hard to stay on it. Rather it is narrow because God has chosen to save people by only one means, Christ Himself, rather than through a multitude of religions.

Only two kinds of people exist in the world today—saved and unsaved. The Bible tells us that the majority of people don't know Christ. While this makes it our job to tell others about Christ (we will cover how to win your friends and family to Christ in further chapters), it also brings home the truth that often in your Christian experience you will have friends and perhaps even family who do not understand your desire to become more Christlike. Those who are not believers simply will not understand the believer's desire to grow in his or her spiritual walk.

Second Corinthians 4:4 enlightens us: "In whom the god of this world hath blinded the minds of them which believe not, lest the light of the glorious gospel of Christ, who is the image of God, should shine unto them." Don't be surprised when an associate makes fun of your beliefs. Understand that the person is only reacting that way because he or she may be depending on works for salvation. Pray daily for that person and go out of your way to be kind to him or her. Don't become discouraged when your colleagues don't hold the same views about eternal life. Instead, pray for opportunities to witness further to them. But you need to realize that those who don't know Christ won't understand your fervor.

The day Andrea trusted Christ was the happiest day of her life. A college friend took the time to explain the plan of salvation to her. The following morning Andrea drove four hours to spend some time with her family over the weekend. Thrilled with her decision, Andrea lost no time in telling her family members that she was "saved."

"Saved?" Andrea's brother Bob snorted. "I didn't know you were lost."

"I mean that I don't have to worry about going to hell anymore. I'm saved from my sin," Andrea said.

"Andrea, please!" Bob begged. "I'm sick of this stuff. I'm sure you'll get over this religious kick in time."

To say that Andrea felt hurt would be an understatement. She didn't understand why her family didn't want to hear about her Lord. She felt discouraged, but her friend from college explained that it would take time for her family to see the difference in Andrea. She involved herself in a church near her college campus. Slowly the family's attitude changed. While many of her family still are unsaved, a year or so later Andrea experienced the joy of leading her brother Bob to Christ.

Are you one of the few Christians in your workplace? Do others in your family consider your beliefs a bit strange? Take a moment to understand that just as the sower could have felt alone in his sowing, so the believer will sometimes feel lonely and even rejected by others in his or her walk with Christ.

The sower could also be compared to the preacher of a local church. He can feel lonely at times as he patiently sows the Word of God. But the man who sows by himself often blesses many. Thousands reap what was sown by one alone.

Take a moment to pray this prayer: "Lord, thank You for giving me a desire to live for You, but help me to recognize that those around me may not understand why living for You is so important to me. Help me to be patient with my friends and family and not give up offering them the Gospel."

PARABLE PRINCIPLE #6—Ready, set, prepare.

Land was at a premium in the days of Jesus, just as it is today. Anyone who has traveled to Israel knows that there is more rocky soil than fertile soil. On a recent trip there, a farmer who owns thousands of acres in the United States told me how astounded he was that there was so little good soil in Israel. He was surprised at how resourceful the people are at utilizing the land they do have. Modern technology has made the country quite a fertile place.

I am not a farmer or even a gardener. I enjoyed planting seeds when I was a child, but I've spent little time really working the soil. Yet I do know one thing—soil has to be prepared in order to receive the seed in the first place. Imagine planting without plows! What if people randomly dumped seeds on top of rock-hard soil, expecting it to grow? I think every person would agree—it is necessary for the land to be prepared.

Guess what? The same is true in your Christian life. The single best indicator that the seed will grow properly is preparation of the soil ahead of time. The field needs good, soft dirt that will readily receive the seed and allow it to produce.

This is how Parable Principle #6 can completely change a ho-hum Christian life. Prepare your own heart *before* you receive the Word of God. Take time to pray, "Lord, I want to receive Your Word and what it has to say. Turn over the caked earth of my own heart and make it soft and ready to receive Your wisdom. I want to understand Your words and apply them to my life."

Stand back and watch God work. Now when you read a portion of Scripture or listen to sound preaching, the Holy Spirit will powerfully affect your life. You will see habits and situations in your own life that need to change. And when you make the changes, you will see progress in your walk with the Lord—no doubt about it.

Commentator John Henry Burns explains, "There is failure in a man's life through an unprepared condition of the soil. Secular traffic hardens all the better feelings of the heart. A man's soul, which should be penetrable, plastic, accessible to the light and love from heaven, becomes callous, repellent, indurated—until it has reached the final stage—'past feeling.' In the proper condition of the mind, it is exquisitely suited to the reception of living seed; it is the seeds' home and rest."[1]

Sarah and Michael have attended First Baptist for about a year. Coming from another denominational background, they were unprepared at first for the differences at their new church. The preaching was the biggest contrast. Their first church was theologically liberal, and the preacher never preached strongly. This never bothered them before they got saved, but now they realized they needed to learn more about the Word of God. So when a friend invited them to try her church, they didn't hesitate.

The preacher at First Baptist encouraged everyone to bring a Bible to church, and when Michael asked Sarah where their Bible was, Sarah was embarrassed to admit that she didn't know. She hadn't looked at their Bible since the day they were married and had recorded that important date on the front page. After much searching, Sarah finally found the Bible under a stack of old *National Geographic* magazines.

The first week they brought their Bible to church, they listened as the preacher asked the congregation to turn to the book of Ecclesiastes. Sarah opened the Bible and thumbed through the strange names, attempting to find Ecclesiastes. Finally she gave up and handed the book to Michael. He flipped through the book ten times in his attempt to find it. Finally, suppressing a grin at their predicament, Sarah opened the book to the index. Running her finger down the book titles, she finally found it. She shot a triumphant glance at her husband as she noted the page number and turned the pages until she reached the correct one. Then the preacher announced that he wanted everyone to turn to Leviticus. Michael and Sarah almost groaned out loud! Leviticus! They had just found Ecclesiastes!

If you could see Michael and Sarah in their pew at First Baptist now, you would never know that at one time they hardly knew where their Bible was, much less where any of the books in the Bible were located. They flip through the pages like pros, helping each other as they follow the pastor's message.

Michael and Sarah have learned one of the secrets of growth. They didn't allow their own embarrassment to keep them from trying to learn the Word of God. They took time to prepare the soil of their hearts and to learn where each of the books was located. Even though it was difficult at first, their effort resulted in a better opportunity for growth during the sermon. Never underestimate the importance of preparing yourself for growth.

PARABLE PRINCIPLE #7—Give it time.

When the sower sowed seeds, he had something already programmed into his brain that not many of us modern-day Americans understand! There is a period of time between planting and harvesting. Hard work that the sower put into the soil would eventually pay off in the survival of his family. That fact kept him going in spite of the heat, rain, and daily hardships of his life.

Do you sometimes feel like an impatient sower? No matter how many verses you memorize or how much you pray, there doesn't seem to be fruit for your labor. You want instant results. You don't want to wait for spiritual growth. Some people view their Christian lives the way they see a box of instant mashed potatoes—add hot water and go! But the Christian life starts with the seed of the potato. It takes time for the seed to properly germinate and grow to fruition. Just as it was the sower's work to remain faithful to his task of sowing, so it is the Christian's work to remain faithful in the things that will help him or her develop spiritually. In other words, it is the believer's job to remain faithful; it is God's job to bring the harvest.

I know when I first trusted Christ, I felt impatient for my own spiritual growth. I wanted to do all the things that I saw spiritual leaders around me doing. As I stuck with it, I saw God working in my life. I got excited as I began to understand that He desired to use me to further His kingdom. The same can be true for you regardless of the stage of your spiritual development.

Three-year-old Josh attended our preschool many years ago. In those days we provided for each class a large plot in which to cultivate flowers and vegetables. Josh loved the feel of the dirt. He enjoyed helping the teacher dig a hole to plant his seeds. He pushed the dirt back over the top of the seeds and ran to get a watering can. The next day when his class visited the garden, he ran to their plot. "Teacher," he whined, "how come I don't have any flowers yet?"

The teacher tried to explain to Josh that it took time for the seeds to grow, but when she wasn't looking, Josh dug a hole and checked each of the seeds.

"Not growing yet," he said wistfully.

Do you feel like Josh when it comes to your Christian life? You're not alone. Every believer wishes for instant results. All of us are like children sometimes, eager to see results before sufficient time has passed. Know that just as the child needs to wait for the plant to grow, so we need to wait for God's harvest. Don't be discouraged as you wait. Instead, continue to sow the seed of the Word of God. He has guaranteed us the harvest, but this harvest is up to Him, not us. First Corinthians 3:6-7 says, "I have planted, Apollos watered; but God gave the increase. So then neither is he that planteth any thing, neither he that watereth; but God that giveth the increase."

Don't give up, Christian! God will produce wonderful results in your life, but faithfulness is the key. Your faithfulness will be met, matched, and exceeded by the faithfulness of our great God!

PARABLE PRINCIPLE #8—You will reap what you sow.

This principle from the first verses in Mark 4 might seem basic, but it still needs to be covered. I have bought Jericho oranges from my local grocery store. I've enjoyed beautiful bouquets of flowers from the Jordan Valley, sold not five minutes away from my home. Picture the farmer with a seed bag over his shoulder, walking (no John Deere tractors in those days) in the fields sowing his precious seeds. These seeds probably had been taken from last year's crops and carefully stored so that no mildew or mold would ruin them. As the means of the farmer's livelihood, these seeds were precious to him. But the day would come when he would begin to put the seeds into the prepared ground. Whatever he planted, he expected to see grow. In other words, if he planted eggplant, he didn't expect to reap eggs! So it is in our lives. Get ready for Parable Principle #8—You will reap what you sow.

Sounds simple, doesn't it? Actually on paper all of us would agree that when a farmer plants corn, he reaps a harvest of corn. If a gardener plants wildflower seeds, then one day she is going to see attractive wildflowers dotting her yard.

Lindsey, a woman in my congregation, called a maid service and arranged to have someone come and clean her home. The year before, following the trend of planting wildflowers and prairie grass in parts of her yard, she had sowed some packages of seeds, waiting expectantly for the beautiful flowers. One day in late May (yes, Chicago winters keep most flowers from blooming before then) she looked out her window and to her delight saw lovely purple and gold wildflowers.

Since it was the first year for these flowers, only a few bloomed. Early one morning when the maid showed up to clean her home, Lindsey got into her car to go to work. The service had called the day before and explained that the maid had only been in the United States for a short time and understood little English. However, they were confident that she would do a terrific job.

Lindsey got home after the maid had left, and she realized that the service was right. The maid had done a great job. The house was sparkling, the floors were washed, the windows shone. Everything looked absolutely perfect. Lindsey was thrilled until she entered her kitchen. Stuck in a vase on the dining room table stood her few wildflowers from the backyard.

The next week the same thing happened and the next and the next. On top of all this, Lindsey has found that she is allergic to these particular wildflowers. Now she dreads entering her home after the maid comes. Because of the language barrier, Lindsey can't explain to the maid that while she loves the job she is doing, she would rather the woman left the flowers in the yard.

Lindsey definitely learned the principle of sowing and reaping from all this. She sowed, and the maid reaped! Yet Jesus made an important point in this eighth parable principle. You may think that the decisions you make every day aren't really that important. However, they are vital.

What kinds of seeds are you sowing today? Are you sowing good seeds? Just what are good seeds? Think about the habits you have in your everyday life. Are they all geared toward attaining your goal of Christian growth and development? You might be thinking, *How could ordinary things such as brushing my teeth or exercising be a help to my Christian life?*

Consider the example of John, a man who exercises every day. If he isn't running around the local track, he lifts weights at the YMCA. During this time he also does something very important—he prays while he exercises. That's right. Prayer and sweat work together as he nurtures his own walk with the Lord. John understands that he needs to focus his energy on the Lord, and he found an easy way to do this in the midst of his daily activities. John is sowing good seeds in his life, and he is sure to reap a bountiful harvest.

We are going to study some of the things that will really impact our Christian lives and bring us on to maturity in our Savior. We are going to look at good seeds and how to nurture them through every day habits.

When I was a boy working in the Oklahoma fields, I couldn't wait to hear what kind of wheat crop was harvested. Our goal was to get thirty bushels per acre, and I wanted to see what the yield was going to be. I understand now that farmers get a lot more than thirty bushels per acre, but at the time our goal was the magic thirty. When the harvest comes in a believer's life, he feels the same excitement the diligent farmer feels when he realizes that all his effort was worth something.

Psalm 126:5-6 says, "They that sow in tears shall reap in joy. He that goeth forth and weepeth, bearing precious seed, shall doubtless come again with rejoicing, bringing his sheaves with him." Second Corinthians 9:6 adds, "But this I say, He which soweth sparingly shall reap also sparingly; and he which soweth bountifully shall reap also bountifully."

There once was a beggar who would sit every day in the street and beg for rice. As people passed, they would drop a kernel or two into his bowl. Each day he received just enough to survive.

One day the beggar was sitting with his little collection of rice when a maharajah walked past. The beggar was sure that the maharajah would be generous and fill his bowl full of rice.

The maharajah came to the beggar and said, "I want what you have in your bowl."

The beggar thought, *I have nothing, and this rich man wants me to give him the only rice I have.*

The beggar took one kernel of rice from the bowl and threw it at the wealthy man in disgust. The maharajah said, "I want more."

The beggar took one more kernel of rice and threw it at the maharajah. Again the maharajah said, "I want more."

Again the beggar threw him another kernel. The maharajah then took out of his pocket three gold coins. He gave the beggar a gold coin for every kernel of rice given to him. As the maharajah returned to his carriage he thought, *Could not this man have spared more?*

Many times we act like that beggar. We cling to our own ways instead of trying God's way. We grasp our own ideas instead of studying Scripture to understand His ideas. And as a result, we fail to experience the blessing of growth in our lives. Remember, the more we surrender to the Lord, the more spiritual blessings He showers upon us

CRUNCH TIME

Once when Michigan State was playing UCLA in football, the score was tied at fourteen with only seconds to play. Duffy Daugherty, Michigan State's coach, sent in place-kicker Dave Kaiser, who booted a field goal that won the game. When the kicker returned to the bench, Daugherty said, "Nice going, but you didn't watch the ball after you kicked it."

"That's right, Coach," Kaiser replied. "I was watching the referee instead to see how he'd signal it. I forgot my contact lenses, and I couldn't see the goal posts."[2]

Kaiser was fortunate in making the crucial points, especially since he forgot to wear his contacts! He knew that the referee had the ultimate authority about whether his kick was good or not. Hosea

10:12 states, "Sow to yourselves in righteousness, reap in mercy; break up your fallow ground: for it is time to seek the LORD, till he come and rain righteousness upon you." Friend, seek the Lord! He is the referee! He wants you to succeed. The beauty of His love is that when we seek Him, He helps us triumph.

The Word of God is powerful when nurtured in our hearts. If it is unable to penetrate deeply, your life will stagnate. One commentator says, "These instructions are then, like the seed, received into the understanding, will, and affections; and after a while, having had their due operation there, bring forth, in various degrees, the acceptable fruits of love and obedience."[3]

Take this sowing and reaping principle to heart. Pray that you will allow only good seed to be planted in the garden of your life. Resist the bad seeds so that when it comes time for harvest, you will have matured in your Christian life, walking ever closer to your Savior.

TOGETHER WITH GOD

The Christian life is a partnership. Famous missionary Hudson Taylor said, "I used to ask God to come and help me. I realized how wrong that was, and now I ask, 'God, may I come and help You? May You do Your work through me.'" I saw a bumper sticker that said, "If God is your copilot, change seats!"

God's action is another part of the sowing and reaping principle. God does the miraculous part, but we must prepare ourselves first. When we sow the right kind of seeds, the right kind of fruit is produced. This process takes time, and sometimes the weeding will hurt. The seed of the Word of God will reach into our lives like a laser beam, highlighting the areas that need changing. Sometimes you are going to have to do something that is good for you spiritually, even though you may not like it.

My five-year-old grandson Jamie likes a lot of foods that some kids don't, but sometimes he comes across something he doesn't like. The other day it was mussels. They were an item on a delicious buffet at a Japanese restaurant. When I put some on his plate, he gave me a look of disgust. I asked him if he had ever tried this dish, and he said no. I encouraged him to taste it. I told him, "Jamie, if you eat mussels, then maybe you will get muscles!" (I know it's corny, but it worked!) Jamie is an athletic boy, and one of his desires is to have strong muscles. So he popped the meat into his mouth. I was surprised when he said he liked it. Now mussels are one of his favorite foods! The waitresses looked surprised. They must not see too many children eat mussels.

When we feed on the Word of God, we develop strong spiritual muscles that will help us to continue serving the Lord even when hardships and trials come. First Peter 2:2-3 says, "As newborn babes, desire the sincere milk of the word, that ye may grow thereby: If so be ye have tasted that the Lord is gracious."

It used to be said that strength training was only for the young, that people middle-aged and older couldn't really benefit from lifting weights. Now numerous studies indicate that strength training helps no matter what age a person is. It is the same way in the Christian life. No matter where you are, whether you've been saved for six days, six years, or even sixty years, now is the time to develop spiritual muscle. It's never too late to begin, and you will love the results.

REV UP FOR REVIEW

Look again at the parable principles we've studied so far.

Parable Principle #1—Jesus taught in parables so that Christians could apply truth in practical ways to their lives.

Parable Principle #2—Devote time every day to Bible reading.

Parable Principle #3—Make it a habit to attend a Bible-believing, Bible-teaching church.

Parable Principle #4—Doctrine is essential to Christian growth.

Parable Principle #5—Other people may not value your desire to grow in Christ.

Parable Principle #6—Ready, set, prepare.

Parable Principle #7—Give it time.

Parable Principle #8—You will reap what you sow.

Consider for a moment the great flexibility of Jesus. He didn't get stuck in a rut with His ministry. His goal was to make His teaching understandable to all who listened. As we know more about the actual parables Jesus taught, I think we are going to understand more about the kind of teacher He really was. This understanding will, in turn, affect how we minister to others.

Then of course we need to recognize that doctrine is essential to spiritual development. Unless we know doctrine, we will not have the capability of growth. We will lack the necessary tools, the essential elements, and the very ingredients of the spiritual life.

Remember that at times you are going to feel lonely as you serve Christ, but He has said He will never leave you nor forsake you. There are definitely going to be times when you feel forsaken by other people. When you think about the lonely sower, consider his joy when he sees the fruit of his labor. And so it will be with you. Don't forget to give yourself time to grow. Great Christians aren't made overnight. There is no secret formula that brings instant maturity.

Now mull over the principle of sowing and reaping as it applies to your life. Are you aware that every action you take affects your spiritual life? Perhaps you need to do some soul-searching and look at the things that could possibly be hindering your spiritual growth. Weed these things out. Do this with diligence. It is important that you sow the seeds of Bible study and prayer into your life. Sow habits that will produce fruit for all eternity.

The most important principle of this study so far is to prepare yourself for spiritual growth. Look at your own heart. Do you pray constantly that God will break up the soil of your own life in order for His will to be accomplished? Are you taking the necessary steps toward preparing for spiritual growth? If you are, watch out! You will experience remarkable progress in your Christian life—growth that will astound you and make you humbly grateful to the Lord. It is His hand that is guiding you, keeping you, and helping you go forward, with your life a testimony for Him.

5

SPIRITUAL RX

A Christian should be a striking likeness to Jesus Christ.

C. H. SPURGEON

MARK PRAYED FOR AN opportunity to speak to one of his fellow engineers about Christ. However, it seemed that the chance never came. One day Mark decided to take Fred out for lunch, and he brought the conversation to spiritual matters.

Fred listened for a little while but soon interjected his own comments. He asked far-out questions, effectively sidetracking Mark. When it was time to go back to work, Fred thanked Mark for the lunch but said, "Listen, Mark, this religious stuff is okay for you, but it isn't my cup of tea. I would appreciate it if you didn't talk to me about it anymore."

Mark felt disappointed, but he honored Fred's wishes. Later Mark shared with me his conversation with Fred. Because of my study in the parable of the sower, I saw that Mark faced one of the situations Jesus had already addressed. When the seed of the Word is sown, some of it falls on the sides of the path, the caked-down part. The hardness of the earth keeps the seed from entering the ground, and Satan often snatches the Word away, keeping that person from trusting Christ.

I encouraged Mark to continue to pray for more witnessing opportunities and not to be discouraged. Just as the sower's job is to sow the seed, so that is every Christian's job. Some seed will fall by the wayside; there is no way to avoid this. But if we diligently persevere, we can be assured that the precious seed will find nurturing soil.

PARABLE PRINCIPLE #9—When you hear the Word, obey it.

Mark 4:4 says, "And it came to pass, as he sowed, some fell by the wayside, and the fowls of the air came and devoured it up." The soil by the wayside was packed from traffic over many years. No plow softened that soil and prepared it for the sown seed. Can our own hearts become like that of the wayside? You better believe it. Remember, it is up to the hearer to make sure the Word penetrates into his or her life. The hearer is Fred. The hearer is a million other people who have heard the Scriptures presented. If they are saved, then they have an obligation to allow the Word to change their way of life. If they are unsaved, the Word has to transform their thinking, making them recognize that it is only Jesus' blood that will get them to heaven.

The hearer is you. When you hear the Word, do you allow it to penetrate deeply into your heart? Great preaching is wonderful, but even more important is eloquent hearing. It isn't the quality of the speaker, the quality of the sower, that determines the outcome. Rather it is the quality of the soil, and that quality is up to you.

I remember a fellow preacher sharing with me about this particular preacher who gave the most boring sermon he had ever heard. Yet at the end of the service, five people trusted Christ as their Savior. This preacher, though perhaps not as interesting as other speakers, still brought the salvation message forth in such a way that the greatest work on heaven and earth was done—souls were won to Christ.

Joseph Exell said, "It is well that our students should be instructed how to preach, but it is equally important that the people should be taught how to hear; for if it be true, as is sometimes cynically said, that good preaching is one of the lost arts, it is to be feared that good hearing has largely disappeared and wherever the fault may have begun, the two act and re-act on each other."[1]

What is the condition of your soil? Do you sit in church and wish the sermon would end so that you can go about your daily business? Beware, dear friend. Watch out for the symptoms of Wayside Hearers' Disorder.

WAYSIDE HEARERS' DISORDER

Years ago I had a neighbor who labored on his yard early every morning. There was no comparison between the amount of time we each spent on our yards. One day I saw that my neighbor's yard looked strange. Rings of dead grass besieged the entire lawn. The rings were small but numerous, and each day they got bigger. It was a disease of some sort, and my neighbor valiantly fought it, using every technique available. The "waysides," or the rings in his lawn, were diseased, and no grass grew in those areas.

Is your spiritual life like my neighbor's unhealthy lawn? Numerous advertisements on TV and radio promote combinations of vitamins and minerals that promise good health, strong bones, improved memory retention, and more. Here's your Spiritual Rx. These three "vitamins" (no minimum dosage) guarantee freedom from Wayside Hearers' Disorder.

Focus Factor Multivitamin

This capsule combines the vitamins of superior hearing with the minerals of excellent attention. It will help the hearer focus anytime the Word is taught. When taken regularly, the hearer will stir himself up to listen. He will train his mind to follow the preacher as he preaches. He will think of hearing the Word as an opportunity to learn more about Christ.[2]

Reflective Supplement

What the good hearer hears, he keeps. In other words, the hearer rigorously reflects on the message from the preacher. He writes the truths down and meditates on them. Every time of hearing the Word should be followed by a time of meditation. Reflect on what you have heard. Contemplate its meaning.

Application Nutritive Formula

A good hearer is not just a hearer of the Word; he is also a doer (James 1:25). The good hearer acts upon what he hears and ably applies it to the situations he faces daily. When regular doses of application are used in the believer's life, he will see spiritual growth.

Take the time to focus, reflect, and then apply the teaching of the Word to your life. Maybe you have succumbed to Wayside Hearers' Disorder. Go for the cure! When you hear the Word of God preached or you study the Bible, focus! Write down what you have learned so that you can then reflect on it throughout the week. Ask God to show you situations where you can use the knowledge you have learned and then apply that understanding. This three-step course of action will give you fresh spiritual energy.

Spiritual Battle

Parable Principle #10—You engage in spiritual warfare when you share the Gospel with others.

Mark 4:15 says, "And these are they by the wayside, where the word is sown; but when they have heard, Satan cometh immediately, and taketh away the word that was sown in their hearts."

Mark may not have realized it, but when he decided to witness to Fred, he embarked on a spiritual battle! Satan doesn't want people to listen to the Gospel, and he is doing all he can to stop people from trusting Christ alone for salvation. These Wayside Hearers hate doctrine and so find fault with the teachers. When the Bible is opened to them, they trample it underfoot.[3] They distance themselves from instruction in the Word, not only by stamping on it themselves but by talking disparagingly about the Word to other unsaved people. How does Satan hinder the precious seed of the Word? In two ways.

Interruptions

Satan desires to keep people from hearing the Word. He fills the world with commonplace interruptions and entertaining diversions to keep people from realizing their need for salvation. Busyness can really prevent people from thinking about the Lord. Many sports events are scheduled for Sundays. Many people don't consider church to be an option anymore; they are so tired from their myriad to-do lists.

Forgetfulness

When the unsaved man or woman does hear the Word, Satan does his best to make sure the person doesn't remember it. The famed preacher D. L. Moody told of an architect in Chicago who had attended church for many years but had never really heard a sermon in all that time. When the minister gave the text and began to preach, he would settle himself in the pew and work out the plans of his current project. He prepared most of his plans for the two companies he worked for during the service. One day the architect finally heard the Word as it was taught, and the scales of unbelief fell from his eyes. Moody went on to say that he has often preached to people and was amazed to find that they could hardly repeat one word of the sermon.[4]

The Never-Fail Tools

According to legend Satan once had a garage sale. Displayed in little groups were all of his bright, shiny trinkets. On the right side were tools that make it easy to tear others down for use as stepping-stones. On the left were some dual-purpose lenses for magnifying one's own importance. If you looked through them the other way, you could also use them to belittle others.

Against the wall was the usual assortment of gardening implements guaranteed to help your pride grow by leaps and bounds—the rake of scorn, the shovel of jealousy to dig a pit for your neighbor, the wheelbarrow of gossip and backbiting, of selfishness and apathy. All of these were pleasing to the eye and came complete with fabulous promises and guarantees. Prices were steep, but not to worry—free credit was extended to one and all.

"Take it home, use it, and you won't have to pay until later," old Satan cried as he hawked his wares. As one visitor browsed, he noticed two well-worn nondescript tools standing in one corner. He found it curious that these two tools had higher prices than anything else. When he asked why, Satan just laughed and said, "Well, that's because I use them so much. If they weren't so plain-looking, people might see them for what they are." Satan pointed to the two tools saying, "You see, that one is doubt and that one is discouragement—those will work when nothing else will."

Satan uses all of these tools to keep the eyes of the unsaved blinded to the truth of Scripture. Make no mistake, Satan is real. He isn't parading around in a red suit with horns. Second Corinthians 11:14 says, "And no marvel; for Satan himself is transformed into an angel of light." One writer said, "Satan's walk is a siege that goes about the fort to find the weakest soul to battle. The motive, cause, and main intention of his journey is to win man."[5]

Judas is an example of a person in whom the Word of God never took root. He stayed with Christ for three years. Much precious seed was given to Judas during that time from the Master Sower Himself. Yet Judas never accepted the Lord as his Savior. In John 17:12 Jesus calls Judas "the son of perdition." "While I was with them in the world, I kept them in thy name: those that thou gavest me I have kept, and none of them is lost, but the son of perdition; that the scripture might be fulfilled."

Judas never trusted Christ, though he had ample opportunity to do so. This disciple was a true Wayside Hearer. He allowed Satan to snatch away the Word, making it of no effect in his life. Satan used Judas right to the end when he betrayed the Lord. Remember, Satan's goal is always to destroy.

In Your Face

Satan's work isn't limited to trying to keep the unbeliever from hearing and receiving the Gospel. He also hinders believers. Paul wrote in 1 Thessalonians 2:18, "Wherefore we would have come unto you, even I Paul, once and again; but Satan hindered us." Paul understood that Satan was alive and well, and Satan's goal was to hinder him from doing work for Christ. Every believer should grasp this startling truth.

But there is good news! The devil can be resisted! We have the promise of Scripture on that. Know that he will try to wreak havoc in your witnessing opportunities. He wants to be in your way and in your face! Yet James 4:7 says, "Submit yourselves therefore to God. Resist the devil, and he will flee from you." How do you resist him?

When doubts and fears rise up in your mind—resist with the promises of God. Quote Scripture. Let God's Word heal your doubts.

Thomas Brooks said, "Satan promises the best, but pays with the worst; he promises honor, and pays with disgrace; he promises pleasure, and pays with pain; he promises profit, and pays with loss; he promises life, and pays with death. But God pays as He promises; all His payments are made in pure gold."[6]

Not too long ago after a late night of counseling several people at church, I arrived at home exhausted. I battle diabetes, and my blood sugar was low. The pressures of the day weighed heavily on my spirit. I had preached twice that day, giving it my best, and I didn't have much energy left. I sat down in a chair and started to pray.

"Lord, I'm exhausted. I'm discouraged. I feel like I can't make it. I need Your strength." Then I remembered that Satan wanted to discourage me. He was using one of his tools on me. I did what I always do when I sense an attack of Satan. I prayed the Lord's promise. "Lord, I remember Your promise: 'Greater is He that is in me than he that is in the world'" (1 John 4:4). I drank some orange juice to raise my blood sugar and read my Bible for a while.

Are you discouraged about the circumstances in your life? Does it seem that your colleague will talk about everything in her life except the Lord? Maybe a family member tests your faith by asking questions that tell you he isn't paying attention when you witness to him. Whatever the situation, remember this: You engage in spiritual conflict when you tell others about Jesus. Satan hates your witness more than anything else. Continue to fight. You are on the winning team! The Lord will give you strength. You only have to ask.

PARABLE PRINCIPLE #11—Don't think you are "perfect too soon."

Janet enjoyed her busy life. Shuttling her kids to soccer games and school, she managed to develop friendships with many of the other mothers who were in the same position as herself. As she cheered for her daughters, she prayed that she would have opportunities to share her faith.

One day in a casual conversation with another mother named

Serena, Janet finally had her chance. She described first her own inward emptiness before she knew Christ. She explained that she wondered if she even had a purpose in life.

Janet was surprised that Serena listened attentively to the sharing of the Gospel. As the soccer game ended, Janet asked her friend if she wanted to receive Christ. Serena immediately said yes. After making sure that Serena understood the Gospel, Janet led her in a prayer of commitment. That night as Janet drove her daughters home, a deep joy resided in her heart.

Serena couldn't seem to talk to Janet enough after that. Every soccer practice and game, the two earnestly conversed with a Bible open between them. Serena began attending Janet's church, and the two spent even more time together. Serena really seemed to want to grow in Christ. Janet learned that Serena had been married twice before and now was trying to raise two daughters from her first marriage.

As the two grew close, Janet prayed daily for Serena that she would continue to grow in her faith. Then one day Serena didn't show up for church. Concerned, Janet called her friend. Not finding her at home, she called again the next day. But it seemed that Serena and her daughters had dropped off the ends of the earth.

A month later Janet called and was surprised when Serena answered. At first Serena seemed hesitant to talk, but finally she told Janet what had been going on. A man from her past had shown up, and on impulse Serena began to date him. A whirlwind courtship ensued, and now they were married. Serena didn't seem interested in talking very long, and Janet was at a loss for words. She asked Serena if she was planning to come back to church, and Serena said she was thinking about it but didn't think she would. She said that church attendance had been taking up too much of her time, and while she wasn't against coming occasionally, she said she thought she needed to get on with her life. She was offended that Janet was pushing her to attend. As Janet hung up the phone, she felt devastated. How could Serena have made such a bad decision, marrying a non-believer?

Janet would be comforted to know that Jesus talked about just such a person when He spoke about the stony ground. He described Serena and thousands like her (both men and women) who become "perfect too soon."

Mark 4:5 states, "And some fell on stony ground, where it had not much earth; and immediately it sprang up, because it had no depth of earth." Mark 4:16-17 explains this situation: "And these are they likewise which are sown on stony ground; who, when they have heard the word, immediately receive it with gladness; and have no root in themselves, and so endure but for a time: afterward, when affliction or persecution ariseth for the word's sake, immediately they are offended."

These verses speak about people who receive the Word with gladness. They experience a great spurt of growth in the beginning of their Christian experience, but then they wither away. This is the danger new believers can experience when they grow in Christ very quickly. They think they are "perfect too soon." Their pride in their spiritual development might cause them to actually stop growing.

First Timothy 3:6 describes this well: "Not a novice, lest being lifted up with pride he fall into the condemnation of the devil." If the plant is not rooted and grounded in sound doctrine, when the inevitable hardships come, the excitement will die off, and the once vibrant Christian will wither away.

Does this mean that the peaked-out believer loses his salvation? The Bible is clear that once a person has trusted Christ, he or she is saved forever. Nothing can loosen the grip of God's hand. John 10:28 says, "And I give unto them eternal life; and they shall never perish, neither shall any man pluck them out of my hand." But growth in Christ will stop, and the person will fail to experience the blessings God wants to bestow.

PARABLE PRINCIPLE #12—Sometimes you will be offended.

Seventeen-year-old Jerry proudly showed me his driver's license the day he got it. His father Stan told me about the time when Jerry first got his permit. Excited to get behind the wheel, Jerry drove while Stan sat in the passenger seat. Stan's nerves were on edge, but after a while he realized that Jerry really was a pretty good driver.

Then the sky got darker, and Stan saw that it was going to storm. He warned Jerry that the first few minutes of rain are the most dangerous because the oil on the road makes it slippery. Concentrating on the approaching storm, Jerry didn't notice the signs that proclaimed they were in a construction area.

Forgetting that he had heard on the radio just that morning about a zero-tolerance policy going into effect for failure to heed construction warnings, Stan didn't tell Jerry to slow down. Flashing lights behind them panicked them both. Jerry pulled the car to the side of the road and looked inquiringly at his dad. What was it that he had done wrong? He was traveling the speed limit. The police officer explained that Jerry should have slowed down as soon as he saw the warning sign. To Stan's chagrin, Jerry got a ticket because of the new policy that had just been passed. It took Jerry an extra year to get his driver's license after that. So you can understand why Jerry was proud when he finally got it!

Just as Jerry missed the warning because of an approaching storm, it is easy to miss God's warnings. We cruise down life's freeway, oblivious to the orange signs until we see the flashing lights. Then we pull over and take a personal assessment, realizing that we had been given warning after warning but had failed to heed them.

What is the warning in Parable Principle #12? Friend, there are times in your Christian life when you will be offended. The word *offended* in Mark 4:17 is the Greek word *skandalizo,* and it means to "entrap or trip up." Persecution or difficulty is like a tiny cable stretching across your path. If you fail to heed God's warnings, the wire is sure to make you lose your footing.

All of us will be offended from time to time. It is an undeniable fact of our daily life. Your boss is going to say something that rubs you the wrong way. Your spouse will utter a sarcastic comment after you've had a particularly bad day. Your child will say something that embarrasses you in front of your friends. But you don't have to let these offenses take hold of your mind and carry you away from God's purpose and plan.

The tendency to take offense can measure the depth of our spirituality. A woman in our church named Paula provides an illustration.

Newly saved, she told me how excited she was to come to church. But one day another Christian offended her. Paula wouldn't even tell me what was said to her, but I could tell that some seeds of the Word were hitting stony ground. She seemed stagnant in her spiritual walk after that, coming to church sporadically and never staying to fellowship with others. The day I preached a sermon from Mark 4:16-17, she told me, "I realize that the comment that offended me has really affected my growth as a Christian. I'm not going to let that happen again." Paula now recognizes that there are times when she will be offended, and she is determined to handle the situation differently.

The people described in this Scripture passage get excited in the beginning of their walk of faith. When they first trust Christ, they are like Serena, eager to serve the Lord. But as soon as something happens to deter their faith, or a fellow church member makes a cynical statement, they back away from the Lord. Jesus explained that their lack of solid roots keeps them from staying grounded in spite of the offense. While they are still saved, they have not let the Word change their lives.

USEFUL, NOT USELESS

When Irving S. Olds was chairman of the U.S. Steel Corporation, he arrived for a stockholders' meeting and was confronted by a woman who asked, "Exactly who are you, and what do you do?"

Without batting an eye, Irving replied, "I am your chairman. Of course, you know the duties of a chairman—that's someone who is roughly the equivalent of parsley on a platter of fish."[7] Do you feel as useless as parsley on a platter of fish? Do you add visual interest but nothing else to the body of Christ?

Understand that when you let something offend you, your usefulness in the work of the Lord may end. Until you deal with that offense and determine not to let it stop you in your walk with the Lord, you will be fundamentally unproductive for Christ.

Luke 8:6 tells us more: "And some fell upon a rock; and as soon as it was sprung up, it withered away, because it lacked moisture." So the problem is twofold. First the roots have not gone far below the surface, and, because of that, moisture didn't nourish the roots.

From my summers in Oklahoma, I understand how important moisture is to a crop. We would take a special piece of farming equipment called a "one-way" and go over that whole field. Our purpose was to break up the dirt so that the water stayed in the ground. As a result, the wheat would have more moisture and produce a better yield.

How do we let the "one-way" of God's Word keep us from the terrible scenario of the lack of roots and moisture? First, we need to pray that God would give us a soft heart toward His Word. We need to stay in a humble frame of mind so that the life-giving power of God's Word can transform us from the inside out.

Dear friend, daily cares and difficulties can contribute to the stony ground that lacks moisture. They can work together to offend you and keep you from serving Christ. Someone will offend you and probably soon. Get ready for it right now. This person could be your pastor (gasp!), a close Christian friend, or a saved family member. Don't let a prideful spirit keep the Word of God from working in your life.

Take a moment right now and ask God to humble your own heart. Ask for His healing to counteract the world's affliction, His strength to handle the offenses that are sure to come your way. You can be sure when you do this that the seed of the Word will sink roots in your own heart so that you can rise to perform great service for Him.

TWO ORDINANCES

A practical way to ensure deep roots in your faith is to observe the two ordinances our Lord gave to every believer. The first is the Lord's Supper, or Communion. I wrote about this earlier. A Bible-believing, Bible-teaching church will have this ceremony at least several times a year. We do it once a month. The Bible isn't specific about how often we should do it. Rather it states that we should do it as often as we like until He comes again. First Corinthians 11:26 explains, "For as often as ye eat this bread, and drink this cup, ye do shew the Lord's death till he come."

The second ordinance that every Christian needs to observe is water baptism. We should be baptized because our Lord was baptized when He lived on this earth. Matthew 3:16 states, "And Jesus, when he was baptized, went up straightway out of the water: and, lo, the heavens were opened unto him, and he saw the Spirit of God descending like a dove, and lighting upon him."

Water baptism is a way that we can identify with our Lord in His death, burial, and resurrection. Romans 6:4 says, "Therefore we are buried with him by baptism into death: that like as Christ was raised up from the dead by the glory of the Father, even so we also should walk in newness of life." Water baptism is an outward sign of what has happened on the inside—when the Lord cleansed us from all sin.

Anna was a Christian before she married Carl. She thought she was so in love with him that it didn't matter that he didn't know Christ. But after their three children came along, she found that it did matter—a lot. She wanted to take the children to church, but Carl resisted her at every turn. Night after night she cried after she tucked her daughter and two sons into bed. She hadn't been to church for so long that she could hardly remember how to pray. Her prayers with her children were halting and stilted. She wanted so much to experience the fellowship and blessing she had felt when she had attended church as a teenager, but Carl was dead set against it.

One day a shaken Carl came home early from work. One of the safety belts that kept his window-washing associate safe had come loose. Plunging twenty stories, the man tore through a large awning on the third floor. Fortunately this broke the man's fall enough that he ended up with only a few broken bones. As Carl hurried down his own scaffolding, he thought his friend was dead. He told Anna that at that moment he realized there was something missing in his life.

The family started attending a Bible-believing church, and after a few weeks of hearing the Gospel, Carl accepted Christ. A month or so later, at the end of the morning service, the pastor gave an invitation for water baptism. Carl had never heard of this ordinance before and asked Anna about it. She explained that she had been baptized when she was a teenager and that water baptism was a way to tell the world what Jesus Christ has done for a person. Carl decided that he wanted to be baptized, but it took him four more Sundays to get up the courage to walk forward and share his request with the pastor.

Later as the preacher said, "Carl, based on your profession of faith in Christ, I baptize you in the name of the Father, the Son, and the Holy Spirit," Carl felt tears come to his eyes. He was beginning to understand that knowing Jesus Christ had made an enormous difference. As he came up out of the water, he felt exhilarated, glad that he had made this decision to follow the Lord.

In our church you can either come forward on a Sunday morning, indicating you want to be baptized, or you can come privately to one of our leadership staff. A church will welcome your desire to be baptized because this decision is important in the life of growth. Following this ordinance from our Lord will help your roots anchor tightly so that when difficulties come, you will better withstand their unavoidable assault. "And have no root in themselves, and so endure but for a time: afterward, when affliction or persecution ariseth for the word's sake, immediately they are offended" (Mark 4:17).

PARABLE PRINCIPLE #13—Guard your reaction toward trials.

STONY GROUND

Not long ago I traveled with my great friend Jack Turney to India. My son-in-law Neal and two other men from our Bible College also went with us. Jack brought a well-drilling rig with him in the hopes of drilling a well near the compound where we stayed. The rig was completely unassembled, and it took Neal and the other two guys an afternoon to put it together. When the drilling began, it seemed at first that it was going great. But fifteen feet or so down, they hit solid rock, and the drilling slowed to inches per hour. Eventually it was decided that this type of well-driller would work only in a place that didn't have so much rock.

Many people are like the ground beneath that compound in India. At first the Word of God gets through to them, and they get excited. But a few weeks or even years later, they harden their hearts to the Word. Perhaps they get tired of the ridicule from other people at work. Maybe they don't like their own family's lack of understanding of their faith. Instead of digging deeper and breaking up the rocky soil of their heart, they stop growing in their walk with Christ. Stone is a figure used in Scripture to signify the stubborn hatred of what is holy and good. Here are three ways that you can keep Stony Ground Syndrome at bay. Ask yourself:

Do I earnestly seek the Lord? Have you lost your first love? John sent a letter to the church of Ephesus in Revelation. He listed their accomplishments for the Lord, and they were many. Yet Revelation 2:4 says, "Nevertheless I have somewhat against thee, because thou hast left thy first love." What was their first love? Their excitement when they first got saved. Their enthusiasm and love for the Lord were a testimony to all. Have you lost your own excitement? Are you still enthusiastic about your service to Christ? These are important questions to ask in an age of Stony-Ground Believers.

What is my reaction to trials? Do you have a tendency to say, "Why me, Lord?" when a trial comes into your life? Stony ground surface alert! Watch out! I have a friend who calls me up whenever he is facing a hard time. I am guaranteed to hear at some point, "Why do I always have to go through these rough times? Why does it always have to be me?" The truth about trials is that the Bible says they are a normal part of a believer's life. It is abnormal to be free from trials. Stop thinking that God is singling you out for mistreatment and instead welcome the trial as an opportunity to see lasting growth in your life.

Make a continuing diagnosis. Here are some thoughts from Puritan preacher Richard Baxter on service to Christ. All will help heal the Stony Ground Syndrome.

1. You will be most careful to understand the Scripture, to know what doth please and displease God.

2. You will be more careful in the doing of every duty, to fit it more to the pleasing of God than men.

3. You will look to your hearts, and not only to your actions; to your ends, and thoughts, and the inward manner and degree.

4. You will look to secret duties as well as public and to that which men see not, as well as unto that which they see.

5. You will reverence your consciences, and have much to do with them, and will not slight them: when they tell you of God's displeasure, it will disquiet you; when they tell you of His approval, it will comfort you.

6. Your pleasing of men will be charitable for their good, and pious in order to the pleasing of God, and not proud and ambitious for your honor with them, nor impious against the pleasing of God.

7. Whether men be pleased or displeased, or how they judge of you, or what they call you, will seem a small matter to you, as their own interest, in comparison to God's judgment. You live not on them. You can bear their displeasure, censures, and reproaches if God be but pleased. These will be your evidences.[8]

Have afflictions and persecutions kept you from fully serving Christ? Have you stopped attending church as regularly as you used to because of Stony Ground Syndrome? You think that you can't handle any more problems and that your trials are too hard to bear? God is with you in the midst of your trials, and He will comfort and help you. Take a moment and pray, "Lord, I know that my reaction to trials isn't always what You would have it to be. Help me to understand that You are with me and that it is the hard times that are actually shaping me to be more like You."

REV UP FOR REVIEW

Parable Principle #9—When you hear the Word, obey it.

Parable Principle #10—You engage in spiritual warfare when you share the Gospel with others.

Parable Principle #11—Don't think you are "perfect too soon."

Parable Principle #12—Sometimes you will be offended.

Parable Principle #13—Guard your reaction toward trials.

Reclaim any territory you might have lost by succumbing to Wayside Hearers' Disorder. Determine to be a Willing Hearer rather than a Wayside Hearer. Use the tips contained in this chapter to improve the way you receive the Word. Perhaps Stony Ground Syndrome has taken over part of your life. Understand that while it will take some diligence, it is possible to break up the offense you might still be harboring. Allow the Word to take deep root in your life. When you take the proper spiritual medicine, the refreshing water of God's Word will flood your newly softened heart with peace.

6

DANGER! THE BIG THREE WANT TO CHOKE YOU!

A servant of God has but one Master.

—GEORGE MUELLER

IN ONLY TEN MONTHS, twenty-eight pedestrians were killed crossing the streets of San Francisco, making it the state's most dangerous city for walking. The city's rate of pedestrian deaths and injuries, 124 per 100,000 residents, is nearly triple that of second-place Los Angeles.

"We're the center of a rushed dot-com industry," says City Supervisor Mabel Teng, sponsor of various pedestrian initiatives. "This is a city in transition, but it needs to remain livable."[1]

The high rate of pedestrian deaths is yet another example of our rushed culture. Many counties are passing laws banning the use of cell phones while driving because of people failing to pay attention to what is going on around them. Countless "labor-saving" devices have been invented since the Industrial Revolution, and yet in some ways these have created more work than ever. The rush to trade on Wall Street, keep up with the Joneses, and live what we call the "good life" crowds out important core values and keeps believers from serving the Lord the way they should.

Of course, recent events in our world have caused many people to focus on things that are more important. In the aftermath of the World Trade Center disaster, a TV journalist stopped a woman on the streets and asked about her business. She said, "I'm not interested in making money anymore. My family and my relationships are the most important things in life."

A well-dressed European woman was on a safari in Africa. The group stopped briefly at a hospital for lepers. Intense heat and buzzing flies bothered everyone. She noticed a nurse bending down in the dirt, tending to the pus-filled sores of a leper. The woman remarked with disdain, "I wouldn't do that for all the money in the world!"

The nurse quietly answered, "Neither would I."[2]

As Jesus stood on the shore of the Sea of Galilee and spoke to His disciples and the masses of people thronging Him, He explained a crucial truth about spiritual growth. Believers would be tempted to let their old natures choke the holiness in their lives. His warnings are critical in a world increasingly bent toward evil. Every believer, whether newly saved or saved for years, needs to look at his or her own life. What is your focus? What controls you? What drives you forward? Do you still crave the things of the world? Is there a difference between you and the culture around you? Is anything keeping you from developing into the person God would have you to be?

PARABLE PRINCIPLE #14—Your old nature hates holiness.

PARABLE PRINCIPLE #15—Your greatest spiritual help? The Holy Spirit.

These two crucial parable principles must be studied together. To fully understand how to grow in the Christian life, believers must understand that they are involved in a significant battle. That conflict is between our old natures (with which we were born) and the Holy Spirit who indwelt us the moment we trusted Christ as our Savior (Ephesians 1:13).

Jesus discussed this battle in the next part of His parable: "And some fell among thorns, and the thorns grew up, and choked it, and it yielded no fruit" (Mark 4:7). He explained a few verses later that these thorns are "the cares of the world," "the deceitfulness of riches," and "the lust of other things." The cares of the world are our tendency to worry about things God has promised to provide. The deceitfulness of riches is our inclination to look at riches as the road to happiness, and the lust for other things is whatever takes our focus off the Lord. But why do these three nefarious weeds have such impact on our lives? Our human nature itself is sinful. Our corrupt soil attracts these weeds and gives them a liberal dose of Miracle-Gro.

Even the great apostle Paul understood what it was like to battle his human nature, his sin nature. He spoke of this in Romans 7:19-25:

> *For the good that I would I do not: but the evil which I would not, that I do. Now if I do that I would not, it is no more I that do it, but sin that dwelleth in me. I find then a law, that, when I would do good, evil is present with me. For I delight in the law of God after the inward man: But I see another law in my members, warring against the law of my mind, and bringing me into captivity to the law of sin which is in my members. O wretched man that I am! who shall deliver me from the body of this death? I thank God through Jesus Christ our Lord. So then with the mind I myself serve the law of God; but with the flesh the law of sin.*

For years when the guys brought porn into the office, Al didn't mind. But the day he trusted Christ as his Savior, he started to be bothered by it. He tried to avoid the material as much as he could, but found it difficult because it was so readily available. He came to one of our pastors for counseling, and through much prayer and Bible study, Al began to understand that the Christian life is a battleground.

Although Al has the Holy Spirit living within him, he still has a carnal nature also. Until Al goes to heaven and receives his glorified body, he will have to deal with his old nature. This part of Al is called the "flesh" in Scripture. This doesn't refer to the skin covering our bodies but to the part of our being that wants to sin instead of obeying Christ.

When Al recognized that there was now a battle going on inside of him, he began to see that by gratifying his flesh, he was weakening his effectiveness to serve. He was letting the temptations of this world keep him from victorious living. But as he studied Scripture and attended church, he learned how to allow himself to be led by the Spirit. This helped him grow stronger in his faith.

One day Al asked the guys to stop using porn around him. He didn't think they would listen. To his surprise the men respected his request. One of his colleagues talked to Al later and shamefacedly explained that he was a Christian but that nobody else would know it by the way he lived. He asked Al if they could hold each other accountable. Al agreed, and now during breaks the two men spend time studying Scripture. They know that at any time they could fall back into their old lifestyles. Yet they continue to fight the battle within, knowing the Holy Spirit will give them grace and help when they need it.

Bible teacher and author Charles Ryrie said, "But the word *flesh* also has a metaphorical sense when it refers to our disposition to sin and to oppose or omit God in our lives. The flesh is characterized by works that include lusts and passions (Galatians 5:19-24; 1 John 2:16); it can enslave (Romans 7:25); and in it is nothing good (Romans 7:18). Based on this meaning of the word *flesh*, to be carnal means to be characterized by things that belong to the unsaved life (Ephesians 2:3)."[3]

There is much confusion about the two natures. I venture to say that if you can understand this concept, you are well on your way to understanding the Bible.

ALL THINGS NEW?

Shortly after I first trusted Christ as my Savior, I attended a service on a college campus. A football player stood up and said, "I'm so glad I don't sin anymore. The Bible says that old things are passed away, and all things are become new."

A friend and I looked at each other. We had just seen that man drunk at a party the night before. We looked up the verse he mentioned: "Therefore if any man be in Christ, he is a new creature: old things are passed away; behold, all things are become new" (2 Corinthians 5:17). If all things were new, then why did we see him in his obviously "old" mode the night before? We dug into our Bibles to find the answer.

THE FIGHT IS ON

Imagine the old nature as my left fist. No matter what I do, I can't make this nature that I got when I was born fit for heaven. I can dress it up, but it still sins. I can baptize it, but it is still filthy. The old nature never gets any better no matter what I do to it.

Imagine my right fist as the new nature I received at my new birth. This is the nature I received when I trusted Christ as Savior. This nature cannot sin. This nature is spirit. While the old nature can be subdued, it never gets any better. But I can choose to live in the power of the nature I received at the new birth.

THE MOMENT YOU BELIEVE

Some teach that you can never know exactly when you trusted Christ. You can only know you're saved if you live the Christian life and exhibit spiritual fruit. However, just as the mother knows when a baby is born, so we can know when we are born again. While some people can't pinpoint the day of their salvation to the minute, they still know that at one point in their life they were trusting in something other than Christ to make it to heaven.

Why is there such confusion about salvation? If you believe that only in service is salvation, then it would stand to reason that if you aren't serving Christ (even if you made a profession of faith at an earlier time), you aren't saved. So you think you need to accept Christ "again" and hope that now you will be successful and serve Christ. If this were true, then wouldn't salvation be of works? The Bible is clear that it is "not by works of righteousness which we have done, but according to his mercy he saved us, by the washing of regeneration, and renewing of the Holy Ghost" (Titus 3:5).

It is His grace that saves us and keeps us! It is His mercy that cleanses us from all sin—past, present, and future. If we had to do anything to maintain our status in God's eyes, then wouldn't that mean salvation is of works?

I believe a lot of the confusion would be cleared up if we just understood the two natures. The Bible clearly teaches that the new nature cannot sin but that the old nature, which is not eradicated until we receive our new bodies in heaven, can do little but sin.

COME FORWARD OR ELSE!

When I was in junior high, a famous evangelist came to our church in Morehead, Kentucky. He painted the flames of hell as being *hot*! He told the congregation that if they didn't come forward and receive Christ, chances were great they would go there.

Being a Methodist preacher's son, I felt embarrassed to walk forward. It might hurt my image, but I didn't want to end up in hell either. I came forward, but the sad thing was that no one explained the plan of salvation to me. I left the altar just as unsaved as when I came to it.

My family and I went to eat with the evangelist after the service, but he never once asked me about my salvation. I assumed that I could reform myself to avoid hell. I promised God I was going to live a faultless life, starting from that moment. By the end of the first day, I was miserable. By the end of the third day, I was so wretched that I said, "There is no way I'm ever going to heaven. I'm going to hell, and so I might as well have fun along the way."

If I had understood salvation, I could have been spared a lot of misery. I hadn't trusted Christ as my Savior. I didn't have the Holy Spirit. There was no way I could have reformed myself. It was several more years before anyone explained that salvation is a free gift, apart from works. There was no way to regenerate myself that would make me worthy of salvation. Rather Jesus came to save sinners—people like me.

BAFFLED RULER

There was a man of the Pharisees, named Nicodemus, a ruler of the Jews: The same came to Jesus by night, and said unto him, Rabbi, we know that thou art a teacher come from God: for no man can do these miracles that thou doest, except God be with him. Jesus answered and said unto him, Verily, verily, I say unto thee, Except a man be born again, he cannot see the kingdom of God. Nicodemus saith unto him, How can a man be born when he is old? can he enter the second time into his mother's womb, and be born? Jesus answered, Verily, verily, I say unto thee, Except a man be born of water and of the Spirit, he cannot enter into the king-

dom of God. That which is born of the flesh is flesh; and that which is born of the Spirit is spirit. (John 3:1-6)

Nicodemus was confused about the new birth. Jesus explained to him that he must be born again. Look at the words of Jesus again: "That which is born of the flesh is flesh; and that which is born of the Spirit is spirit." There is a distinction between that which is born of flesh (your first birth) and that which is born of the Spirit.

BORN FROM ABOVE

Some people might ask, "But why doesn't God stop me from sinning? Couldn't I just trust Christ as my Savior and stop sinning?" If God had to stop you from sinning, He would have to stop you from thinking evil thoughts. If He stopped you from thinking, He would control everything about you. If God did that, then obviously we would no longer have a free will. We make choices about what we are going to let control our lives.

Here is an excellent verse about the two natures: "This I say then, Walk in the Spirit, and ye shall not fulfill the lust of the flesh. For the flesh lusteth against the Spirit, and the Spirit against the flesh: and these are contrary the one to the other: so that ye cannot do the things that ye would" (Galatians 5:16-17).

Your old nature says, "I want to do the things I used to do. I don't want to go to church." Your new nature counters, "I want to go to church. I want to pray. I want to read my Bible." It's your choice as to which one will win. If the new nature continues to win, the old nature is subdued.

What happens when we don't live righteously, when we indulge our flesh? God will never send us to hell, but He will discipline us. Like a loving parent who cares about a child's well-being, so God cares about how we live. Hebrews 12:7, 11 explains, "If ye endure chastening, God dealeth with you as with sons; for what son is he whom the father chasteneth not? . . . Now no chastening for the present seemeth to be joyous, but grievous: nevertheless afterward it yieldeth the peaceable fruit of righteousness unto them which are exercised thereby."

Chris knew his parents were disappointed with some of his behavior. His grades were slipping. His attitude was terrible. One night his parents sat him down.

"Chris," his mother said, "we will not tolerate what you've been doing lately."

"Yes," agreed his father. "We love you, but you're going to be punished because of the way you've been acting."

So the Lord is displeased when we fail, but His love for us doesn't change. He may have to chasten us just as Chris's parents did. But just as Chris will always be the son of his mother and father, once we trust Christ as Savior, God is always our Father.

When God disciplines the believer, he does it to produce the peaceable fruit of righteousness in the person's life. The Christian doesn't have to fear that God will get so mad that He will say, "Forget it—you are no longer my child!" We are secure in Him.

THE WAY TO BE CONSECRATED

Paul says, "For to be carnally minded is death; but to be spiritually minded is life and peace" (Romans 8:6). The word *carnal* means fleshly or worldly. When we center our thoughts and actions on the things of this world, we will stop being effective for the kingdom of God. How do we stay spiritually minded? We build up our spiritual natures, learn the doctrines of the Bible, and apply spiritual truths to our lives. Romans 12:1-2 states, "And be not conformed to this world: but be ye transformed by the renewing of your mind, that ye may prove what is that good, and acceptable, and perfect, will of God."

John Mason Brown was a drama critic and speaker well known for his witty and informative lectures on theatrical topics. One of his first important appearances as a lecturer was at the Metropolitan Museum of Art. Brown was pleased, but also rather nervous, and his nerves were not helped when he noticed by the light of the slide projector that someone was copying his every gesture. After a time he broke off his lecture and announced with great dignity that if anyone was not enjoying the talk, he was free to leave. Nobody did, and the mimicking continued. It was another ten minutes before Brown realized that the mimic was his own shadow!

Was Brown's shadow real? Of course. Does a shadow have the power to control a person's actions? Of course not. It can only mimic the person. But in Brown's case, his shadow did take control momentarily. Why? Because he allowed himself to be so distracted by it that he completely forgot what he was supposed to be about. That's a good description of the sin nature we carry within us as redeemed people.[4]

Don't let the "shadow" of your flesh control you. Instead, open yourself up to the Word of God. Stay away from a covetous attitude. Put a lock on your old nature. Deal with those nasty habits.

"This I say then, Walk in the Spirit, and ye shall not fulfil the lust of the flesh" (Galatians 5:16). Too many people reverse this verse, and consequently they are backwards in their thinking about the Christian life. The verse does not say, "Do not fulfill the lust of the flesh, and you will walk in the Spirit." Rather it says, "Walk in the Spirit, and ye shall not fulfil the lust of the flesh."

You serve Christ by grace just as you were saved by grace. You cannot live the Christian life on your own! The Holy Spirit is your greatest spiritual help, a gift that will make it possible to live a separated life.

Do you know which nature controls your actions? Do you allow the Holy Spirit to guide you, or does your old nature guide you? Determine to let the Holy Spirit of God control you, and you will experience great joy in your Christian life.

How to Avoid Sin

Bible teacher R. A. Torrey once said:

> I often think there is little use in telling young Christians you must not dance; you must not play cards; you must not go to the theatre; you must not do this, that and the other thing. There is a far better way: Get them to let the Holy Spirit have full right within, and they will have no desire for such things—they will stay away from the theatre and the dance, and the rest, not merely because they ought, but because they will not desire to go. Who

that knows of a clear, crystal spring will sneak off to a green, slimy pool to drink?

When Mr. Moody was holding meetings in Philadelphia, a lady came to him one day at the close of one of his meetings and said: "Mr. Moody, I don't like you!"

"Why?" he asked.

"Because you are so narrow."

Mr. Moody replied, "Why do you think I am narrow?"

"Because you don't believe in the dance, you don't believe in cards, you don't believe in the theatre, you don't believe in anything nice!"

"Let me tell you something," he said. "I go to the theatre whenever I want to."

"What!" she exclaimed. "You go to the theatre whenever you want to? Oh, I do like you, Mr. Moody! You are much broader than I thought."

"Yes," he replied, "I go to the theatre whenever I want to. I don't want to!"[5]

THE BIG THREE

Mark 4:18-19 identifies three things that would wrap around your newfound growth and choke it into oblivion: "And these are they which are sown among thorns; such as hear the word, and the cares of this world, and the deceitfulness of riches, and the lusts of other things entering in, choke the word, and it becometh unfruitful."

Now that we understand the old nature and the new nature, perhaps we can learn how to pour herbicide on the nasty weeds so the Word will not be hindered anymore. Jesus is giving us major muscle for new-nature buildup!

PARABLE PRINCIPLE #16—Worry is a choker.

What are the "cares" of the world of which Jesus speaks? In Scripture the word *care* often relates to worry. The cares of this world relate to obtaining the necessities of life—food, clothing, shelter. How can worry over those things choke out the Word?

Jesus said in Matthew 6:25, "Therefore I say unto you, Take no thought for your life, what ye shall eat, or what ye shall drink; nor yet for your body, what ye shall put on. Is not the life more than meat, and the body than raiment?"

Does this mean that the believer is never to think of what he or she is going to wear, or what kind of home he is going to live in, or what she is going to eat for dinner that night? Jesus understood that people need these things, but He encourages all of us to recognize that the cares of the world can choke our growth. Why? We can easily look to those things too much—not realizing that they are blocking our view of God. Their influence can blind our minds to eternal truth.

How often do you worry about your financial situation? Do you obsess over your retirement or your children's college education? While Christians can and should plan for the future, it is most important to understand that this earth is temporary and that God's kingdom is eternal.

Does any of this apply to you? If there isn't something to worry about, do you worry that there is nothing about which to worry? I am tempted to worry as much as anyone. Yet I've learned an important secret in my worry war. God has shown me over and over again that He cares about me and will provide the answers to anything I am worried about. When I have His perspective, I also feel secure and tend to feel less anxious.

It is natural to worry. In a sense, worry is trying to take control of a situation over which we have no control. In some ways it gives us a feeling of power over the situation. To have to sit back and let God take full control—now that is difficult!

When we worry, we are grabbing the situation from the hand of our God and saying, "I can deal with this better than you can, God!" And then we blame Him when the problem isn't resolved! We have to learn to trust, and some days that means a moment-by-moment decision.

Missionary Joy Ridderhof said this about faith: "What are people who are living by faith going to do when money gets tight and depression comes?"[6] The thought came to me that the real question is: "What are people who are not living by faith going to do?"

Isaiah 40:8 always helps me: "The grass withereth, the flower fadeth: but the word of our God shall stand for ever." Over the years in ministry, I have a practice that has helped me to put my burdens on the Lord more than anything else. When I am faced with what seems like an insurmountable difficulty, I write something on a piece of paper. What do I write? I write down the worst thing that could happen. When I see it on paper, it is easier to recognize that God continues to guide me, and He will help me through whatever situation arises. Why don't you try that the next time "the cares of the world" start to overwhelm you. Write down the worst thing that could happen on a piece of paper and then ask God to take care of you. You will stop the Worry Choker in its tracks!

PARABLE PRINCIPLE #17—If you love the world, you do not love Christ.

He was so excited. He knew he was going to heaven. He had never been happier. Getting to know the apostle Paul was wonderful because Paul was the first person to really care about him. Demas enjoyed working with him, helping him in many ways. But he kept thinking about what he wanted for his life. He desired a certain level of prestige, and it didn't seem that being a Christian brought him the success he craved. We read in 2 Timothy 4:10, "For Demas hath forsaken me, having loved this present world, and is departed unto Thessalonica . . ."

Jesus said that the deceitfulness of riches hinders the growth of the Word of God in our lives. This even happened to a man who worked beside the apostle Paul! Preacher and author Alexander Maclaren said, "The 'cares of this world' and the 'deceitfulness of riches' are but two sides of one thing. The poor man has cares; the rich man has the illusions of his wealth. Both men agree in thinking that this world's good is most desirable. The one is anxious because he has not enough of it, or fears to lose what he has; the other man is full of foolish confidence because he has much."[7]

Unlike those with Stony Ground Syndrome, these people understand the truth, and the Word does take root and bear fruit in their lives. But eventually the cares of the world and the desire for the things of the world choke out their fruit. In other words, they crown the old nature and allow it to rule their lives.

All of us act this way at times. We may understand a lot of Scripture and obey it. Perhaps our comprehension of truth has grown throughout the years, and we feel that we are going along pretty well. But the subtle sins of worry start to rob us of our spiritual joy. The desire for worldly success clouds our desire to serve. Suddenly our old nature is reigning, choking out the tiniest sign of spiritual growth. Don't swallow the worldly sentiment that wealth is more important than anything else. Be on guard at all times and avoid the Demas Disease.

PARABLE PRINCIPLE #18—Possess your possessions.

The third thing that can choke the growth of the Word of God is our longing for anything that is not spiritual. This counterfeit craving blinds us to what is truly important. These three chokers are all related by a common root—worldliness in thought and action.

Dave Roper gives a good definition of worldliness: "Worldliness is reading magazines about people who live hedonistic lives and spend too much money on themselves and wanting to be like them. But more importantly, worldliness is simply pride and selfishness in disguise."[8]

Worldliness is like a beautiful oasis that you see far off in the desert. Because you see water ahead, you go ahead and finish your canteen. But as you stagger forward, you discover that what you thought was a placid pond is really scorching sand. That is also what lust is like. This sin is more than just immoral sensual desire. Lust is a powerful emotion that entices our physical being with thoughts of grandeur and power. Is wealth wrong? There were many men and women in the Bible who had great riches. Obviously the answer is no. Yet our desire should not be for more wealth. Rather our desires should be focused solely on the spiritual.

I have known many fine Christians who used their resources for the Lord. Whenever there was a need, they were quick to volunteer their time and personal wealth to help. But there are other believers to whom riches matter far too much. The actual economic status of these Christians doesn't seem to matter. They can be rich or poor.

But they have let their own lust for money run rampant to the point that it has consumed and ruined their Christian lives.

When I was young, I had some friends who were multimillionaires. One day they hit a chicken while driving. They stopped the car, picked up the chicken, and took it to the gas station to trade it for gasoline. These people also worried constantly that they would not have enough money to pay their taxes. This is an example of people whose effectiveness for Christ was ruined by their craving for wealth.

Dear friend, I challenge you to analyze your own life. Are you using your money wisely for the work of the kingdom? Or are you squandering it here on this earth? Decide today to keep The Big Three—the creeping cares, the sham of worldly success, and counterfeit cravings—from disabling your walk with Christ.

You Are Wealthy (Spiritually)

What is the strategy for keeping The Big Three at bay? Possess your possessions. You might say, "I thought I was not supposed to want possessions. I need to desire to be consecrated." That is true. I mean your real possessions.

Bible teacher H. A. Ironside once said that believing God's testimony is like endorsing a check and cashing it. A man went into the home of a very poor woman who had applied for relief. He saw something on the wall that attracted his attention. It was a piece of paper in a neat frame.

He asked, "What is that on the wall?"

She replied, "I just don't know what it is, but it's a paper my uncle sent me, and I don't like to throw it away. So I keep it in remembrance of him."

He exclaimed, "Don't you see what it is!"

"No, I don't understand it."

"Well, it's a bank check. Look! There is the name of the bank on which it is drawn, and it says, 'Pay to Jennie Johnson the sum of $5,000.00,' and there is your uncle's name at the bottom of it."

"I can't believe it," she said. "He intended for me to have that money, and here I've been living in abject poverty for years."[9]

You already have great wealth, but it isn't here on this earth. You could be the richest person in the world, and that would be nothing compared to what you will possess in heaven. Jesus Christ has given you eternal life. He wants you to possess your possessions—your true possessions. Your eternal check is written on the Bank of Heaven. Jesus wants you to recognize that the desire for the world is sinful. Instead, look at what you already have. Romans 11:33 states, "O the depth of the riches both of the wisdom and knowledge of God! how unsearchable are his judgments, and his ways past finding out!"

THE BIG THREE BLESSINGS

Instead of worrying about the Big Three Chokers, why don't you think about the Big Three Blessings? These gifts from God are pure and perfect. They will not fade or tarnish.

All Spiritual Blessings

Ephesians 1:3 tells us, "Blessed be the God and Father of our Lord Jesus Christ, who hath blessed us with all spiritual blessings in heavenly places in Christ." Dear friend, you are blessed with all spiritual blessings in heavenly places in Christ! You already have them, and so go ahead and possess them!

Sealed with the Spirit

"In whom ye also trusted, after that ye heard the word of truth, the gospel of your salvation: in whom also after that ye believed, ye were sealed with that Holy Spirit of promise, which is the earnest of our inheritance until the redemption of the purchased possession, unto the praise of his glory" (Ephesians 1:13-14). Like earnest money a person gives with the intention of buying a home, so the Holy Spirit is the earnest of your inheritance—eternal life. You were sealed with the Holy Spirit when you trusted Christ. The Holy Spirit helps you to understand Scripture and will lead and guide you if you let Him.

Christ's Power Working in You

"The eyes of your understanding being enlightened; that ye may know what is the hope of his calling, and what the riches of the glory of his inheritance in the saints, and what is the exceeding greatness of his power to us-ward who believe, according to the working of his mighty power, which he wrought in Christ, when he raised him from the dead, and set him at his own right hand in the heavenly places" (Ephesians 1:18-20).

Now that you know Christ, His mighty power is working through you. He is the fountain of all riches and authority, and He gives all that to you freely. Instead of thinking about what you don't have, look toward what you already possess—great riches in Christ. Don't concentrate on your temporal belongings. Look to Christ. Focus on His great gift to you. Consider the blessing of eternal life. Doesn't that make the discomforts of today seem easier to bear? You have tomorrow, and you have eternity in heaven in your future! Thank the Lord for the blessing of the Holy Spirit. Praise Him for working His mighty power through your life. Your Big Three Blessings will give you victory over the Thorny Big Three.

REV UP FOR REVIEW

Parable Principle #14—Your old nature hates holiness.

Parable Principle #15—Your greatest spiritual help? The Holy Spirit.

Parable Principle #16—Worry is a choker.

Parable Principle #17—If you love the world, you do not love Christ.

Parable Principle #18—Possess your possessions.

As you walk in the Spirit, you will stop fulfilling the lusts of the flesh. Instead of the lust for other things crowding your life day in and day out, you will want the precious seed of the Word to permeate your life. You will find that when you let the Holy Spirit have control, your desire will be to glorify Christ. The Big Three will no longer have power over you.

The parable principles about the old nature and the Holy Spirit are important for you to understand. When you recognize that you are letting your old nature rule, confess your sin to God. He has promised to hear you and forgive (1 John 1:9). When fellowship is restored, you can continue to crave holy things, actively seeking and cultivating a relationship with the Lord.

Don't forget to watch out for The Big Three! Worry will keep you from true joy. Loving the world will keep you from loving Christ. Instead crave what is consecrated. Your final lesson? Possess your possessions. Christ wants you to understand that you already own the eternal riches of heaven. He wants to envelop you with His treasures. He wants you to recognize that you already possess every tool you need to live a successful Christian life.

Take a moment and pray this prayer: "Lord, You've given me so much. I pray that I will crave what is consecrated. I ask that you will help me to focus on the eternal—that I will see that what I possess on this earth is only temporary. Only what You have already given me is eternal. Help me to grasp the truth that Your Holy Spirit is my constant guide and companion and my greatest resource for spiritual success."

THE GOOD-SOIL CHRISTIAN

Pray for great things, expect great things, work for great things, but above all, pray.

—R. A. TORREY

A PRESCHOOL TEACHER wrote a song about popcorn and taught it to her class. She had all the children crouch down on the floor, and at the appropriate point in the song, they all popped up like crunchy kernels of popcorn. Soon the children jumped all over the room as they sang the popcorn song. One little boy named Greg remained crouched on the floor. The teacher asked him, "Why don't you pop up like the other children?"

Greg replied, "I'm stuck on the bottom of the pan."[1]

I've had days like that—days I've felt stuck to the bottom of the pan. I think all of us have, especially when it comes to our spiritual lives. We've studied the way Satan chokes the seed of the Word so that our lives are stagnant, unproductive, and in the end wasted. We've seen that trials are more the norm than the exception in the Christian experience and that the way we react to those hardships is a key component in avoiding Stony Ground Syndrome. And in the last chapter we saw that our old nature fights to keep us from experiencing the peace of God. Our flesh wants to control us, and we must continue to build up our new nature to keep that from happening. If all this makes you feel stuck to the bottom of the pan once in a while, don't be discouraged. There is a way to rise above the difficulties of life. There is a way to defeat the devil. The parable principles in the following chapters will help us develop habits that promote spiritual growth. These behaviors will help us to walk closer to our Savior.

WHAT'S YOUR POV?

Some professional people have a different viewpoint from the rest of us. Filmmakers and videographers look at life through a camera that frames the footage they want to capture. Their goal is to focus on the point of view (POV) or the person or object they are shooting. They want to portray what that person is looking at, what he or she is thinking, where he or she wants to go. Filmmakers don't focus on their own desires, their own thoughts, their own needs. Rather they tell a story with the camera using the other person's POV.

Our POV as Christians also has to be different from the POV of people around us. To crave the things of God, we can't focus on the trials or give into Satan's vile ways or our old nature. Instead our POV needs to change. We need to focus on the Lord and what He would have us to do. We need to concentrate our energy on the things that will bring the most glory to Him.

When you focus on Him, the great blessings you enjoy each day are suddenly apparent. A Christian named R. C. Chapman was asked how he was feeling. "I'm burdened this morning!" was his reply. But his happy countenance contradicted his words.

The questioner exclaimed in surprise, "Are you really burdened, Mr. Chapman?"

"Yes, but it's a wonderful burden—it's an overabundance of blessings for which I cannot find enough time or words to express my gratitude!" Seeing the puzzled look on the face of his friend, Chapman added with a smile, "I am referring to Psalm 68:19, which fully describes my condition. In that verse the Father in heaven reminds us that He 'daily loads us with benefits.'" (Source unknown.)

Chapman had a different POV from the one we frequently have. He knew that when he focused on the eternal, he would see blessings flooding his daily life. In His parable Jesus also talks about the good ground—soft, rich, ready for the Word, and prepared to produce wonderful eternal growth. This is the kind of soil that produces a bountiful, glorious harvest. It is possible for you to be a Good-Soil Christian. You only need to change your POV.

THE RIGHT INGREDIENTS

Every Wednesday afternoon I check on our church kitchen to see how everything is going. Jon Laegeler, who runs this huge operation, is always in motion, mixing up massive batches of dough, helping take steaming pizzas out of the oven, and supervising the other workers.

Jon organizes and cooks hundreds of meals a day. All of our students, from preschool through Bible college, and staff eat nutritious homemade lunches every day. In addition to this, on Wednesdays the kitchen staff prepares hundreds of pizzas and other short-order items for dinner. Church members and school parents can order a pizza for carryout, or they can eat it in our dining hall.

I enjoy watching Jon add the yeast to the rest of the ingredients for the pizza dough. He usually puts in about four ounces of yeast for a hundred twelve-inch pizzas. It seems like such a little bit of yeast to make that many pizzas, but a few hours later a mountain of dough waits to be formed into pizza crusts.

Compare what Jon does week after week to what happens in the Christian life. A lot of ingredients are necessary to help a Christian grow: Bible study, prayer, church attendance, fellowship, and witnessing. When you mix in the yeast of the Holy Spirit, the ingredients form a wonderfully productive Christian.

THE GOOD-SOIL CHRISTIAN

Jesus talks about the good soil in the Parable of the Sower. This soil is only good because it has been broken up. No rocks hamper the seed from taking root, and the weeds are persistently pulled. Jesus knew this analogy would transfer easily to the spiritual realm. A Good-Soil Christian has first-class soil only because he continually breaks it up by asking the Lord to help him to receive the Word willingly when it is preached. He works hard to pound those rocks just below the surface, asking the Lord to keep him from being offended by other Christians. He pulls the weeds of care and lust out of his life by confessing his sin and thereby maintaining fellowship with His Savior. Hence, the Good-Soil Christian doesn't just "happen" by accident. Instead, this person has a deliberate plan for spiritual growth.

What should be the goal of one who has Wayside Hearers' Disorder? Break up the packed ground to change it to soft, ready soil. How about the aspiration for one with Stony Ground Syndrome? Feed the new nature and break up those rocks that are preventing the seed from anchoring properly. Consider those thorny Christians who have let worry, the world, and covetousness choke out their spiritual development. What should they do to see growth? They need to be on the alert for anything that blocks their spiritual sight.

Imagine a farmer thinking that good soil just happens—that all he has to do is scatter seed on the ground. He probably wouldn't produce enough of a crop to feed a family of mice, much less his own family. The farmer knows it takes work to produce a crop. Therefore, we shouldn't be surprised that it takes effort to see spiritual growth. Hosea 10:12 states, "Sow to yourselves in righteousness, reap in mercy; break up your fallow ground: for it is time to seek the LORD, till he come and rain righteousness upon you."

Look at the Good-Soil Christian verses in Mark 4:8 and 20: "And other fell on good ground, and did yield fruit that sprang up and increased; and brought forth, some thirty, and some sixty, and some an hundred." "And these are they which are sown on good ground; such as hear the word, and receive it, and bring forth fruit, some thirtyfold, some sixty, and some an hundred."

Commentator Joseph Exell said, "Those who produce are those who understand the Word. They keep the Word. The seed once lodged in the heart remains there. It is not caught away by the wicked one, it is not destroyed by the scorching beams of persecution, it is not choked by the thorns of worldly cares and pleasures. It is laid up in the understanding, memory, and affections; and guarded with attention and care, as the most invaluable treasure."[2]

Celebrate, Christian! Rejoice! The parable principles are working together to produce a wonderful harvest.

PARABLE PRINCIPLE #19—Don't compare your spiritual growth to that of other believers.

Shelly was excited about her spiritual growth. She had finally found a church that taught the Word of God. Week after week, she absorbed the Word as the pastor gave it. Day after day she began to set aside time to pray. She had been saved since she was a young child, but had fallen away from the Lord during college. Now she was making progress and had never been happier.

One Sunday Shelly met a woman who had attended the church for some time. Sarah invited Shelly out for lunch, and when they started talking about spiritual things, Shelly was surprised at all Sarah knew about the Bible. She seemed to have practically memorized the entire New Testament.

Shelly kept thinking about Sarah's knowledge of Scripture all week. It made her feel pretty discouraged. Although she had made some spiritual progress, she thought that she would never come close to knowing as much about the Bible as Sarah.

If Shelly had understood the Parable of the Sower, perhaps she wouldn't have compared herself to Sarah. Jesus says clearly that while it is our job to prepare the soil and receive the Word, it is God's job to bring the harvest. Shelly doesn't need to worry. God will use her in mighty ways, but she needs to stop comparing herself to Sarah.

Let's glean again from Mark 4:8: "And other fell on good ground, and did yield fruit that sprang up and increased; and brought forth, some thirty, and some sixty, and some an hundred."

The word *yield* in the Greek is *didome*, which means "to bring forth," "to deliver," or "to have power." If you put God's Word in your mind, it will generate thirty-, sixty-, or one hundredfold. The yield begins at thirtyfold. If you are a Good-Soil Christian, you are guaranteed at least that much.

Recognizing God's part in the harvest lifts the burden we feel when we compare ourselves to other Christians. It is our goal to break up the soil of our own heart and prepare for growth. It is our job to make sure we receive the Word with gladness, but it is God who takes care of the harvest. He knows and understands that some Christians are going to produce more than others. He is the ultimate judge. If you are doing your part to prepare for growth, let God do His part and bring forth the harvest.

God gave us our abilities and talents in the first place. He wants us to use those talents for his service no matter how meager they might seem. Some may start out with just one talent; others may start out with a hundred talents. But I don't believe there is a Christian in the world who can't produce thirty-, sixty-, or one hundredfold. Every Christian can experience victorious living because bearing fruit comes through faithful obedience to God. Not everybody has a perfect voice to stand in front of the congregation and sing a solo. However, everybody can join in congregational singing, ministering to others by their own excitement for the Lord. Not everybody can stand in front of people and preach the Word, but everybody can be a witness to a neighbor. Not everyone has the ability to teach a Sunday school class of two-year-old children, but everyone can share the love of Christ with a child.

A close friend, Ralph Kowalski, was born with quite a few physical limitations. He was small in stature, and his body shook with spasms throughout all the tasks he performed. I first met him when Linda and I started Quentin Road Ministries in the city of Chicago. Somehow he had heard of me and knew the name of the street where our church was located. He walked along the street knocking on every door until finally he came to our small storefront. It was a Saturday, and we didn't usually meet that day. However, we had a special service this particular Saturday, which made it a double miracle because otherwise Ralph might never have found us. Ralph and I struck up an instant friendship, and he became one of our first members.

Ralph didn't let anything stop him from using the opportunities he was given. Ralph was one of the greatest soul-winners I ever knew. One day I got a call from him. He was working as a janitor at a public school. He had witnessed to a teacher there and called me to come help him lead the teacher to Christ. I drove to the school and found the teacher ready to trust Christ as his Savior.

A few years ago Ralph suffered a fatal heart attack. I will always have a special place in my heart for this great man of God. He didn't let anything stop him from growing. I know a lot of people with many more talents and abilities than Ralph ever dreamed of possessing, but who still complain that they don't have enough ability to be used of God. Ralph knew what some people don't. God can use anyone. I imagine him standing in heaven cheering us all on to finish the race. If he could, he would say to you, "Don't let anything stop you from finishing your course. Especially don't compare your spiritual growth to that of other people. God is the final judge, and He is the only one you need to please."

FABULOUS FRUIT

My son Jim and his wife took their girls, Amy (eight) and Erica (seven), apple picking last year. The girls held onto either handle of the bushel basket as they eagerly walked into the orchard.

"I'm going to pick the most apples," Erica boasted.

"Oh yeah?" Amy teased. "Try and beat me!"

The two girls picked as many apples as they could reach. Then Amy spied the perfect apple.

"Daddy, do you see that apple? Would you mind getting it for me? It's too high for me to reach."

Jim will do anything for his girls. He climbed a ladder that was already in the tree and reached as high as he could. His fingers closed around the apple, and he handed it down to Amy.

"Thanks, Daddy," Amy said as she took a huge bite. "This one tastes the best!"

What if my son's family went to the apple orchard at the right time of year but found no apples? "Sorry," the orchard management would say, "we didn't have a harvest this year. None of the trees produced any fruit." Tragically, sometimes we also fail to produce fruit in our Christian lives. Galatians 5:22-23 lists the fruit we should produce: "But the fruit of the Spirit is love, joy, peace, longsuffering, gentleness, goodness, faith, meekness, temperance: against such there is no law."

The Christian who grows in Christ will be more loving, joyful, peaceful, longsuffering, and gentle. As he or she matures and changes, these characteristics will develop. And remember, you don't have to bear only one kind of fruit in your life. Unlike the apple tree that can only produce apples, the Christian can and should produce every one of the fruits of the Spirit.

The Word of God is more than a book of facts. You can't put a timer on how God will produce growth in your life. You can't study for thirty hours in order to produce thirtyfold, sixty hours for sixtyfold, a hundred hours for one hundredfold. These verses of Scripture aren't meant as an exact equation. Let's look at some of the habits you should cultivate each day that will help you in your spiritual growth. It is essential that you take each of these parable principles into account.

PARABLE PRINCIPLE #20—Fellowship with people who share your desire for spiritual growth.

Angie learned that one of the ways to be a Good-Soil Christian was to take a look at the kind of people she hung around. She had always made friends easily and enjoyed their company at parties and bars before she got saved. After she trusted Christ, she witnessed to her friends, but they laughed at her. One day one of her friends invited her to a party.

Angie hesitated. She had started to read her Bible and had realized that her old life wasn't pleasing to God. But she still wanted to be with her friends, and so she reluctantly said she would go.

As she got ready, she felt bad. She knew there would be drinking and that her friends would start acting really stupid. Just before she left, Faye, one of her new friends from church, called asking Angie to help her with the church's soup kitchen that night. Angie quickly agreed, her heart feeling lighter than it had all week. She called Ashley back and told her that she couldn't go to the party after all. Ashley didn't even seem disappointed. Angie realized that her friends didn't really want her around because she had changed so much. As she helped Faye dish out food, she understood that her new way of life would involve some choices about her friends.

When Angie made that important decision, she was working on the soil of her heart, developing habits that would help her grow spiritually. She knew that if she wanted to grow as a believer, she needed to think about the kind of impact her friends were making on her life. This decision didn't mean that she would cut off her old friends and fail to witness to them and bring them to Christ. But it would mean that if she didn't want to continue her old ungodly habits, she needed to be around people who had the same spiritual desires she did.

It is quite true that a bundle of logs burns much longer than a single log. But how do you find people of like mind who desire to grow spiritually? In a local church, you will find a cluster of believers who are helping each other burn brightly for Christ. Angie made a decision about which friends to spend time with, and it is important that you make the same kind of decision if you want to grow spiritually. Your outlook has been transformed, and your lifestyle has changed, but if you continue to hang around those who don't have the same desire for spiritual growth, you will find your longing for the things of God tapering off. You will find yourself burning less and less brightly until one day the garish lights of worldliness will choke out all that good seed of the Word. Hang on to Parable Principle #20 and remember that it is important to fellowship with like-minded believers if you want to be a Good-Soil Christian. I know one thing: Thanks to her decision, Angie is going to grow!

PARABLE PRINCIPLE #21—Develop the habit of prayer.

When researchers with the Gallup organization surveyed Americans regarding the role of prayer in their lives, they discovered that 82 percent of the female respondents and 69 percent of the men said prayer was important.[3] But while a pretty high percentage of people say prayer is important to them, there isn't much evidence in their lives that supports what they say. Writer Dallas Willard must have observed the same thing. He said, "The 'open secret' of many 'Bible-believing' churches is that a vanishing small percentage of those talking about prayer . . . are actually doing what they are talking about."[4]

Janna pulled up to the front of her apartment and jumped out of her car. She held her briefcase over her head to keep off the drizzling rain as she sprinted to her door. Worried about being late for an important job interview, she was mad at herself because she had forgotten her good shoes. She fumbled through her purse searching for her apartment key. She had taken it off her main key ring the other day, intending to get copies made. Now she couldn't find it.

Glancing at her watch, she dug in her purse frantically. She needed this new job. The continued backbiting of her coworkers combined with the pressures of a long commute made her current job intolerable. Janna rushed back to her car to see if she had left it on the dashboard. Then she remembered. The key was in her pocket. She had put it there early this morning.

When she walked into her job interview fifteen minutes later, a huge smile crossed her face. She had made it and on time! The key had been in her pocket all along.

When a warrior goes out to fight, you can be sure that he doesn't forget any of his weapons! When a person wants to do a good job on a business presentation, he or she gives much thought to the points that need to be covered, the media to be used, and even the clothing worn. But the most important spiritual key, the one that will help more than any other preparation, is *already* in one's pocket. It is the greatest weapon. It will unlock the door of God's blessing and power.

But how do we use this key, this great power called prayer? How do we take advantage of this tool that will give us great strength to face our problems with dignity and fortitude?

Prioritize

One thing you will notice if you study the biographies of great Christians down through the ages is their prayer life. They understood the importance of prayer, and they made it a priority. When asked the secret of his spiritual power, famous preacher Charles Spurgeon said, "Knee work! Knee work!"

C. S. Lewis said this about prayer: "The moment you wake up each morning, all your wishes and hopes for the day rush at you like wild animals. And the first job each morning consists in shoving it all back; in listening to that other voice, taking that other point of view, letting that other, larger, stronger, quieter life come flowing in."

The Purpose

James Gilmour, a missionary to Mongolia, was once asked to treat some wounded soldiers. Although he was not a doctor, he did have some knowledge of first aid, and so he felt he could not refuse the request. He dressed the wounds of two of the men, but a third had a badly broken thighbone. The missionary had no idea what to do for such an injury. Kneeling beside the man, he asked the Lord for help. He didn't know how God would answer his prayer, but he was confident that his need would be supplied.

He couldn't find any books on physiology in the primitive hospital, and no doctor arrived. To complicate matters, a crowd of beggars came to him asking for money. He was deeply concerned about his patient, and yet his heart went out to those ragged paupers. Hurriedly he gave them a small gift, plus a few words of spiritual comfort.

A moment later he stared in amazement at one weary beggar who had remained behind. The half-starved fellow was little more than a living skeleton. The missionary suddenly realized that the Lord had brought him a walking lesson in anatomy! He asked the elderly man if he might examine him. After carefully tracing the femur bone with his fingers to learn how to treat the soldier's broken leg, he returned to the patient and was able to set the fracture. Years afterward Gilmour often related the way God had provided him with a strange and yet sufficient response to his earnest prayer. When we raise our petitions, we too can be certain that the Lord will help us—even though the answer comes by way of those who "have no power."

There are many Christians who misunderstand the purpose of prayer. They think that God is like a cosmic Santa Claus who will shower them with gifts and wealth if only they ask. And yet the purpose of prayer is far greater than the obtaining of monetary, tangible blessings. If I were going to rewrite the story of James Gilmour, the missionary to Mongolia, my personal ending might have been a bit different. I might have said, "And the poor beggar turned out to be a medical doctor who immediately set the soldier's leg." Yet God's answer to Gilmour's prayer was more glorious and more grand than any ending I could have conjured up. The answer was for Gilmour himself to learn how to set the man's leg. Who knows how much that knowledge helped Gilmour in his further missionary endeavors?

James 4:2-3 states, "Ye lust, and have not: ye kill, and desire to have, and cannot obtain: ye fight and war, yet ye have not, because ye ask not. Ye ask, and receive not, because ye ask amiss, that ye may consume it upon your lusts."

Prayer is not getting God to adjust His program to what we want. When we pray, it isn't God who changes; it is us! The purpose of prayer is to glorify God through His work here on earth. We are not to use prayer as a tool to change the will of God. Rather prayer is a tool to use to see His will performed on this earth. The more we learn Scripture, the more we seek our Father's face, the more we seek to do His will, the more our prayers will be prompted out of our deep understanding of what the will of God is.[5]

LEARNING TO PRAY HIS WAY

When my granddaughters Amy and Erica were younger, they sometimes asked their parents for things that weren't good for them. Amy may have asked my son to let her use his pocketknife just because she saw him using it. Jim knew that Amy was too young to use a knife, and of course he said no. As the girls got older, they learned more about their mom and dad and what things they should ask for. Erica knows that if she says, "Daddy, can I have some money to buy my sister a present?" her daddy will probably give her the money.

Just as children learn more about what to ask their parents for, when we get to know our heavenly Father better, we learn how to pray to get our prayers answered.

Dear friend, let your prayers line up with the will of God. Ask Him to give you opportunities to witness to friends and neighbors. Ask Him for strength to endure your coworker's barbed comments. Ask Him to teach you how to encourage others. Study His Word and learn what His will is. Then your prayers and your study will help you to become a spiritual person. Preacher Robert Law wrote, "Prayer is a mighty instrument, not for getting man's will done in heaven, but for getting God's will done on earth."

FEEL LIKE PRAYING?

Earnestness in prayer is not indicated by language, loudness, or length of the prayer. Rather prayer needs to be a discipline in our lives. Don't expect always to "feel" like praying. Instead develop the habit of

The Good-Soil Christian   131

prayer based not on how you feel but on the promises of God. He will hear you, whether you feel that He is listening or not!

Imelda was learning to develop this habit of prayer in her life. Yet she found that it was more difficult than she had thought. She decided to get up half an hour earlier each morning to pray. She bought a special notebook and on the front cover wrote, "Prayer Journal."

Her plan was a good one. She was going to write down systematically the areas of her life that needed prayer, and her journal would help her to be organized about it. The first morning Imelda slept through her alarm. When she woke up, she thought, *I missed my time of prayer!* She grabbed her journal and Bible and prayed for a few minutes before she started to get ready for work.

The next day her oldest son was sick throughout the night, and Imelda didn't get any sleep. Once again she missed her time of prayer. Morning after morning Imelda found things getting in the way of her prayer time. So she decided to rearrange her schedule. Instead of praying first thing in the morning, she prays during her break at work. This is much more doable for her specific circumstances.

PRAYER HELPS

Here are some biblical guidelines for when to pray.

Pray without ceasing. Seek to develop an unbroken consciousness of God's presence and care. "Rejoicing in hope; patient in tribulation; continuing instant in prayer" (Romans 12:12).

Pray in the midst of discouragement, doubt, and fear. "Yet the LORD will command his lovingkindness in the daytime, and in the night his song shall be with me, and my prayer unto the God of my life" (Psalm 42:8).

Pray about everything. We often pray only during the crises of our lives, but we need daily strength, guidance, and protection. "Evening, and morning, and at noon, will I pray, and cry aloud: and he shall hear my voice" (Psalm 55:17).

Pray at a special time each day. We can be busy in service "for the Lord" and yet not set aside time to pray every day. We need this daily spiritual boost to keep ourselves on track. "But we will give ourselves continually to prayer, and to the ministry of the word" (Acts 6:4).

Undergird your spiritual growth with prayer. Our external life must have a deep internal groundwork of prayer, or else our lives will be feeble, weak, and fruitless. Every plant has a root system that is essential to its survival. If prayer is not a daily habit in a believer's life, then strong, deep spiritual roots will not develop. "Continue in prayer, and watch in the same with thanksgiving" (Colossians 4:2).

PRACTICAL PRAYER POINTERS

Here are some handy helps for you in developing a rich and powerful prayer life.

1. *If someone asks you to pray for him or her, take a moment right away to do it silently.* That way you have at least done it once. If the request is something you need to remember again, take a moment to write it down.

2. *Keep a prayer notebook near your Bible.* During your devotional time when you read your Bible, go through your prayer list. Write down the date you receive an answer next to the request. If you are discouraged, take some time to go through your past requests. You will be surprised at how many times God has specifically answered your prayers.

3. *Realize that the answer to your prayer is not limited in any way.* God will sometimes answer your prayer in a totally different way from what you might imagine.

4. *Be persistent!* Don't give up. I have known many Christians throughout the years who have prayed for their family's salvation. Though at times it seemed hopeless that the family would ever listen or be open to the Gospel, after years of constant prayer, miraculous answers came. One woman prayed for her unsaved parents for many years. Not too long before her mother's death, she received confirmation that her mom was saved. Her father has also trusted Christ. What would have happened if she had given up? She would never have experienced the blessing of seeing her parents come to Christ.

5. *Make sure your prayers are spiritual.* Pray not only for your phys-

ical needs but for opportunities to witness. Pray not only for your health but that you will have a servant's heart.

6. *Pray for your pastor every day.* He needs your prayers more than anything else. There are many people who say, "Pastor Scudder, can I do anything to help you?" And I always ask them to pray for me. Prayer is one of the most important helps we can give one another.

7. *Pray for those in governmental authority.* Pray for your boss too.

8. *Take time to pray.* Make it an important appointment. Not everyone can take time in the morning, though for a lot of people that is the best time. For some people, taking part of their lunch break to get away and quietly pray is the ticket. Other people pray in the evening.

9. *Confess your sins when you pray.* First John 1:9 says, "If we confess our sins, he is faithful and just to forgive us our sins, and to cleanse us from all unrighteousness." If you become accustomed to confessing your sins, then you may remain in constant fellowship with the Father. When you accepted Christ's payment on the cross for your sins, your offenses were forgiven. Yet your daily walk with Christ is hurt by both deliberate and unintentional sin.

GET RESULTS

Romans 15:30 states Paul's desire for believers to pray for him: "Now I beseech you, brethren, for the Lord Jesus Christ's sake, and for the love of the Spirit, that ye strive together with me in your prayers to God for me."

Developing a strong prayer life is crucial. When we learn to pray to our heavenly Father, we will learn how to stay strong. The cares of the world will be less likely to make an impression on us. The delusion of wealth won't have the same impact on our souls. The constant yearning for things other than God will diminish. Prayer brings God's provision into difficult situations.

Dr. Helen Roseveare, missionary to Zaire, tells of a remarkable answer to prayer:

> A mother at our mission station died after giving birth to a premature baby. They tried to improvise an incubator to keep the

infant alive, but the only hot water bottle we had was beyond repair. They asked the children to pray for the baby and for her sister. One of the girls responded, "Dear God, please send a hot water bottle today. Tomorrow will be too late because by then the baby will be dead. And dear Lord, send a doll for the sister so she won't feel so lonely." That afternoon a large package arrived from England. The children watched eagerly as we opened it. Much to their surprise, under some clothing was a hot water bottle!

Immediately the girl who had prayed so earnestly started to dig deeper, exclaiming, "If God sent that, I'm sure He also sent a doll!" And she was right! The heavenly Father knew of that child's sincere requests in advance, and five months earlier He had led a ladies' group to include both of those specific articles. (Source unknown.)

Spend time working the discipline of prayer into your life. You will find a well of constant strength and encouragement that will fortify your internal spiritual root system. Why don't you make a decision right now to give the highest priority to prayer? Decide on a time of day to pray. Find a notebook to use for your prayer time. Write down your spiritual goals. Do you wish for more control over your temper? Do you desire to lead a family member to Christ? Write these goals all down. Date each request. Pray for these things daily. You will find that prayer is the spiritual key you've had in your pocket all along. Why don't you take it out and develop its discipline today?

REV UP FOR REVIEW

Parable Principle #19—Don't compare your spiritual growth to that of other believers.

Parable Principle #20—Fellowship with people who share your desire for spiritual growth.

Parable Principle #21—Develop the habit of prayer.

Friend, I know you desire to be a Good-Soil Believer. I know you want to keep the soil of your life soft and ready to receive the Word. I know you want to experience spiritual victory, and you will. Just don't compare your sixtyfold to someone else's one hundredfold. Be glad when you produce thirtyfold. Be thankful you have produced anything at all. Instead of dwelling on the success of others, why don't you thank the Lord for giving you success? This will take the focus off the place it should never have been, other people, and instead focus it on the Lord. You should praise Him for the mighty blessings He has given you. Stop worrying about how far you have to go and concentrate on thanking the Lord for what He has already done through you. Joy will overflow from your thankful heart.

I hope you will take seriously the need to have friends who share your desire to grow spiritually. This support will help you avoid Wayside Hearers' Disorder. Ask the Lord to show you other believers who want to grow and then be a true friend to those people. Together you will make a difference for His name.

The habit of prayer can never be emphasized enough in the Christian life. While it is important to pray throughout the day, it is also of utmost importance to dedicate some special time each day to prayer. It is absolutely essential that you develop that pattern, for it is through prayer that you experience God's power and daily care. A prayer time sets your mind toward the things of God and helps you to focus on what He would have you to do. Good-Soil Christian, I know you are ready for the harvest. You are working to maintain that wholesome soil that receives the Word with gladness. You are developing the disciplines that will help you produce maximum results. As you continue to maintain your Willing Hearer/Doer status, I know one thing for sure: God is working to produce a bountiful, incalculable, joy-filled yield in your life. Happiness. Peace. Contentment. Everlasting help. It's all yours today.

Don't Be a
Burned-out Bulb

When I am gone, say nothing about Dr. Carey; speak about Dr. Carey's Savior.

—William Carey

I DON'T PICK UP hitchhikers anymore. I realize it is too dangerous. Yet many years ago while attending Bible college, I was young and brash and picked up hitchhikers to witness to them.

One day I stopped for a young man named Gary. He didn't know his life was going to change forever the day he stood by that lonely road in Florida. He asked for a ride to the University of Miami campus. As we drove, I shared the Gospel with him. Gary listened attentively. When I asked him if he wanted to trust Christ as his Savior, he said yes. Gary and I prayed, thanking God for sending His Son to die for our sins. Gary and I talked for a few more minutes before he got out of the car. I told him that the Holy Spirit now lived inside of him and would help him to live the Christian life.

A week or so later I got a phone call. It was Gary. His voice sounded desperate. "Can you call God off?" he pleaded.

"What do you mean, 'call God off'?" I asked.

"I live on the Miami campus stealing food to get by. Now that I'm saved, I feel guilty when I hit someone over the head to rob them."

Gary said he wanted to meet with me. We sat in a small park, and he shared a rather shocking story with me. He was AWOL from the army and had murdered his own father. The police were trying to find him.

I took a deep breath. I hadn't known that I'd been talking with a murderer! I looked Gary straight in the eye and said, "You need to turn yourself in."

He jumped back, and his eyes grew hard. "Never!" he said.

I stood to go, hoping I wouldn't be his next victim.

"Gary, I'm going to pray that God makes you so miserable that you have to turn yourself in," I said.

"I won't go to jail," Gary said between clenched teeth.

I didn't hear from Gary for about a month. Linda and I hadn't been married very long. We were living in a trailer not too far from the Bible college. One day the phone rang. It was Gary.

"I'm ready to turn myself in," he said. "I'm about to starve to death because I can't steal, and I know I can't keep living like this."

"Okay, Gary," I said.

"I have just one favor to ask you."

"What's that?"

"Would you go with me? I don't think I can do this by myself."

"Sure," I said.

"One more thing," he said, "would you buy me a meal before I turn myself in?"

Linda and I drove out to the Miami campus to pick him up. Now that I look back, I can't believe I brought my wife on such an excursion. But we knew the power of God and that He had changed Gary. We took Gary to a restaurant not too far from the jail. Linda and I didn't have enough money to order anything for ourselves, but we sat and watched him while he hungrily bolted down a plate of food. As he finished, he looked at both of us and asked, "Can I have something more?"

We both dug in our pockets and found enough change for him to have more food. He wolfed that down and then stood up. "I'm ready to go," he announced calmly.

When we arrived at the jail, I walked in with Gary. He told the officers his name, and they immediately came around the counter with handcuffs.

I said, "Listen, be careful with Gary. He's a changed man. The

Lord Jesus Christ saved him, and Gary wants you to know that." I then proceeded to give the Gospel to all the police officers.

I didn't see Gary for a while after that. Because they thought he was mentally ill, he was sentenced to a center for that type of prisoner. I visited him once while he was there. He was so happy to see me. He took me around and introduced me to many people he had won to Christ. He had given out hundreds of gospel tracts and was known for his love for the Lord.

I often think about what my life would have been like had I not been so excited about the Gospel. I know for sure I wouldn't have had such interesting experiences. I believe that this drive to share with others the good news has enriched and blessed my own life. I want the light of my own life to point others to the wonderful Gospel, the life-saving message of salvation, the timeless truth that all can trust Christ and know for sure they are going to heaven.

Would you also like to know how to share the Gospel with others? When you talk to someone who doesn't know Christ, do you know how to turn the conversation toward spiritual matters? When you try to tell a close family member about the Lord, do you find yourself at a loss for words?

This next parable principle and the following guidelines will give you insight and help in sharing the Gospel.

PARABLE PRINCIPLE #22—It is a privilege to share the light of the Gospel with others.

"And he said unto them, Is a candle brought to be put under a bushel, or under a bed? and not to be set on a candlestick?" (Mark 4:21). Jesus switches from talking about the farmer and his seed to a common object then and now, a candle, whose primary job is to shine. Light, of course, is essential to planet earth. That is why Jesus so often compared believers to light. If the sun were to suddenly burn out, we would have eight minutes of light and heat left, and then our planet would slip into a permanent deep-freeze.

In the Pacific Northwest, where it's overcast many days, lots of people suffer from light deprivation. This condition results in mood swings and depression. There's even a scientific name for this problem: Seasonal Affective Disorder, or SAD. People suffering from SAD have to set up special light panels in their homes and get heavy doses of illumination in order to be happy campers. We need light. It's hard to survive without it.

Mark 5:21 and the verses that follow it seem to reinforce the lessons from the Parable of the Sower. These short, pithy, proverbial sayings were sure to be remembered by the hearers.[1] Even later that evening, they would light their own oil lamps, instantly bringing to mind Jesus' illustration of how believers were to shine in the darkness of the world.

The Greek word for candle means "a portable lamp." In my office right now, I have several such lamps from Jesus' day. Made of clay, they had a place for a wick and a small well for oil. Sometimes these lamps would be put up on sticks so that they could give more light. Imagine the foolishness of setting a lamp under a basket or a bed. For the lamp to be useful, it had to be raised up and free of any covering so that it could provide light for all in the home.

There is probably no single object of everyday use that better illustrates what the Christian must do in the world. A tiny pinprick of light in the darkest room brings hope. Consider how many ships a lighthouse has saved!

Jesus calls John the Baptist a light in John 5:33-36: "Ye sent unto John, and he bare witness unto the truth. But I receive not testimony from man: but these things I say, that ye might be saved. He was a burning and a shining light: and ye were willing for a season to rejoice in his light. But I have greater witness than that of John: for the works which the Father hath given me to finish, the same works that I do, bear witness of me, that the Father hath sent me."

John was a burning and shining light. There could be no greater compliment than that for a Christian. This is my own desire, and I know it is yours. I want others to see my light and desire that same light in their own lives. The Gospel has great power to reveal. We are to display to others the precious treasure that we have found and persuade them to seek it for themselves. We are to tell them the good news that we have heard and seek to give a clear enough message so that they may believe it themselves.

Perhaps you are thinking, *I want others to know about Christ. I want my friends and neighbors to go to heaven. Yet I don't really know how to go about witnessing to them. I don't even really know what to say. Sometimes instead of being a light to the world, I feel like a burned-out bulb.*

You don't have to remain in that condition. In the next section you will find out how to share the light of the Gospel with others. Then your light will shine boldly and brightly.

STRUCK BY THE LIGHT

He was struck down by a blinding light on the road to Damascus. A voice out of heaven shouted, "Saul, why are you persecuting me?" Paul's conversion was unique, and he knew it. No other means could have so effectively turned his attention away from the Christians he was persecuting to the Christ he persecuted more.

Paul said, "Who art thou, Lord? And the Lord said, I am Jesus whom thou persecutest: it is hard for thee to kick against the pricks. And he trembling and astonished said, Lord, what wilt thou have me to do? And the Lord said unto him, Arise, and go into the city, and it shall be told thee what thou must do" (Acts 9:5-6). Later in Scripture when Paul preached, he included his own testimony. He described the day he was struck by the light and told how that light changed him forever.

I think the first help you can glean from Paul is to use your own testimony when you witness. How did you trust Christ as your Savior? Where were you? What were you thinking and feeling? How did the truth of the Gospel challenge your thinking? What kind of works did you think you had to do for salvation before you found out it was a free gift? Jesus knew when He shared parables and stories that people would listen. So use your own story, how you understood the Gospel, as an opener when you witness. This can be an effective way of ministering to others.

Paul gives us more tips on witnessing, and he is a great one to teach us. His whole purpose was to share the good news of Jesus Christ with as many people as he could. He took this job seriously, and his example challenges us to do the same. First Thessalonians 2 mentions many qualities Paul had as a soul-winner. His conduct gives us insight into his success.

1. *Paul was bold in his witness.*

"But even after that we had suffered before, and were shamefully entreated, as ye know, at Philippi, we were bold in our God to speak unto you the gospel of God with much contention" (1 Thessalonians 2:2).

Often I have been surprised at how well people respond to boldness in sharing the Gospel. I am not saying that you need to be rude or in someone's face. Yet a crucial element of witnessing is courage. Sometimes circumstances such as the events of September 11, 2001, make people more open to the Lord. Take advantage of those times, and in a gentle and loving way, but with boldness, share the Gospel with others.

I remember one time I had offered to the woman sitting beside me on a plane a gospel tract. She rudely refused to take it. A little while later after an emergency landing because of engine trouble, she turned to me and said, "Could I have that pamphlet, please?"

2. *Paul used no deceit or trickery.*

"For our exhortation was not of deceit, nor of uncleanness, nor in guile" (1 Thessalonians 2:3). Paul didn't use any false gimmicks when he shared the Gospel. This principle should go without saying, and yet there are many Christians who use trickery or even spread a false gospel for their own benefit. These people make it difficult for us to share our faith without someone saying, "Oh, I know about you Christians. You say you are so holy. Well, what about So-and-So on television?" It is important that people understand that we are sincere in our efforts to share the Gospel.

3. *Paul fulfilled his trust and pleased God.*

"But as we were allowed of God to be put in trust with the gospel, even so we speak; not as pleasing men, but God, which trieth our hearts" (1 Thessalonians 2:4). Paul's sacred trust was the Gospel. He knew that sharing Christ with others was his most important duty. When he explained God's truth, he knew he was pleasing God. Friend, do you realize that every time you hand out a gospel tract, you are pleasing God? When you take a moment to share the Gospel with another person, God is pleased that Parable Principle #22 has become an important part of your life. As you share the Gospel, you are fulfilling a sacred trust.

4. *Paul shared the Gospel without desire for personal gain.*

"For neither at any time used we flattering words, as ye know, nor a cloak of covetousness; God is witness" (1 Thessalonians 2:5). Paul gave the Gospel to others without worrying about whether people could give something back to him. He simply did his duty, fulfilling his sacred trust.

5. *Paul didn't care about the praise of men.*

"Nor of men sought we glory, neither of you, nor yet of others, when we might have been burdensome, as the apostles of Christ" (1 Thessalonians 2:6). Paul knew his commission was from the Lord Himself. Therefore, he didn't seek human praise for his actions. Rather, he focused on the need for others to hear his message.

6. *Paul was gentle.*

"But we were gentle among you, even as a nurse cherisheth her children" (1 Thessalonians 2:7). I remember another time that a college friend and I picked up a hitchhiker (Florida again!). We sat him between us and drove over the mile-long Key Biscayne Bridge. Right in the middle of it, Bill looked at him and said, "Do you know where you're going when you die?"

The hitchhiker's eyes got wide as he stared out the window at the water below us. "Are you going to kill me?" he asked.

We both learned from that experience that we needed to be more careful when we gave out the Gospel. Paul was gentle in his approach to soul-winning. He cared about those he witnessed to. There is no greater mark of a successful soul-winner.

Show love when you witness. If the message is rejected, know that you have planted the seed of the Gospel. Just as it takes time for a seed to germinate and grow, so the gospel seed will grow even if you don't personally see the harvest.

7. *Paul showed great love for the lost.*

"So being affectionately desirous of you, we were willing to have imparted unto you, not the gospel of God only, but also our own souls, because ye were dear unto us" (1 Thessalonians 2:8).

Late one night a salesman drove into a strange city and tried to get a room in a hotel. The clerk informed him that there was no vacancy. Disappointed, he started to leave the lobby when a dignified gentleman offered to share his room with him. Gratefully the traveler accepted this kindness. Just before going to sleep, the man who had shown such hospitality knelt and prayed aloud. He prayed for the stranger by name and asked the Lord to bless him. Then when he awoke the next morning, he told his guest it was his habit to read the Bible and commune with God at the beginning of each day and asked the salesman if he would like to join him.

The host gently explained the Gospel, and it wasn't long before the salesman accepted Christ. As the two were ready to say good-bye, they exchanged business cards. The new believer was amazed when he read the card. It said, "William Jennings Bryan, Secretary of State."

Bryan understood that he was not simply a representative of the United States government, but more importantly he was an ambassador for Jesus Christ. He was a common laborer in the field of God who desired to share the love of Christ with others. Bryan welcomed a stranger to share his room—a kindness that opened the salesman's heart to the Gospel.

There were four of us who left the University of Kentucky to attend Florida Bible College. Bill Adams, Ed Sutton, Rance Darity, and I were so excited about witnessing to others. The Lord brought many unsaved people our way. In retrospect, I realize that sometimes our enthusiasm brought harm to God's kingdom. One time we took gospel pamphlets and stuck them in all of the hymnbooks of a certain denomination that didn't teach salvation by grace.

Another time Bill Adams and a group of his friends decided they weren't reaching enough people. They spent several afternoons tightly rolling up tracts in pieces of tinfoil. They loaded up a van and drove fifty-five miles per hour down the highway, throwing the miniature "bombs" out by the hundreds.

As time went on, we began to see that there are many effective ways of proclaiming the Gospel that bring glory, not disgrace, to the kingdom of God. It is important to show love for the lost when you witness to them. Don't hit them with a fifty-five-mile-per-hour gospel "bomb!"

8. *Paul labored diligently.*

"For ye remember, brethren, our labour and travail: for labouring night and day, because we would not be chargeable unto any of you, we preached unto you the gospel of God" (1 Thessalonians 2:9). Paul didn't get discouraged in his labor. Rather, he continued giving his best for the sake of the Gospel, understanding that God would bless his hard work.

Is there a family member who continues to listen as you explain the Gospel but won't accept it? Perhaps you know a teenager who likes to talk to you about spiritual things but still hasn't accepted Christ. Know this: Your diligence, just like Paul's perseverance, will pay off. It will be worth it, but you must be diligent.

9. *Paul's testimony kept him from being a burned-out bulb.*

"Ye are witnesses, and God also, how holily and justly and unblameably we behaved ourselves among you that believe" (1 Thessalonians 2:10). It is so important to keep your life pure and clean so that others will listen to what you say.

10. *Paul discipled his new converts.*

"As ye know how we exhorted and comforted and charged every one of you, as a father doth his children, that ye would walk worthy of God, who hath called you unto his kingdom and glory" (1 Thessalonians 2:11-12). Paul continued to help those who trusted Christ.[2] He taught them more about Scripture. These verses say he comforted them and helped them. He did this because he knew that they would then be ready to do the work of an evangelist themselves. They would be prepared to give the Gospel to others, thereby multiplying Paul's own efforts.

LEARN TO SPEAK

A witness has something to declare. Are you saying it? Some believers say, "I don't have to talk about my faith; I just have to show my faith." These same people have no problem talking about their job, their favorite restaurant, the football game last Sunday, or the latest computer upgrade, but witnessing for their Lord and Savior? Out of the question!

In many churches there are many workers, but few are soul-winners. There are many leaders, but few who are witnesses. Yet every Christian can and should be a soul-winner.

In a book entitled *The Day America Told the Truth,* these were the responses to "Why do you think you will go to heaven?"

60%	I'm basically a good person.
15%	I've done the best that I could.
10%	I believe in God.
8%	I go to church.
5%	I obey the Ten Commandments.
2%	I don't know.

Notice that not one of these answers is correct. Most people don't know how to go to heaven. They may call themselves Christians, but if they don't know how to go to heaven, then they certainly are not believers. That is why it is so important that we witness. Psalm 71:24 says, "My tongue also shall talk of thy righteousness all the day long."

WITNESSING HOW-TO'S

A young boy named Zach went to his Sunday school teacher after class. "I don't know how to tell other people about Jesus," he said.

"Yes, you do," his teacher responded. "Do you know John 3:16?"

"Of course!" the boy said proudly. "That's the first verse I learned!"

"That verse is enough to tell someone about Jesus. Do you think you could explain that verse to them?"

"Sure I could." Zach smiled. "I'll try it this week."

You don't have to be a theologian in order to witness to others. In fact, you could just witness with John 3:16 like Zach. Here are some straightforward witnessing how-to's that will help you lead someone to Christ.

1. First, say that everyone is less perfect than a holy God. But be careful. Don't look the person in the eye and say, "You're a sinner!" Rather, explain that everyone is a sinner, including yourself, and that it takes only one sin to be less than perfect. Look up Romans 3:23 and

read it aloud: "For all have sinned, and come short of the glory of God." Explain that the word *sin* means to miss the mark of God's perfection. Even one sin is enough to keep us out of heaven.

2. The Bible says that even our good deeds are unclean in God's sight. Our good deeds can never pay the price for our sin. Isaiah 64:6 states, "But we are all as an unclean thing, and all our righteousnesses are as filthy rags; and we all do fade as a leaf; and our iniquities, like the wind, have taken us away."

3. Since our good deeds are unable to take away sin, and sin keeps us from perfection, we are all under the penalty for sin—death. Explain that eternal death means separation from God forever. Look up Romans 6:23 and read it aloud: "For the wages of sin is death; but the gift of God is eternal life through Jesus Christ our Lord."

4. Because we have all sinned, we deserve to be separated from God forever. God hates sin, for it separates us from Him, but He loves us, the sinners. Revelation 21:27 is a good verse to use at this point: "And there shall in no wise enter into it any thing that defileth, neither whatsoever worketh abomination, or maketh a lie: but they which are written in the Lamb's book of life."

5. Explain to your friend that one can only go to heaven by God's grace. Grace means unmerited favor or undeserved mercy. Give an illustration of a present you bring to a birthday party, and explain that a gift is not earned. Now read Ephesians 2:8-9: "For by grace are ye saved through faith; and that not of yourselves: it is the gift of God: not of works, lest any man should boast."

6. Share that Christ made the perfect payment for the person's sin on the cross. Second Corinthians 5:21 is a great verse to use now: "For he hath made him to be sin for us, who knew no sin; that we might be made the righteousness of God in him."

7. Recap that we are all sinners and that the penalty of sin is eternal separation from God. Say again that God loves the person and offers the gift of eternal life. God requires that he or she trust in that payment. Say that all the person has to do to have eternal life is believe in Jesus Christ. Read John 3:16 to your friend: "For God so loved the world, that he gave his only begotten Son, that whosoever believeth in him should not perish, but have everlasting life." Assure your

friend who trusts Christ that Jesus' blood cleanses him or her from all sin. Speak also of the death, burial, and resurrection of our Lord. A good verse to use is 1 Corinthians 15:3-4: "For I delivered unto you first of all that which I also received, how that Christ died for our sins according to the scriptures; and that he was buried, and that he rose again the third day according to the scriptures."

8. When you are sure your friend understands the plan of salvation, then say, "Will you place your trust in Jesus Christ to save you? To trust Him means to rely totally on Him, not on your own good works to get you to heaven. Will you do this right now?"

9. If your friend says no, then ask what he doesn't understand. Answer his questions. If the person doesn't want to receive Christ, then know that you have planted a seed. If your friend says yes, explain that since he has trusted Jesus Christ as Savior, he can know he has eternal life. Finish with 1 John 5:13: "These things have I written unto you that believe on the name of the Son of God; that ye may know that ye have eternal life, and that ye may believe on the name of the Son of God."

Think about the joy you will feel when that person says, "Yes, I understand what you are saying. I believe that Jesus paid for all my sins so that I can go to heaven." If you wish, you might pray with your friend at the close of the conversation. Explain that it isn't necessary to pray to go to heaven because that would be a good work. Yet it is helpful to close in prayer. You could say something like this: "Father, I am so glad that my friend has just trusted You as his Savior. I am happy that he understands that You died for him and paid for his sins. He now understands that nothing he could do could pay for his own salvation. I praise You that he is now Your child and can know for sure he is going to heaven. In Jesus' name, amen." If your friend wishes, he could pray as well.

ADDITIONAL TIPS

Highlight Salvation Verses

As a further help, look up the above verses in your Bible before you witness. Highlight them. After Romans 3:23 write in the margin next to it "Isaiah 64:6" and so on. That way when you are giving the Gospel, you can turn to the next verse easily. It also helps to memorize these verses on salvation. This will build your confidence, and then you can witness even if you don't have your Bible with you.

Ask for an Interpretation

If you find as you are witnessing that the person doesn't understand the Gospel, ask her to read the verse herself. Then ask her what her interpretation of that verse is. This is a great way to keep her engaged in the conversation and for you to make sure that she understands what you are saying.

Don't Get Sidetracked

Try not to get into a deep philosophical discussion when you are witnessing. Stay on the Gospel. That is where the power is. Romans 1:16 says, "For I am not ashamed of the gospel of Christ: for it is the power of God unto salvation to every one that believeth; to the Jew first, and also to the Greek." Remember that I said that before I trusted Christ, I had no interest in spiritual things? The person you are talking to needs to get saved before he can understand spiritual things. That's why I can't stress enough how important it is that you stay on the Gospel. If the person brings up other religions, evolution, or just wants to argue, be polite and answer the questions, but don't get into a dispute. Pray that someone else will reap what you have sown.

Use Illustrations

We have seen throughout this book that the Lord used illustrations as He explained spiritual truths. You can use them too. They should have subject matter familiar to the person and ought to be concrete, rather than abstract, forming a picture in the person's mind. Keep them short and to the point. Don't get so carried away with illustrations that they usurp the proper place of Scripture in your presentation. Always bear in mind that your illustrations are a means to an end—to throw additional light upon the Scriptures—and not an end in themselves.

Agree When You Can

When a person is right, agree with him or her. And when you must disagree, do so in as pleasant a way as you can. Don't turn someone off to the Gospel by insensitivity or brashness.

Don't Use Too Many Verses

When one verse clarifies the point, leave it there. Usually the person's problem is not that he needs more verses, but rather that he does not understand or believe the verse you just showed him.

Use Questions

As an example, for the verse: "Whosoever believeth in him should not perish, but have everlasting life," you might ask: "Does this verse say, Whoever works, whoever joins the church and pays a tithe, will not perish? Does this verse say that those who believe will have life until they start sinning again?" Questions will help your friend think with you about the verses and understand them.

Be Honest

If you can't answer a question, say so! Don't bluff. Say you don't know and offer to find the answer to give to the person at a later date.[3]

OH, MY ACHING BACK!

We've studied much about the farmer and his expected harvest. When you sow the seed of the Word in others, you are assuming a new role, that of the sower. Remember that you will sow seeds in all types of people. Some will be like the good ground, ready to receive the Word and trust Christ. Others will have Wayside Hearers' Disorder, and still others will have Stony Ground Syndrome. Don't let this discourage you. Understand that when you are diligent, God will bring a harvest.

A story reminds me of how hard it is sometimes to witness. Gregory told about going strawberry picking with his wife's parents. When they got to the fields, many people were already hard at work there. Each person received a cardboard flat to hold the picked strawberries, and the family walked out to the fields. As they headed down the rows, looking for a good place to start, visions of strawberries heaped high and overflowing over a piece of shortcake came to Greg's mind. But as soon as he began picking, the visions started fading. Strawberry picking was hard work, and it seemed as if his cardboard flat would never get full. Ten minutes later his back started to ache. He got to his knees and started to push the flat in front of him as he continued to pick. His back felt better, but his knees started to hurt. Soon he looked at his wife's flat and asked if he could combine his with hers. Everyone in the group decided to call it a day.

Sometimes this is how it can feel to witness. We feel strong as we read the Bible, but when we get out into our everyday jobs, we find ourselves tired and achy, ready to give up. Jesus told us that the harvest is plentiful, but sometimes we want to say, "Oh, my aching back."[4]

Understand that it is normal to get weary when you are doing the work of the Lord. There are no Super Christians, only a Super Savior. It is only through His strength that we can reap the harvest. It is only through the power of the Holy Spirit that we can witness to others and have the energy to persevere when it is difficult. Recognize that while you may sometimes feel like Gregory as he picked strawberries, God will give you renewed strength. All you need to do is ask.

At times we probably think it would be easier if we could be like Lucy in the old Peanuts cartoon. Lucy says to Charlie Brown, "I would have made a great evangelist."

Charlie Brown answers, "Is that so?"

She says, "Yes, I convinced that boy in front of me in school that my religion is better than his religion."

Charlie Brown asked, "Well, how did you do that?"

Lucy answers, "I hit him over the head with my lunch box."

Missionary to China J. Hudson Taylor said, "The harvest here is indeed great, and the laborers are few and imperfectly fitted, without much grace, for such a work. And yet grace can make a few feeble instruments the means of accomplishing great things—things greater than even we can conceive."

When I was recently in China, I asked every Chinese Christian I met if he had heard of Hudson Taylor. They all said that they might not be saved today if he hadn't come to China.

So take the previous witnessing steps and use them to tell others of the plan of salvation. Study the guidelines and use Scripture skillfully as you fulfill your greatest duty as a believer.

PARABLE PRINCIPLE #23—How you live affects your witness for Christ.

A skeptic promised British preacher Alexander Maclaren that he would attend his church for four Sundays on which Maclaren would be presenting the main tenets of Christianity. The skeptic listened intently to the sermons. After the fourth message, he presented himself for church membership, saying he had received Christ as his Savior.

Maclaren was delighted and could not resist the impulse to ask which of the four sermons brought him to this decision. The skeptic replied, "Your sermons, sir, were helpful, but they were not what finally persuaded me." He said that after church one Sunday as he was helping an elderly woman on a slippery sidewalk, she looked up into his face and said, "I wonder if you know my Savior, Jesus Christ. He is everything in the world to me. I would like you to know Him too."

It was the woman's heartfelt plea that brought that skeptic to the cross. Her countenance must have communicated to him just how dear her Lord was. No matter the words we speak, there is nothing like a genuine witness to bring others to Christ.

Look again at Mark 4:21: "And he said unto them, Is a candle brought to be put under a bushel, or under a bed? and not to be set on a candlestick?" If you took a candle and put it under a bushel basket, not too many people would see the light. In our Christian walk, when we let the bushel of selfishness, of false humility, and of embarrassment crowd out our light, those we witness to will not listen. Our testimony affects how others view Christianity, and it is of utmost importance that we remember this. Titus 3:8 says, "This is a faithful saying, and these things I will that thou affirm constantly, that they which have believed in God might be careful to maintain good works.

These things are good and profitable unto men." Here are three bushels that can cover your light as a believer.

THE SELFISHNESS BUSHEL

In a heated exchange with one of her colleagues, Alice said, "I wish you had never gotten that promotion. I was the one who deserved it."

Pam stared at her. "I never knew you were such a selfish person, Alice. I thought you were a Christian."

Alice felt pierced to the heart. She had let the bushel of selfishness and ambition crowd out her witness to Pam.

After a moment, Alice said haltingly, "I'm sorry. You're right. I am being selfish."

H. A. Ironside once said, "If lips and life do not agree, the testimony will not amount to much." Selfish desires not only choke out our spiritual growth, but they also destroy our testimony for Christ.

THE FALSE HUMILITY BUSHEL

If Pastor Rice had heard it once, he had heard it a thousand times.

"I don't have any gifts or abilities," Kevin said despairingly.

"The Lord has given you talents, Kevin," Pastor Rice said.

"No, He hasn't. I'm not worth anything."

Pastor Rice sighed. He knew that Kevin said this in order to hear his pastor assure him that he did have talents. Still he knew Kevin wouldn't stop degrading his own abilities no matter what he said. One day Kevin surprised Pastor Rice by witnessing to his mother. She didn't trust Christ, but she listened intently and said she would think about it. Kevin realized that his previous statements to his pastor were actually made in self-pity. He determined to let the Lord use him by sharing the Gospel with others.

Don't hide your candle under the bushel of false humility. You may not have many talents, but you can serve the Lord with the talents you have. I have seen people with the lowest income and the worst education (at least in the world's eyes) used of God in mighty ways. I have observed people with disabilities become great soulwinners. Don't let anything stop you from witnessing!

THE EMBARRASSMENT BUSHEL

Quentin Road Ministries was just beginning when I led Edward to Christ. He was eager to tell his friends and neighbors about his Savior. However, one day his enthusiasm was almost his undoing. He started to witness to a woman in a grocery store, and she got angry. She picked up the nearest thing she could find, which happened to be a can of stewed tomatoes from a stacked display. She hurled it at Edward, narrowly missing his head. Edward turned and ran, but not before she sent several more cans crashing at his feet.

Edward was devastated. He moped for weeks, not witnessing to anyone and feeling hopelessly embarrassed. I tried to encourage him, but nothing helped. He had decided it was too hard to win people to Christ.

Edward let embarrassment overcome his desire to witness. Don't let this happen to you. If people reject the Gospel, don't worry about it. Remember that it is God who brings the harvest. Your job is simply to sow the seed. Since you are being faithful in doing your job, there is no need to feel embarrassed.

EQUIPPED FOR THE TASK

A man named Mike was a security guard at East Towne Mall in Knoxville, Tennessee. One day he helped a police officer run down a fleeing shoplifter. Mike received a police commendation—and a warning from his boss. It seems Mike was not supposed to get involved. He participated in several other incidents for which his boss also reprimanded him— preventing a strong-arm robbery, intervening in a car theft, and complying with a police officer's request for assistance. His superiors explained that security guards at the mall have no more authority than any other civilian. They are supposed to avoid the situations into which Mike thrust himself. Apparently, the thinking of mall officials is that the appearance of authority (though not real) will help to prevent problems, while avoiding the risks and lawsuits that come with actual authority.

As believers, we don't just have the appearance of authority. We have authority direct from the Word of God. We must not be just "mall guard" Christians, never really witnessing and never really making a difference for Christ. Philippians 1:27 says, "Only let your conversation be as it becometh the gospel of Christ: that whether I come and see you, or else be absent, I may hear of your affairs, that ye stand fast in one spirit, with one mind striving together for the faith of the gospel." This word *conversation* means manner of life. We need to understand that how we live our lives does affect whether others will hear the Gospel. Their eternal destiny is at stake. As much as possible, live in such a way that others will listen as you share the greatest news of all.

REV UP FOR REVIEW

Parable Principle #22—It is a privilege to share the light of the Gospel with others.

Parable Principle #23—How you live affects your witness for Christ.

Take these two parable principles to heart. Being a witness of the grace of the Lord is our most important job as believers. The Lord's last command before He ascended into heaven was for us to take the Gospel to the lost. It is the Great Commission, our most important command to obey. Won't you accept the challenge from our Lord? Will you take the suggestions in this chapter on sharing the Gospel? Will you pray for specific occasions to tell the truth of salvation to others and then take advantage of the opportunities given you? This glorious Gospel is yours to give. You will experience no greater joy than when you share it with others.

Someday the Bugs Will Come Out

We judge of things by their present appearances, but the Lord sees them in their consequences; if we could do likewise, we should be perfectly of His mind; but as we cannot, it is an unspeakable mercy that He will manage for us.

—JOHN NEWTON

THE HEALTH INSPECTOR studied every surface of our town's bakery. She crawled under the utility sink and checked the pipes. She stood on a ladder and examined the ceiling. She poked her finger in a pastry or two. The bakery wasn't very big, but the inspection took over two hours. Finally she declared the business fit to operate.

Six months later the health inspector visited again. When the owner saw the inspector exiting her car, the owner said to one of her workers, "Quick, spread some flour on the counter by the cash register."

The worker looked surprised at the order but did as she was told. The inspector spotted the flour immediately. "Clean up that flour next to the cash register," she said.

The owner cleaned up the flour.

"Everything looks fine," the inspector said as she left.

The owner glanced at her watch. "Only took five minutes that time," she said.

"Why did I have to sprinkle flour next to the cash register?" the worker asked.

The owner laughed. "The inspector's job is to find something wrong. We just gave her something easy to find."

There is a lot of truth in that. Human nature naturally looks for imperfections. Sometimes this tendency even affects our view of God. Perhaps we grew up thinking of Him as a harsh father figure who enjoys squashing sinners with a huge hammer. It could be that your view of God was more of a celestial 911. If you had an emergency, He would help you, but in any other circumstances He couldn't care less.

I'm sure you know that neither of these views is correct. God is a loving heavenly Father who is both just and merciful. He demands perfection but sent His Son to pay for sins we couldn't pay for on our own. Since we trusted Christ as our Savior, we have more than just a heavenly inspector observing us. We have a perfect judge, one who is reviewing our deeds. He isn't pompously recording every weakness. He is a righteous judge who is recording the deeds done by believers for an exciting reason: He wants to reward our faithfulness. He judges us because one day He will present us with what I call the W.D. (Well Done) degree. He will give us crowns and rewards, and we in turn will lay them at His feet. So while we serve the Lord out of gratitude for what He did for us, we also have the excitement of striving for rewards. The Bible compares the Christian life to a race. The runner desires to win. Otherwise he wouldn't run at all.

A world-class runner was invited to compete in a marathon in Connecticut. On the morning of the race, she drove from New York City, following the directions—or so she thought—given her over the telephone. She got lost, stopped at a gas station, and asked for help. She knew that the race started in the parking lot of a shopping mall. The station attendant knew of such a race scheduled just up the road and directed her there.

When she arrived, she was relieved to see in the parking lot a small number of runners preparing to compete. She had thought there would be more runners. She hurried to the registration desk, announced herself, and was surprised by the race official's excitement at having so renowned an athlete show up for their race.

"We're sorry, but we don't have a record of your entry," an official told her, "but hurry and put on this number, and you'll just make it to the beginning before the gun goes off."

She won the race easily, almost four minutes ahead of the first male runner in second place. After the race she was surprised when no one handed her a prize envelope. Then she figured it out. The race she had run in was not the race to which she had been invited. That race was held several miles away in another town. She'd gone to the wrong starting line, run the wrong course, and missed her chance to win a valuable reward.[1]

The Christian life is a race you can win, and you don't have to be a world-class athlete to do it. We don't have to worry that we are running the wrong race because we have the Bible as our guide. Our next parable principle shows what the believer's judgment is all about.

PARABLE PRINCIPLE #24—You will be judged for deeds done for Christ.

In the last chapter we saw that our lives should be a witness. They should shine like a lit candle in a dark room. Keeping the candle out from under the cover of worldliness, selfishness, and a myriad of other distractions is a lifelong process. That is what brings us to the next point Jesus makes in His discourse. Just as the candle shows the objects that are in the room, so shall nothing be hid in our lives. We may be lulled into thinking that nobody sees what we do in secret, but this parable principle dispels that myth. "For there is nothing hid, which shall not be manifested; neither was any thing kept secret, but that it should come abroad" (Mark 4:22).

Thomas Edwards, a Scottish naturalist, went searching for insects. He had an old coat with many pockets that he wore for his expeditions. Each pocket had many cardboard boxes in which to place the various specimens he might find. His day was hugely successful, for he collected many rare insects, each of which he placed within its own little box.

As he traveled home, a storm overtook Edwards. The thunder roared, and the lightning flashed around him. The rain came down in torrents, and he was soon drenched to the skin.

He noticed a farmhouse a short distance away. An elderly woman let him in and offered him a seat by the fire. The warmth of the fire lulled him into sleep. Presently the woman returned to the room. Suddenly she screamed and caught up a broom and shooed him out of the house. Standing outside in the rain once again, he looked down and understood the woman's terror. He was covered from head to foot with his beloved insects. The soaking rain had softened the boxes and set the prisoners at liberty. They remained unseen in his pockets until the warmth of the fire brought them out. I doubt that that dear lady invited any strangers into her home again for a long time!

Dear friend, someday the bugs of carnality and apathy toward Christ will come out. One day all will be made right. We will be judged for our works. Those who haven't served Christ will suffer loss. Are you prepared to face Christ's judgment?

FAST FACTS ABOUT REWARDS

Sometimes schools urge their students to sell magazines to raise money. One man told me that when he was a student, he had hated the awards ceremony at the end of such a fundraiser. He never won anything because he never sold anything. He never sold anything because he never worked like the other kids. But it never failed—when all the prizes were being passed out, he wished that he had done more work.

My grandson Jamie isn't like that. He got his first taste of school fundraising last year. He loved it. Of course, that was mainly because he won a bike for his efforts. The offer of a prize motivated him. He had worked hard going out with his dad to sell tickets to an all-you-can-eat pizza party. He kept telling his mom that he was going to win. Julie was afraid he would be disappointed if he didn't win, and so she explained, "Jamie, you may not win the bike. There are a lot of other kids trying to win it."

"I can still try," Jamie said doggedly. "I'm having fun trying."

It is the same way in the Christian life, only better, because you aren't competing against other believers, and everyone can win. This is a win-win situation for all. Not only can you live your life with the many blessings already available to you in the present (the Holy Spirit, the Bible, the privilege of talking to God, your local church), but you have the wonder of heaven to anticipate. On top of all this, you will be rewarded for your faithfulness on this earth. It doesn't get any better than that!

Let's study a passage of Scripture that gives us some hints about our eternal rewards:

> *According to the grace of God which is given unto me, as a wise master-builder, I have laid the foundation, and another buildeth thereon. But let every man take heed how he buildeth thereupon. For other foundation can no man lay than that is laid, which is Jesus Christ. Now if any man build upon this foundation gold, silver, precious stones, wood, hay, stubble; every man's work shall be made manifest: for the day shall declare it, because it shall be revealed by fire; and the fire shall try every man's work of what sort it is. If any man's work abide which he hath built thereupon, he shall receive a reward. (1 Corinthians 3:10-14)*

These verses say that every man's work shall be made manifest. This is similar in language to Mark 4:22. The fire that this passage refers to does not mean the eternal flames of hell. There is an important distinction between God's judgment of believers and the Great White Throne Judgment. The first judgment is only for believers. Those who have served Christ will receive rewards. Those who cluttered their lives with worldliness and didn't give themselves to the Lord's service will not be punished with hell. Instead, they will not receive the rewards faithful believers get.

Here are some verses that refer to what is known as the Great White Throne Judgment:

> *And I saw a great white throne, and him that sat on it, from whose face the earth and the heaven fled away; and there was found no place for them. And I saw the dead, small and great, stand before God; and the books were opened: and another book was opened, which is the book of life: and the dead were judged out of those things which were written in the books, according to their works. And the sea gave up the dead which were in it; and death and hell delivered up the dead which were in them: and they were judged every man according to their works. And death and hell were cast into the lake of fire. This is the second death. (Revelation 20:11-14)*

All people at the Great White Throne Judgment are punished forever. I believe that according to this passage there are degrees of hell. There will be a judgment of works at this judgment as well, but because those being judged haven't trusted Christ as Savior, the end result is hell.

YOU ARE A WINNER

Jill knew she wasn't a winner. Although the front of the envelope almost shouted, "Jill Smith, you could already have won $1,000,000," she didn't believe it. She had fallen for the sweepstakes game before, filling out multiple entries and hoping against hope that she would win. She had spent hours planning how she would spend her windfall. As she looked at her life, she saw for the first time how much time she had wasted on useless things. Now she knew that all of her dreaming had been a waste of time. She threw this latest offer into the trash.

The Lord operates differently from the world. The world makes false claims and promises, feeding human greed and pride. It causes people to give up everything worthwhile in the hope of winning something better. Yet the consistent winner is always the world and never the individual. Human greed is such that the victim almost never realizes this. The world feeds on uncertainty and insecurity, promising dreams it can never deliver. The world also exploits people's moods. Studies indicate that gambling increases when economic times are uncertain, and people are concerned about their future. Joseph Dunn (director of the National Council on Compulsive Gambling) says, "People who are worried about the factory closing take a chance on making it big."[2] A person is seven times more likely to be killed by lightning than he is to win a million dollars in a state lottery.[3] Yet people continue to place their faith in a scheme that will never give them anything in return.

God's rewards are completely different from the "you could already be a winner" mentality. The biggest distinction? Every faithful Christian wins. The Lord promises to reward every believer according to his or her works. Individual looks, talents, or strengths do not matter. There is no favoritism, no empty promises.

Faithfulness to the call of God ensures not only a better life here on this earth but also a better life in heaven.

Martin Luther said:

> If we consider the greatness and the glory of the life we shall have when we have risen from the dead, it would not be difficult at all for us to bear the concerns of this world. If I believe the Word, I shall on the Last Day, after the sentence has been pronounced, not only gladly have suffered ordinary temptations, insults, and imprisonment, but I shall also say: "O, that I did not throw myself under the feet of all the godless for the sake of the great glory which I now see revealed and which has come to me through the merit of Christ!"[4]

When Luther looked at life from the proper point of view, his feelings about any sacrifice he had to make on this earth made complete sense. There isn't a Christian alive who, when he sees Christ, will say, "I wish I hadn't done so much for You." Instead, we will all say, "I wish I had done more for You, Lord. Nothing I did for You compares to what You did for me."

Friend, take a moment and consider what Christ will say about your life at the judgment seat. Are you living in such a way that you are bringing honor and glory to the Lord Jesus? Is the fruit of the Spirit (love, joy, peace, longsuffering, gentleness, goodness, faith, meekness, temperance) evident in your life? Are you witnessing to others and serving in your local church? These are works made of gold.

GOING FOR THE GOLD

The phrase "judgment seat" comes from the Greek word *bema*. Though *bema* is used several times in the New Testament to refer to the court of a human judge, historically it comes from the Isthmian games, which were forerunners to our modern Olympic games. The city of Corinth was located on an isthmus, part of a peninsula in the southern section of Greece.

The bema was a raised platform on which the judges sat. There

were two reasons why the judges sat there. First, they could see if anyone tried to cheat. Second, from the raised platform they conferred
rewards.

History tells us that the winners of the Isthmian games received
garland wreaths that symbolized wonderful rewards. A winner was
exempt from military duty. He received a paid education for his entire
family. He paid no taxes for life. A bronze plaque with his name on
it was placed on the gates at the entrance to his home city.[5] So the parallel is clear. Christ, our perfect judge, will reward His faithful believers one day from the heavenly Bema Seat. The rewards will mean
much more than a bronze plaque ever could.

TRUTHS ABOUT THE BEMA SEAT

No Exemptions

Not long ago Jane, one of the church secretaries, was called for jury
duty. The summons came at a bad time, and Jane called to ask to be
excused. The officials agreed to postpone her summons, but she still
had to serve eventually. You can get out of a lot of things on earth. You
might be excused from jury duty, a traffic ticket, or homework. But
you can't call up the heavenly judgment office and say, "I'm sorry, but
I can't appear before the judgment seat of Christ. I'm too busy right
now." No believer will be excused from standing before Christ. That
is one appointment you will keep. Paul says in Romans 14:10, "But
why dost thou judge thy brother? or why dost thou set at nought thy
brother? for we shall all stand before the judgment seat of Christ."
The Bema Seat involves the universal body of Christ. All believers
from this age will be present.

You Stand Alone

This judgment is individual. Only you will give witness of your life.
No one can stand for you; neither can you stand for anyone else.
Husbands can't appear for wives. Parents can't appear for children.
You will face your own judgment. Hebrews 4:13 says, "Neither is
there any creature that is not manifest in his sight: but all things are
naked and opened unto the eyes of him with whom we have to do."

Our Actions Determine Future Judgment

One morning a woman opened the door to get the newspaper and was surprised to see a strange little dog with her paper in his mouth. Delighted with this unexpected "delivery service," she fed him some treats. The following morning she was horrified to see the same dog sitting in front of her door, wagging his tail, surrounded by eight newspapers. She spent the rest of that morning returning the papers to their owners.[6]

The little dog thought he understood the rules of the game. Deliver a paper and get a treat. Deliver eight newspapers and get eight treats. The dog didn't even realize that he caused trouble for the woman. The Christian life is not like that. We don't blindly perform works for which we have no guidelines. Rather we have a treasure trove of help and spiritual principles about the types of works that bring glory to the Father. When we follow His guidance and His wisdom, He promises a reward.

First Corinthians 3 stresses the importance that our works be built of the right "materials." The works that count are compared to gold, silver, and precious stones. The actions that don't matter are compared to wood, hay, and stubble. The analogy couldn't be easier to understand. When a home burns down, the gold and silver present in the home can be picked out of the ashes. So these materials are fireproof, and that is why they are compared to lasting good works that we complete for the Lord.

We enjoyed camping when our children were small. Building the campfire is an important part of the camping experience, especially if you need the fire to cook dinner! What if I tried to start a fire with Linda's wedding ring (imagine my wife's horror!)? No one could start a fire with gold or silver because they are indestructible. Wood, hay, and stubble, on the other hand, are quite destructible, burning quickly and easily until only ashes remain.

The Bible shows us how to live for Christ, and when we allow the Holy Spirit to work through us, we are most assuredly building our lives with gold, silver, and precious stones. This idea dovetails with an earlier concept we studied. Wayside Hearers' Disorder and Stony Ground Syndrome can cause our works to be wood, hay, and stubble. When we don't allow the seed of the Word to penetrate our hearts and change our lives, we will suffer loss at the Bema Seat. Look again at 1 Corinthians 3:15: "If any man's work shall be burned, he shall suffer loss: but he himself shall be saved; yet so as by fire." Notice in this verse it says, "he himself shall be saved." You will go to heaven, but you won't receive your W.D. Degree. You won't have any crowns to cast at the Lord's feet, and you will wish with your whole heart that you had done more for Christ.

Christ the Judge

This is the "judgment seat of Christ"—not the judgment seat of my wife, my children, my congregation, or my fellow pastors. Other believers will not judge you; nor will you judge others at this judgment. Christ knows not only your actions, but also the motives behind your actions. He knows not only your deeds, but also the thoughts behind your deeds. It will be a perfect judgment far beyond any human court.

Perhaps you think of another believer as Super Christian. He reads his Bible and witnesses. He answers all the questions in your small-group Bible study. Yet at the judgment seat, Christ is not going to stand Super Christian up and compare him to you. Super Christian will be judged for himself, and you will be judged for yourself. In the human realm, we are guilty of two things, comparing ourselves to other believers and comparing believers to each other. The Perfect Judge will look at your life and try your actions. How you treated others, the priority you gave to church attendance, your opportunities to witness—all of this will be tried and judged. Because He is omniscient, His assessment will be complete and infallible. God keeps a dependable, accurate record of the works that we do.

The first American missionaries to Burma, Adoniram and Ann Judson, labored many years before they saw their first convert. Ann wrote, "One Burman has embraced the Christian religion and given good evidence of being a true disciple. . . . This event, this single trophy of victorious grace, has filled our hearts with sensations hardly to be conceived by Christians in Christian countries."

Adoniram Judson wrote later, "I can assure you that months and months of heart-rending anguish are before you, whether you will or not. Yet take the bitter cup with both hands, and sit down to your repast. You will soon learn a secret, that there is sweetness at the bottom."[7]

There is sweetness at the bottom of the cup of this life! It comes in a small degree now as we experience God's continued faithfulness, but there is more to come! This sweetness is the judgment seat of Christ. Our Lord isn't like the health inspector I wrote about earlier. He isn't hoping we will do something wrong. He is praying that we will live right! The Bema Seat ought to excite us rather than deflate us. Christ's loving heart is actually cheering us on as we faithfully serve Him. Remember, He died for you. That deed alone should show us what kind of judge He is. He has given us the power of the Holy Spirit to help us finish well. He has provided for us all things in heavenly places in Christ Jesus. All of this should urge us forward. It should make us actually yearn for this judgment.

Friend, you can eagerly anticipate your judgment. It can be a blessing. Of course, if you see your life's works burned, you will have a sense of loss. I don't think any Christian lives 100 percent all the time in a way that glorifies Christ. Even the greatest believer will have some wood, hay, and stubble. There will be some regret.

Yet, as I've mentioned earlier, this judgment will bring relief to the faithful believer. The persecuted Christian who languished most of his life in jail in a Third World country will see that his life really counted. Christ will reward him though he may have received no praise or help while he lived on the earth. The faithful pastors who gave their lives for their congregations will finally understand the reasons they had to face such hardships. The believer whose parents disowned her because of her beliefs will be rewarded in heaven though she received disdain on earth. If you are serving the Lord, you don't need to dread this judgment. Of course, there will be times when you fail, but the key is to keep at it! Get back up and persevere, looking toward the great Judge, who is cheering you on to victory.

REWARDS FOR SERVING CHRIST

The Bible refers to five possible crowns the believer could receive. There are also references to "rewards."

The Incorruptible Crown

First Corinthians 9:25 mentions an incorruptible crown: "And every man that striveth for the mastery is temperate in all things. Now they do it to obtain a corruptible crown; but we an incorruptible." When Paul wrote this letter to the believers, they knew about the Olympic-style games and that the athletes strove for rewards that didn't last. The crown in this passage is called incorruptible because it will not fade away. It seems to be awarded for faithfulness.

The Soul-Winners' Crown

"For what is our hope, or joy, or crown of rejoicing? Are not even ye in the presence of our Lord Jesus Christ at his coming?" (1 Thessalonians 2:19). This crown of rejoicing is the Soul-Winners' Crown. We will rejoice when we see people in heaven as a direct result of our ministry on earth. This crown is a reward for those who let the candle of their life bring light to others.

The Crown of Righteousness

Read Paul's famous life motto: "I have fought a good fight, I have finished my course, I have kept the faith: Henceforth there is laid up for me a crown of righteousness, which the Lord, the righteous judge, shall give me at that day: and not to me only, but unto all them also that love his appearing" (2 Timothy 4:7-8).

Paul knew that he would receive this crown for finishing his course. He resisted Stony Ground Syndrome and Wayside Hearers' Disorder. He continued to break up the soil of his life to allow the seed of the Word to put down deep and lasting roots. He didn't do this just once in his ministry. He didn't just get saved and then say, "I've arrived. I don't need to continue to work on my spiritual development." His life goal was to finish the race, and to finish he must continue to run well.

Will you receive this crown? The longer I am in ministry, the more I wish to simply finish my course well. The devil is still after me. I still have hardships and trials that war against the soul. But I know one truth—I desire to echo these words of Paul at the end of my life more than anything else: "I have finished my course, I have kept the faith." I know that is your own desire.

The Crown of Life

James 1:12 describes this crown: "Blessed is the man that endureth temptation: for when he is tried, he shall receive the crown of life, which the Lord hath promised to them that love him." When we endure trials stalwartly, this is the crown that will be awarded us. So the next time a coworker says something rude, remember this crown awaiting you. When your children break your heart and you are tempted to quit, think about the crown of life. If you are lonely in the ministry, consider the crown of life. The perfect Judge knows what you are facing. He won't forget your faithfulness when you stand before Him at last.

The Crown of Glory

Faithful ministers of the Word, this crown is for you! First Peter 5:4 says, "And when the chief Shepherd shall appear, ye shall receive a crown of glory that fadeth not away." This crown is for dedicated pastors, those who labor in the Word and doctrine. I want to encourage you pastors who are reading this book. Continue on! Keep feeding, nurturing, and guiding your flock! In the trials in which you felt totally alone, Christ recorded your faithfulness. For all the conflicts with people that distressed your soul, Christ has prepared for you a special reward—the crown of glory.

Astonishing Rewards

Here are some verses that could possibly be referring to other rewards we will receive at the judgment seat.

> Knowing that of the Lord ye shall receive the reward of the inheritance: for ye serve the Lord Christ. (Colossians 3:24)

> Cast not away therefore your confidence, which hath great recompense of reward. (Hebrews 10:35)

And, behold, I come quickly; and my reward is with me, to give every man
according as his work shall be. (Revelation 22:12)

SUFFERING LOSS

The Scriptures say much about those who will not receive crowns or
rewards. Reread 1 Corinthians 3:15: "If any man's work shall be
burned, he shall suffer loss: but he himself shall be saved; yet so as by
fire." If your life isn't lived for Christ, you will suffer loss at the judgment seat. Second John 8 convicts all of us: "Look to yourselves, that
we lose not those things which we have wrought, but that we receive
a full reward." Colossians 2:18 says, "Let no man beguile you of your
reward in a voluntary humility and worshipping of angels, intruding
into those things which he hath not seen, vainly puffed up by his
fleshly mind."

We need to guard our walk with the Lord so that we receive a full
reward. There is no failure you could undergo on earth that could
compare to how you will feel if you suffer loss at the judgment seat.
When you look at Christ, you will recognize what He did for you, and
you will feel heart-rending regret. You will understand that your life
could have brought more people to heaven. The agony at the thought
of people going to hell because you failed to witness to them is
incomprehensible. You will perceive that the candle of your life was
covered by the bushel of selfishness. The deeds you are doing right
now are determining the kind of judgment you will receive. Will it
be a joyous reward ceremony? Or will it be a time of regret? My
desire is for you to make the choice right now that will cause you to
anticipate the Bema Seat eagerly.

YOU CAN DO IT!

All the rewards and crowns that we have studied are heavenly in
nature. Yet it is easy to get caught in the worldly trap of wanting our
rewards immediately. If we do something over and beyond the call of
duty at work, we want instant recognition. If we help someone, we
want to be thanked. If we do a good deed, we want other people to
notice. Christ's judgment of fire will expose all the secret drawers,
recesses, and hiding places of our hearts. Our thoughts, desires,

motives, passions, and affections will be sifted before the eyes of the universe.[8] Matthew 6:1-2 says, "Take heed that ye do not your alms before men, to be seen of them: otherwise ye have no reward of your Father which is in heaven. Therefore when thou doest thine alms, do not sound a trumpet before thee, as the hypocrites do in the synagogues and in the streets, that they may have glory of men."

It should excite you that you are going to be rewarded for your faithfulness. I've heard people say, "I don't really care about the rewards I'm going to receive. I just serve the Lord out of love." While it is true that we should serve our Lord out of gratitude, He has promised rewards to those who serve Him faithfully. It is not wrong to get excited about those rewards; otherwise why would the Bible talk about them so much? If you are to receive a prize at work for winning a contest, should you not get excited about your reward? You helped the company by working hard, and that is good. But as an added incentive, the company wishes to personally recognize your faithfulness.

As believers, we labor for a far greater Boss than any earthly supervisor. At the end of your life, He will personally recognize your perseverance and your passion for the things of God. Go ahead—get excited about it!

CASTING OUR CROWNS AT HIS FEET

How will we react when we receive our crowns? When we see the Lord in all His glory, we will do what the elders who sat around the throne did. Revelation 4:10-11 states, "The four and twenty elders fall down before him that sat on the throne, and worship him that liveth for ever and ever, and cast their crowns before the throne, saying, Thou art worthy, O Lord, to receive glory and honour and power: for thou hast created all things, and for thy pleasure they are and were created." A believer wrote the following poem:

> *When I stand at the judgment seat of Christ,*
> *and He shows me His plan for me,*
> *The plan of my life as it might have been*
> *Had He had His way, and I see*
> *How I blocked Him here and checked Him there,*

and I would not yield my will,
Will there be grief in my Savior's eyes—
Grief, though He loves me still?
He would have me rich, and I stand there poor,
Stripped of all but His grace,
While memory runs like a hunted thing
down the paths I cannot retrace.
Then my desolate heart will well nigh break
with the tears that I cannot shed;
I shall cover my face with my empty hands,
I shall bow my uncrowned head. . . .
Lord of the years that are left to me,
I give them to Thy hand.[9]

Do you think that no one appreciates your hard work for the Lord? Do you perform the same task week in and week out in your church, and no one notices unless you don't do it? As you continue to teach your children the Bible, do you find that sometimes they don't seem to listen? Has someone dear to you turned her back on you, and you don't know why? Take heart. A judgment is coming. Someday the bugs will come out, and you will be rewarded.

It would have been more than enough just to be delivered from sin. It would have been more than enough to have a home in heaven. It would have been more than enough to have the Holy Spirit dwelling within us. It would have been more than enough to have the Bible, the privilege of prayer, and the fellowship of believers. But our God is the kind of God who piles on the chocolate sauce, the whipped cream, and the sprinkles for His children when He rewards us for our faithfulness.

A TASTE OF GLORY

One Sunday night after preaching and then counseling with many people, I saw a dear Mexican family walk toward me.

"Pastor, I have made dinner for you," Maria said with a smile.

After my first bite, I decided that Maria is a master chef. Following the hard work of the day, it was almost as if the Lord were saying, "Jim, I have you in My hand. I am taking care of you. This meal is a reminder that you are loved."

What I experienced that evening was actually a taste of heaven. These moments are mini-rewards, a taste of glory, if you will. But one day Jesus Himself will be waiting for you with outstretched arms. When you see Him, you will fall at His feet. Tears will flow because of your overwhelming gratitude for what He has done for you. And finally you will understand everything you have faced in this life.

First Corinthians 13:12 states that now we see through a glass darkly. Currently, we can't really understand why everything happens the way it does in this life. But face to face with our Savior, we will know. We will understand. It will be enough.

10

THE EXTREME HEARER

It doesn't matter, really, how great the pressure is; it only matters where your pressure lies. See that it never comes between you and the Lord—then, the greater the pressure, the more it presses you to His breast.

—HUDSON TAYLOR

HE DOESN'T JUST RETURN the lost wallet; he adds cash before he returns it. Oscar Brogden, a Manchester council worker in England, started tracking down the owners of wallets brought into his office by street cleaners. He puts at least two pounds in each purse or wallet he returns. If it belongs to someone on a fixed income, he puts in ten pounds.

Oscar said, "Being robbed is a terrible thing. It's like someone giving you a good hitting, and it's upsetting in itself." Oscar mainly started to return the wallets because of the sentimental value of photos and other items. He returned forty-four wallets in one three-month period alone, reported *The Manchester Evening News.*

Jennie Fleetwood said she was staggered when Oscar returned her purse with a cash gift. "I received my purse, with most of my cards still inside as well as some money. As you can imagine, I was delighted. I hadn't expected to see the purse again."[1]

Oscar's giving attitude is refreshing in today's culture. People live for what they can gain rather than what they can give. The attitude in our world is "I deserve it," and today's advertising reflects this view. A recent TV commercial flashed the words, "You gotta have this car," as the screen pictured the vehicle from different angles. The following ads are commonplace today:

"Become a world-class violinist instantaneously."

"Melt ten pounds in ten minutes! . . . A workout so easy, you do it in your pajamas!"

"Delivers so much peace of mind it should be covered under your health plan." (Ad for a popular car.)

"Look better and feel younger in just minutes a day. . . . The key to a healthier, happier life." (Ad for an oxygen chamber. Price tag $3,999.95.)[2]

The parable principles describe a mind-set that is radically different from the attitude displayed by society in general. The world wants you to buy into its philosophy so that you will buy its stuff. If you buy, they profit. Advertising reflects what the advertisers hope is the consumer's mind-set. If they can get you to believe that you deserve the good life, then you will purchase what they are selling.

Yet Christ tells us to deny ourselves. Instead of satisfying our every whim, we need to focus on hearing more of His Word. Instead of the "me attitude," we need to have the "Christ attitude," desiring to hear as much of the Word as we possibly can.

PARABLE PRINCIPLE #25—You will be judged by how much of the Word you use.

Look at Mark 4:24: "And he said unto them, Take heed what ye hear: with what measure ye mete, it shall be measured to you: and unto you that hear shall more be given." The perspective in this verse differs from the view believers often have. People are trained in our Christian culture to go from conference to conference, seminar to seminar, and church to church. Often the perceived quality of these events is determined by the style of the preacher.

"Brother So-and-So does a good job, but he could be a bit more dynamic," one person might say. "I thought he preached a good message, but his illustrations were terrible," another observer might add.

And yet this verse and many others in Mark 4 concentrate solely on how we *listened*, not on the preacher's delivery. This is an important distinction. While there are various skill levels when it comes to delivery, in the end it isn't the preaching that matters. Rather it is the listening.

The assumption of this parable principle is that the preaching you hear is Bible-based. If you listen to preaching that isn't fundamentally sound, then of course, it is of no benefit to anyone. However, the Bible does speak more about how well we hear than how well the preacher spoke. On this earth people talk about the preacher's delivery. At the judgment seat, Christ will ask how well you listened. He will evaluate whether the sermon brought needed changes to your life. James 1:25 verifies this: "But whoso looketh into the perfect law of liberty, and continueth therein, he being not a forgetful hearer, but a doer of the work, this man shall be blessed in his deed."

There are athletes called "weekend warriors" because they do nothing athletic all week, but on the weekends they exercise as though they had worked out every day. This often results in injury. Then there is the moderate athlete who consistently works out a few days a week. The third level is the extreme competitor, such as Rodd Millner, a former Australian commando. He is preparing to jump from a balloon floating in near-space, twenty-five miles above the ground. His goal? To become the world's highest skydiver.

Rodd hopes to freefall for six minutes before opening his parachute and to touch down within thirty miles of Ayers Rock in central Australia. He said, "A man in space has never achieved this, but research indicates the transition will be safe and smooth."

He appears undaunted that some scientists disagree. They say the descent through near-space could be so fast that his head could explode. Rodd plans to make the jump wearing a pressurized space-suit and will have a camera attached to his body so that millions of viewers can watch on television. In 1960 an American set the unofficial world record at 102,000 feet. Boeing 747s rarely fly higher than 35,000 feet. Rodd plans to jump from 130,000 feet.[3]

Christ isn't calling us to be extreme athletes like Rodd, but He is calling us to be extreme hearers. The weekend-warrior believer will never know what it is like to live throughout the week for the Lord. He attends church faithfully, but his life doesn't change as a result of the sermons he hears. The people who know him will never see a transformed life.

The moderate hearer tries to be faithful and does make a few adjustments in her life, but she never develops the spiritual discipline to make much of a difference.

The extreme hearer does three things—he regularly breaks up the ground of his heart, he never misses an opportunity to hear the Word, and he actively makes the changes in his life commanded by the Word.

Commentator Joseph Exell said, "Hear, praying that the Word may be blessed to you. Hear practically, obeying the exhortation which has come to you. This hearing is to be given not to a favorite set of doctrines but to the whole of the Word of God."[4]

This parable principle tells us that we are to be extreme hearers, for we are going to be judged on how well we listened. Did you know that during last week's church service, God wanted you to really listen? He had something for you in that message that could have changed your life, but if you didn't hear it, it never will. In your daily devotional time when your mind wandered, God desired for you to remember what you read. He wants you to be an extreme hearer, a hearer whose primary goal is to learn, obey, and apply as much of the precious seed of the Word as possible.

SAMUEL THE HEARER

He thought he heard a voice. He sat up. Was someone calling him? He ran to the next room. "Eli," he asked breathlessly, "did you need me for something?"

"No," Eli answered, "I didn't call you. Go back to sleep."

But Samuel heard the voice again . . . and again. The third time Eli caught on and told Samuel, "Go, lie down: and it shall be, if he call thee, that thou shalt say, Speak, LORD; for thy servant heareth. So Samuel went and lay down in his place. And the LORD came, and stood, and called as at other times, Samuel, Samuel. Then Samuel answered, Speak; for thy servant heareth" (1 Samuel 3:9-10).

In the quiet of his room, young Samuel learned how to be an extreme hearer. He was excited that God wanted to speak to him, and he listened well.

Samuel's willingness to say, "Speak, Lord, for thy servant hears you," should echo our own heart's cry. We need to have that same willingness, eagerness, and enthusiasm to hear God's words. The more you hear, the more you will gain. The more you gain, the more you will desire to serve others. God has promised you the abundant life, a wonderful life, but you need to put yourself in a position to constantly hear the Word to obtain the blessings of that life.

Too many believers have the same philosophy toward Christianity that the medical profession has toward the flu vaccine. When you get a flu shot, you are injected with a very small amount of the sickness. It is so small that it shouldn't make you sick, but it should keep you from getting full-blown influenza. Many people in the church just want flu-shot Christianity. They are glad they have been delivered from hell, but they don't want so much religion that they turn into extreme hearers.

What about you? Do you need to go from being a weekend hearer to an extreme hearer? Do you need to say with Samuel, "Speak, Lord, for thy servant hears you?" God has promised to give His abundant blessing to those who make hearing and obeying the Word a priority. Why don't you go to the next level of hearing right now?

PARABLE PRINCIPLE #26—The more you hear, the more you gain.

Let's read this verse again: "If any man have ears to hear, let him hear. And he said unto them, Take heed what ye hear: with what measure ye mete, it shall be measured to you: and unto you that hear shall more be given" (Mark 4:23-24).

The girls huddled together in their timeout.

"I want you to remember all the hard work you've put into this sport," the coach said, "and give it everything you've got."

Marissa remembered. She thought about all the balls she had kicked, laps she had run, and every one of the goals she had made. Practice after practice, she had given 100 percent, and now she was ready. She sprinted toward the net and scored the winning goal. Marissa's teammates ran to her, shouting in excitement. She just smiled. All her hard work had paid off. The hours she had put into soccer were beginning to show their fruit.

In the Christian life listening isn't just practice; it's the game. The more you open yourself up to the Lord and the more you serve others, the more God will use you. Perhaps you have been hesitating about starting a local Bible study. It could be that your pastor has asked for volunteers for a particular project. Maybe the Lord has laid it upon your heart to contribute to the church's building fund. Whatever mission you have been given, what is stopping you from going all the way? If it has been an unwillingness to fully dedicate your life to the Lord, then I pray that you will surrender yourself right now. A life of joyous service awaits your decision.

THE HUNDREDFOLD CHRISTIAN

Jesus again emphasizes listening in Parable Principle #26, and I think that we cannot put too much emphasis on this subject. Earlier we saw that the Word comes to us in two main ways—through Bible study and attending a Bible-teaching church. We have seen how to break up the soil of our hearts so that when we do hear the Word, it penetrates deeply into our souls. And then we were admonished to obey the Word that we hear so that we will grow. Now we see once again how important hearing the Word is, with one added bonus: Jesus says that the more you hear of the Word, the more you will gain from it. This is an exciting truth, and it tells us the secret of the hundredfold Christian.

Look again at Mark 4:20: "And these are they which are sown on good ground; such as hear the word, and receive it, and bring forth fruit, some thirtyfold, some sixty, and some an hundred." Do you really want to produce in your Christian life? Do you want to go far beyond the minimum of the thirtyfold promised to the Good-Soil Christian? Then this parable principle gives us the secret. The more you open yourself up to the Word of God, the more you will produce.

Preacher Charles Spurgeon said, "When you hear, you shall have more desire to hear, more understanding of what you hear. You will be more convinced of its truth and have more personal possession of the blessings of which you hear. You will have more delight in hearing, and more practical benefit from it. God gives more to those who value what they have."[5]

ONE MILE TO EMPTY

Jake's eyes were on the road. They had to be. It was pouring down rain, and the traffic was terrible. A sign warned him of an upcoming curve, and he gripped the steering wheel tightly. Suddenly his fuel light blinked.

"My gas tank is almost empty, and there isn't a gas station for miles," Jake muttered. "I should have filled up when I had a chance this morning."

When it comes to hearing God's Word, we sometimes forget the importance of keeping our spiritual tanks full. Instead, we let them drain out until we are miles from the nearest gas station before we realize that there is a problem. The solution? Take this parable principle to heart. When you put yourself in a position to hear the Word of God continually, then your gas tank will never be empty. The Word replenishes us and revitalizes us as we apply it to our lives, causing us to experience exponential growth.

SIGNS YOU'RE CLOSE TO EMPTY

If you ignore your fuel gauge, you will run out of gasoline. It is even worse to ignore your spiritual fuel gauge. For when you do that, you not only slow to a halt, but you start to slide backwards. I have preached for years that there is no standing still in the Christian life. You are either going forward or backwards.

Someone might think, *It's not a big deal right now that I'm not really attending church. I will finish my education first, and then I'll get back to church.* What you don't understand is that all the time you spend away from church, you are traveling backwards. You are backtracking to the world's entrapments, negating any gain you might have made. It won't be long before Stony Ground Syndrome and Wayside Hearers' Disorder overtake you.

Here are some signs that your spiritual fuel tank is close to empty:

After a tough day at the office you think, *I can't go to church tonight. I'd rather stay home and watch TV.*

You miss your daily devotional time for a week and think, *It's not a big deal that I didn't read my Bible this week. I'll do it another time.*

Your designated time of prayer is cut short for a few days. Instead of getting right back on track, you think, *I'll get to it sometime.*

A friend asks you a question about your beliefs and you think, *If I witness to her, she'll think I'm crazy.*

The pastor asks the congregation to come to a special workday, and you think, *I'm too busy to help out at church.*

Your children ask you to read them a Bible story before they go to bed, and instead of getting excited about the opportunity to share God's Word with them, you get frustrated at the time it will cost you.

Can you think of any more signs that you are not hearing enough of the Word? When our circumstances dictate how much time we spend at church and in the Word, we need to recognize that we are fast approaching spiritual empty. Heed the warning! Get back on track. Make church and Bible study a priority and become a hundredfold believer.

WATCH OUT FOR INDIFFERENCE

Missionary David Brainerd said, "I have ever found it, when I have thought the battle was over and the conquest gained, and so let down my watch, the enemy has risen up and done me the greatest injury."[6]

Brainerd understood a key truth about the Christian life. Not only must we be alert for the warning signs of spiritual neglect, but we also have to guard against something that can be an even greater enemy—indifference. This adversary defeats countless believers and shuts down many churches. When a believer becomes indifferent to the things of God, he slowly stops doing the one thing that has helped him more than anything else—listening. And since he has stopped hearing the Word, he has started listening to his old nature and his archenemy, the devil. Satan is so tricky that many times the believer doesn't even realize that he or she is slipping. The person continues sporadically attending church and opening the Bible occasionally, not understanding that he or she is meandering toward the precipice of spiritual failure.

When Rosina Hernandez was in college, she once attended a rock concert at which one young man was brutally beaten by another. No one made an attempt to stop the beating. The next day she was shocked to learn that the youth had died as a result of the pounding. She could never forget the incident or her culpability as a passive bystander.

Some years later Rosina saw another catastrophe. A car driving in the rain ahead of her suddenly skidded and plunged into Biscayne Bay. The vehicle settled in the water with only the rear showing. In a moment a woman appeared on the surface, shouting for help and saying her husband was stuck inside.

This time Rosina waited for no one. She plunged into the water, tried unsuccessfully to open the car door, and then pounded on the back window as other bystanders stood on the causeway and watched. She screamed at them, begging for help, shouting that there was a man dying in the car.

First one man and then another came to help. Together they broke the safety glass and dragged the man out. They were just in time. A few minutes later it would have been all over. The woman thanked Rosina for saving her husband, and Rosina was elated. She had promised herself that she would never again fail to do what she could to save a human life.[7]

Rosina's story gives us a key to guarding against indifference in our spiritual walk. We need to remember what we have been saved from. Had we not heard the Gospel of Jesus Christ, we would be bound for hell. If we had died in our sins, we would have suffered eternal banishment from God. We would do well to remind ourselves of Romans 8:2: "For the law of the Spirit of life in Christ Jesus hath made me free from the law of sin and death." When we remember what we've been saved from, our hearts remain open to hearing the Word of God. Apathy will not overtake us, and we will see growth. Don't remain indifferent to this great grace you have received.

HOW TO RESOLVE CONFLICT

Conflicts in the body of Christ can keep believers from absorbing the Word as they should. Remember Parable Principle #12: Sometimes you will be offended. And when people are slighted, or when they upset others, conflict will result. People stay home from church to avoid conflict and hence miss out on Bible preaching.

A man named Mr. Carnal and a woman named Miss Backslider have formed a company called The Coalition for Conflict, or CC. This company has developed conflict in the church into something of an art. Mr. Carnal and Miss Backslider regularly argue with each other to hone their skills. The last time they quarreled, they wrote down their insights. Throughout my years in ministry, I have talked to many people who hold to these rules of conduct. So here are CC's rules and some verses that directly counter them. Use these verses as tools to resolve tension between believers in the biblical way.

Perhaps you yourself follow CC's rules and didn't even realize it. If so, use the Scripture Solver Bible verse the next time you are tempted to handle conflict in the wrong way. This will help you to keep your heart from being hardened to the seed of the Word. It will also help keep your church from becoming a CC casualty.

Miss Carnal's Confrontation Rule: Be sure to develop and maintain a healthy fear of conflict. Let your own feelings build up until you are in an explosive frame of mind. Don't go talk to the person who has offended you. It is better to stay away from him and gossip about him to others.

Scripture Solver: "Let all bitterness, and wrath, and anger, and clamour, and evil speaking, be put away from you, with all malice" (Ephesians 4:31).

Mr. Backslider's Ambiguity Axiom: If you must state your concerns, be as vague and general as possible. Then the other person cannot do anything practical to change the situation.

Scripture Solver: "Wherefore putting away lying, speak every man truth with his neighbour: for we are members one of another" (Ephesians 4:25).

Miss Carnal's Down-Your-Throat Edict: Assume you know all the facts and that you are totally right. Quoting someone in authority is helpful. Do most of the talking.

Scripture Solver: "Though I speak with the tongues of men and of angels, and have not charity, I am become as sounding brass, or a tinkling cymbal" (1 Corinthians 13:1).

Mr. Backslider's Authority Adage: Make sure you listen to all talk against authority. Don't refute it even if you know it isn't true. Make sure you don't tell anyone in authority what people are saying.

Scripture Solver: "Against an elder receive not an accusation, but before two or three witnesses" (1 Timothy 5:19).

Miss Carnal's Look-Good Law: Announce your willingness to talk with anyone who wishes to discuss the problem with you. But do not take steps to initiate such conversation.

Scripture Solver: "Brethren, if a man be overtaken in a fault, ye which are spiritual, restore such an one in the spirit of meekness; considering thyself, lest thou also be tempted" (Galatians 6:1).

Mr. Backslider's Jealousy Clause: Latch tenaciously onto whatever evidence you can find that shows that the other person is merely jealous of you.

Scripture Solver: "And be ye kind one to another, tenderhearted, forgiving one another, even as God for Christ's sake hath forgiven you" (Ephesians 4:32).

Miss Carnal's Motive Maxim: Judge the motivation of the other party. Keep track of any angry words.

Scripture Solver: "Wherefore, my beloved brethren, let every man be swift to hear, slow to speak, slow to wrath: For the wrath of man worketh not the righteousness of God" (James 1:19-20).

Mr. Backslider's Squeaky-Clean Rule: Pass the buck! If you are about to get cornered into a solution, blame someone else.[8]

Scripture Solver: "He that covereth his sins shall not prosper: but whoso confesseth and forsaketh them shall have mercy" (Proverbs 28:13).

Friend, avoid the Coalition for Conflict! Learn to deal with conflict in your life, especially when it comes to brothers and sisters in your local church. Perhaps reading this has convicted you about the way you are treating someone in the body of Christ. Then adopt the Scripture Solvers and use them to show love to others. Jesus said that others would know we are believers by our love for one another (John 13:35).

TRIALS, THE ULTIMATE CHANCE TO HEAR

We have looked at several things that can close our ears to the Word of God and hinder our spiritual growth—missing church and daily

Bible reading, indifference to the Word, and conflict within the body of Christ. Now think about one more thing that can keep us from really hearing the Word: trials. Trials can either make us careful hearers, or they can stunt our growth. The choice is up to us. Trials are designed to bring us closer to the Lord and His Word. Yet many times our own hearts can become hardened instead of softened when we face hardships.

The Reality of Trials

Perhaps you've heard the expression, "Clothes make the man." I want to say that it isn't clothing that makes a man or woman. Rather it is trials. I have learned this the hard way.

April 18, 1989, started off like any other day. As I walked past my secretary's office, she motioned that she had something to tell me. She said our school had been kicked out of an association of Illinois Christian schools. We hadn't had any warning, and they didn't even give us a hearing. Two of our pastors had attended a meeting of the association and had been told publicly that our school was not welcome any longer. Our school's athletic programs were at their earliest stages. We had just started playing the schools in this association. I knew this would devastate our students. Our hardworking teams would be prohibited from playing other Christian school teams. This rejection caused some of the deepest pain I've ever felt. I immediately called the head pastors of the two leading schools. The pastors both refused to talk to me.

I knew I could easily win this case in court, but I also knew I could not go to court. We decided we wouldn't fight back. We were in the middle of our basketball season, and when we called to find out about an upcoming tournament, we were told we weren't invited.

The pain I felt that night was intense. I cried out to God and asked Him why our kids had to be punished in this way. It seemed that God had forsaken me, but then He came so close to me that I could feel Him, though not physically. God comforted me that night, and I knew He was with me. I thought of the time when only five preachers out of a hundred supported Spurgeon's withdrawal from the Baptist Union Council. The majority overruled and censured their best-known member. But from the moment of our school's ouster, God started working mightily in my life. Our ministry changed forever.

We called other schools and found that the vast majority of them were sickened by what had occurred. They said to us how much they loved playing our school and how much they loved the free pizza we served to them after the games, win or lose. We branched out, finding other tournaments and eventually starting our own. Recently we held a twenty-team volleyball tournament with many teams on the waiting list. All of the schools that come say our tournament is the best one in several states. Both of the schools that kicked us out of the association now play our teams in volleyball and basketball.

Before we faced this trial, I had never had a desire to be on TV or radio. But after that event, I felt a strong desire to learn more about broadcasting. I went to visit an old friend, Yankee Arnold, in Athens, Georgia. He showed me how we could get on TV with very little money. I started to get excited. When I returned home, the board told me that Linda and I needed to take a vacation after all the troubles we had faced. While seeing my mother in Florida, I went to visit Florida Bible Church. I was surprised that the renowned Dr. Curtis Hutson, former editor of *The Sword of the Lord*, was to preach. The pastor, Jim Sheffield, asked me to come meet with Dr. Hutson after the service. Dr. Hutson was a man I admired because of his emphasis on the clear Gospel. He believed in presenting the message simply and didn't use unclear phrases that cause confusion.

Dr. Hutson said, "Jim, I've always wanted to be in your church." I couldn't believe it. I shared with him the hardships we had recently faced. He said, "Those things are hard. I know those men. They have a reputation for the kind of thing they did to you."

Dr. Hutson preached in our church four times before he died. He encouraged me to fight "tougher" and continue on to serve God even more vigorously than before.

We decided to invest a quarter of a million dollars to launch our own TV broadcast. The Quentin Road Bible Hour aired on a high-power station with both cable and broadcast. We were given the number one slot—nine to ten on Sunday nights and enjoyed that spot for many years. A short time after that, we broadcast on the Acts Network, owned by the Southern Baptists. We also broadcast all over Europe and in Israel. Later we went on WGN cable and many other stations across the nation and the world.

I kept thinking, *Lord, how could You be so good to me?* I remembered what Joseph said to his brothers when they discovered that he whom they had wronged was the second most powerful man in Egypt. Genesis 50:20 says, "But as for you, ye thought evil against me; but God meant it unto good, to bring to pass, as it is this day, to save much people alive."

I wish I could tell you that was the hardest trial I've ever had, but since then others have come that were just as difficult. But I can tell you that no matter how bad the trials are, there is a special blessing for the soul that hangs onto the grace of God. The trials helped me grow, and they can do the same for you. Remember, the greater the testing, the greater the blessing. Hang in there; your blessing is just around the corner.

When we are extreme hearers, we will encounter trials. But instead of pushing us away from the Lord, trials will bring us closer so that we are open to what God wants us to do. If I had allowed myself, I could have gotten so discouraged I would have quit. Instead, the Lord sent Dr. Curtis Hutson to encourage me when I needed it the most.

What is your response to trials? How do you react to difficult times? If you are an extreme hearer, then hardships will maximize your growth. Even though they will be difficult, trials show you the next step you need to take. Here are some helps for managing difficult times.

1. Expect trials.

Hardships are inevitable. James 1:2 says, "My brethren, count it all joy when ye fall into divers temptations." This verse doesn't say "*if* you encounter problems;" it says "*when* you encounter problems." Jesus said in John 16:33, "These things I have spoken unto you, that in me ye might have peace. In the world ye shall have tribulation: but be of good cheer; I have overcome the world." Problems are not an elective; they are a required course. You don't get out of them by trying to avoid them. Instead, accept trials as a part of your Christian experience. First Peter 4:12 says, "Beloved, think it not strange concerning the fiery trial which is to try you, as though some strange thing happened unto you." When you expect trials, you will be better equipped to become more like Christ through them.

2. Trials are unpredictable.

Trials are not planned. We seldom can anticipate the problems we're going to experience in life. If we expected them, then we would run the other way when they come. We wouldn't learn from our trials. We don't plan to have a flat tire; nor do we plan to go through a crisis. Trials are unplanned and irregular, occurring when we least expect them. Accept the fact that problems are inconvenient, and you will react much better to them.

3. Problems develop patience.

Here's some good advice from nineteenth-century preacher A. B. Simpson: "Beloved, have you ever thought that someday you will not have anything to try you or anyone to vex you again? There will be no opportunity in heaven to learn or to show the spirit of patience, forbearance, and longsuffering. If you are to practice these things, it must be now."[9]

One preacher said:

> God's best gifts come slowly. We could not use them if they did not. Many a man, called of God to . . . a work in which he is pouring out his life, is convinced that the Lord means to bring his efforts to a successful conclusion. Nevertheless, even such a confident worker grows discouraged at times and worries because results do not come as rapidly as he would desire. But growth and strength in waiting are results often greater than the end so impatiently longed for. Paul had time to realize this as he lay in prison. Moses must have asked, "Why?" many times during the delays in Midian and in the wilderness. Jesus Himself experienced the discipline of delay in His silent years before His great public ministry began.[10]

James 1:3-4 says, "Knowing this, that the trying of your faith worketh patience. But let patience have her perfect work, that ye may be perfect and entire, wanting nothing." Pressure produces patience, and patience will help us to avoid Wayside Hearers' Disorder and Stony Ground Syndrome. Your trials have a purpose. They aren't sent into your life aimlessly. They come so that you can learn what God has for you.

4. Problems purify faith.

This word *trying* in James 1:3 means "testing." This word was used to describe the process of purifying and testing gold. Heating up the gold burned off the impurities of the dross. Job, who faced trials greater than most Christians could imagine, said, "But he knoweth the way that I take: when he hath tried me, I shall come forth as gold" (Job 23:10). When we face problems and we trust in the Lord through those problems, He purifies our faith. Missionary Clarence W. Jones said, "View your pressures no longer as burdens but as a platform for His glorious sufficiency."[11]

5. Problems produce perseverance.

Another word for patience could be perseverance. This is staying power. This is the ability to keep on, to hang in there when times are tough. Hebrews tells us about the man with the ultimate staying power, Christ. "Looking unto Jesus the author and finisher of our faith; who for the joy that was set before him endured the cross, despising the shame, and is set down at the right hand of the throne of God" (Hebrews 12:2).

We don't like pressure, and we often do everything we can to avoid it. We run from it and try to hide from it. However, God uses problems in our lives to teach us how to handle pressure—how to never give up.

Persistence paid off for American astronomer Clyde Tombaugh, who discovered the planet Pluto. After astronomers calculated a probable orbit for this "suspected" heavenly body, Tombaugh took up the search in March 1929.

Time magazine recorded the investigation:

He examined scores of telescopic photographs, each showing tens of thousands of star images in pairs under the dual microscope. It often took three days to scan a single pair. It was exhausting, eye-cracking work—in his own words, "brutal tediousness." And it went on for months. Star by star, he examined 20 million images. Then on February 18, 1930, as he was blinking at a pair of photographs in the constellation Gemini, he wrote, "I suddenly came upon the image of Pluto!" It was the most dramatic astronomic discovery in nearly 100 years.[12]

When you see your problems producing perseverance, you will know that it has been worth going through them. Even if it seems at the time that your problem is brutal and tedious, hang in there. God is working through you to produce His glory in your life!

REV UP FOR REVIEW

Parable Principle #19—Don't compare your spiritual growth to that of other believers.

Parable Principle #20—Fellowship with people who share your desire for spiritual growth.

Parable Principle #21—Develop the habit of prayer.

Parable Principle #22—It is a privilege to share the light of the Gospel with others.

Parable Principle #23—How you live affects your witness for Christ.

Parable Principle #24—You will be judged for deeds done for Christ.

Parable Principle #25—You will be judged by how much of the Word you use.

Parable Principle #26—The more you hear, the more you gain.

Watch for the early warning signs that could let you know that you are not hearing as much of the Word as possible. Remember that your W.D. Degree requires your faithfulness. It is vital to keep in mind that when you skip church or your daily Bible reading, you are missing opportunities to hear and understand the Word. Another way to keep yourself open to the Word is to constantly remember what you have been spared. Don't forget to thank the Lord for your salvation. This will help you to break up the hard soil of your heart and keep yourself open for growth.

There are other dangers that can keep you from hearing the Word as you should. Conflict between believers can keep you away from church. The Bible is full of help for us as we practice loving our brothers and sisters in Christ. Pray also that God will give you the proper perspective on trials. Make a request of the Lord that the pressures of life will never come between you and Him. Instead, lean on the Lord as the pressure of the trial increases. Then the trial will help you to be an extreme hearer, one who hears and obeys what he hears. Keeping these truths in mind will help you gain maximum benefit from the precious seed of the Word.

1 1

YOUR HARVEST WILL COME

*There are grave difficulties on every hand, and many more are loom-
ing ahead—therefore we must go forward.*

—WILLIAM CAREY

FLAT ON HIS BACK and in serious pain, Bill looked as miserable
as he felt. Ed Sutton and I had decided to visit our friend who had
recently been in a car accident. The accident had resulted in a back
injury, putting Bill on total bed rest for six weeks.

"I wasn't sure God loved me anymore, and so I asked Him for
chastisement," Bill explained. "That is definitely not one of the
smarter things I've ever done."

"You asked God to chastise you?" Ed asked, incredulous. "You're
kidding, right?"

"I wish I was," Bill said. "I was reading in my Bible where it says
whom the Lord loves, He corrects, and I thought, *I haven't been chas-
tised lately. Maybe the Lord doesn't love me.*"

We were all young Christians and did many things much cra-
zier than Bill's prayer. I understood that the Lord corrected His
children, but I was content to let the Lord give it to me when I
needed it. Of course, I don't know if Bill's car accident was the
result of chastening or not. It could have been a trial brought his
way so he could grow. Whatever the case, the fact remains: The
Lord chastens His children. He deals with them as a loving father
deals with his children.

Charles Spurgeon said, "When God chastises his children, He
does not punish as a judge does; but He chastens as a father." As we
continue to study the parable principles, we see that another compo-

nent of Christian growth is chastisement. This important element is often overlooked in the church today.

PARABLE PRINCIPLE #27—God will correct you when you don't obey Him.

"For he that hath, to him shall be given: and he that hath not, from him shall be taken even that which he hath" (Mark 4:25). When we fail to be extreme hearers who listen to the Word and obey it, the Lord will discipline us. The Christian's purpose here on this earth is to bring forth fruit. We are to witness to others. We are to allow the Holy Spirit to control us so that we produce the fruit of righteousness.

When we study the life of Jesus, we see that He wasn't pleased when elements of nature didn't produce as they should. Jesus Christ fashioned nature to produce. Consider His attitude toward the fig tree in Matthew 21:19-20: "And when he saw a fig tree in the way, he came to it, and found nothing thereon, but leaves only, and said unto it, Let no fruit grow on thee henceforward for ever. And presently the fig tree withered away. And when the disciples saw it, they marvelled, saying, How soon is the fig tree withered away!" Jesus wanted the fig tree to produce a crop of figs, and it is His desire for us to bring forth a harvest as well.

Jesus told parables about those who had lost something valuable and then described how hard they searched for it. Luke 15:8 says, "Either what woman having ten pieces of silver, if she lose one piece, doth not light a candle, and sweep the house, and seek diligently till she find it?" This story shows us the love He has even for the person who is "lost" in habitual sin. The Lord, like this woman in the parable, will seek that one diligently, desiring for the person to become a productive part of the body of Christ.

Another parable in Matthew 18:12-13 speaks of a shepherd's love for the lost sheep: "How think ye? if a man have an hundred sheep, and one of them be gone astray, doth he not leave the ninety and nine, and goeth into the mountains, and seeketh that which is gone astray? And if so be that he find it, verily I say unto you, he rejoiceth more of that sheep, than of the ninety and nine which went not astray."

Jesus is compared many times in Scripture to a Shepherd and we as believers to the sheep. His desire was to help the lost soul and bring him back into fellowship.

Jesus told these parables to demonstrate His care and concern for unbelievers. I believe He wanted us to understand that just as a woman would take time to find her lost coin or a shepherd would search for his lost sheep, so He seeks us with even greater tenderness. He wants people to trust Him as Savior. This goal should be our own. As believers, we should seek out those who don't know the true Shepherd and share with them the gospel message.

In all of these parables there is one prevailing theme. Something was wrong or missing, and it brought sadness to the Lord Jesus Christ. When believers do not bear fruit, the Lord may chasten them. He loves His children too much not to correct them when they are wrong.

Perhaps you have had the wrong view of God's chastening hand. Perhaps you think of God holding your head on a chopping block, a huge ax in His hand, waiting for you to do wrong. This picture could not be further from what the Bible teaches. When we trust Jesus Christ as our Savior, we are born into the family of God. We call God our heavenly Father. This is an awesome privilege made possible by the shed blood of Jesus Christ. Because we are now in the family of God, He treats us as His sons and daughters. If He has such great tenderness for sinners, how much more love must He have for His own children. He desires for us to produce. He yearns for us to bear fruit. He wants us to witness to others. We've already discussed the rewards He wants to give His faithful servants. Now it is time to look at the other side of the coin—His chastening hand.

BECAUSE OF LOVE

I remember when my son Jim was old enough to mow the yard—a great day for a father! Maybe the first two or three times, Jim enjoyed mowing the yard. What if after a few weeks Jim had said, "Dad, I don't want to mow the yard anymore"? Would Jim still have been my son? Of course. But I would have had an obligation toward Jim. It was important that he continue to respect my authority. By disciplining him, I would be saying, "Jim, I love you, but since you did not do what I asked of you, I need to discipline you."

Our Father God deals with His children the same way, only He is much greater than a human father. God knows everything and has perfect wisdom. Nothing He brings into your life is for your harm; rather it is for your good (Romans 8:28). He can judge motives like no parent on earth can. He knows what will happen if you make the right decision and what will happen if you make the wrong decision. His perfect wisdom makes His discipline an act of goodness in your life. Hebrews 12:7 says, "If ye endure chastening, God dealeth with you as with sons; for what son is he whom the father chasteneth not?"

Does this mean that the Lord would send you to hell as part of His discipline? When I discipline my son, would I say, "You aren't in my family anymore"? My son cannot become "unborn" out of my family. There might have been times that he wished he wasn't in our family (when he did something wrong!), but he still was part of the family. It is the same with the family of God. God will chasten you, but His punishment will never be hell. Look at John 10:28-29: "And I give unto them eternal life; and they shall never perish, neither shall any man pluck them out of my hand. My Father, which gave them me, is greater than all; and no man is able to pluck them out of my Father's hand." One author said, "The goal of God's discipline is restoration—never condemnation."

We are not to despise this chastening of the Lord. We need to understand that this discipline is done out of greater love than we could possibly imagine. Hebrews 12:5 says, "And ye have forgotten the exhortation which speaketh unto you as unto children, My son, despise not thou the chastening of the Lord, nor faint when thou art rebuked of him."

FACTS ON CHASTENING

The knock sounded loudly on the door on a cold October day. A wrinkle-faced man stood on the stoop, holding a shopping bag.

"Can an old man have a bite to eat?" he asked.

"Come in," Tom said. "We have some leftover stew and biscuits from dinner."

After the man ate, he asked if he could spend the night in the barn. Tom gave permission. The next day Tom walked into his kitchen and saw the old man sitting in his chair in the dining room. He looked at his wife, Anna, but she didn't say anything. Tom tried to hide his irritation. Throughout the day, wherever Tom went, it seemed that he ran into the man, sitting in his favorite chair, rummaging through the closets, or walking around the property. Tom talked to Anna and said, "I'm going to ask him to leave."

Tom approached the visitor with his request. But then the man surprised Tom and Anna by pulling a piece of paper out of his pocket and spreading it on the table. It was the title to Tom and Anna's property.

"You mean you own this property?" Tom asked.

"Yes, I own this property. You've been paying rent to *me* all these years."

"I suppose that means you can do with it whatever you want," Tom said finally.

"Yes, I suppose it does," the man said.

That piece of paper gave Tom a whole new perspective on the man he had first viewed as an interloper.

Our Creator God owns the title to our lives. He owns our bodies. We have been bought with a price as it says in 1 Corinthians 6:20. We might relegate Him to the spare room of our lives as a result of our actions, but we need to understand that we are not our own. He has the right to give us direction, and it is our responsibility to obey. God does not follow a program of benign neglect with His children. Instead, He acts in our lives to train and correct us, whether we consent or not.

Your earthly father may have disciplined you in anger or to vent his frustrations. Some of you may have grown up with an abusive father, and you carry the wounds of that relationship with you even today. You may have experienced so-called discipline that was simply abuse. Because of that, it may be difficult for you to relate to the idea of God as a loving father. It may be tough to accept the idea that discipline can be motivated by love.

However, God does not act toward us in anger. His wrath toward our sin was completely paid for by the death of Christ. God is not angry with those who have put their trust in His Son. Rather, He loves you so much that He wants your life to produce much for Him. Your heavenly Father disciplines you with far greater love than any earthly father ever could.

Ricky knew he was in trouble. He didn't realize how hard he had hit the baseball until it sailed through the neighbor's window. Somehow he got up the courage to knock on the neighbor's door. When Mrs. Smith answered, Ricky almost turned and ran, but instead he told her what he had done. She looked sad and then invited him into the house. Ricky stepped inside, not knowing what to expect.

"Ricky," Mrs. Smith said, "I'm so proud of you for admitting that you broke my window. I'm going to be easy on you because you did come and tell me. I want you to work in my garden to pay for the window."

Ricky was relieved. He wasn't sure he would enjoy working in her garden, but he knew that he could have been in a lot more trouble. However, Ricky was surprised to find himself enjoying the gardening. Even after Mrs. Smith told him that he had worked enough, he still came over to help. Today he owns his own landscaping business, and he proudly cites Mrs. Smith as the reason for his success.

God's chastening may not feel like love. It can actually be painful. It is unpleasant. But God loves us enough to allow the discipline to continue because He knows it is for our good.

THE REASON BEHIND HIS DISCIPLINE

There is a purpose to the chastening God brings into your life. He doesn't do it for the fun of it or because He enjoys watching His children suffer. Rather, He does it for the fruit it produces in our lives. Read again Hebrews 12:11: "Now no chastening for the present seemeth to be joyous, but grievous: nevertheless afterward it yieldeth the peaceable fruit of righteousness unto them which are exercised thereby."

Discipline brings peace. I know that one of the reasons there was peace in our home while our children were growing up was that we disciplined our children. There was a calm atmosphere because the children knew their boundaries. Proper discipline brings peace. Chastisement also brings a renewed desire in our hearts to do right. God chastens because of what it produces in our lives—peace, holiness, and righteousness. Believe it or not, God disciplines us in order to bless us!

Parents, if you've witnessed your children's misbehavior turn into a desire to please you after they are disciplined (Proverbs 22:15), then you can understand the reason behind God's chastisement.

ILLNESS—CHASTISEMENT FOR SIN?

Does this mean that all suffering is chastisement? When you get a fever, do you need to confess your sins to the Lord? If your car has a flat tire, is God trying to tell you something? Understand that on this earth, we may not even know which instance was chastisement and which was simply a trial sent to make us better people. God's Word says that sometimes sickness is a result of sin in our lives, but it also speaks of Job, a man who endured trials for no sin of his own but rather because Satan wanted to tempt him to curse God.

Paul addresses a grievous problem occurring at the church of Corinth. The people were getting drunk when they took Communion together. First Corinthians 11:27-32 says:

> *Wherefore whosoever shall eat this bread, and drink this cup of the Lord, unworthily, shall be guilty of the body and blood of the Lord. But let a man examine himself, and so let him eat of that bread, and drink of that cup. For he that eateth and drinketh unworthily, eateth and drinketh damnation to himself, not discerning the Lord's body. For this cause many are weak and sickly among you, and many sleep. For if we would judge ourselves, we should not be judged. But when we are judged, we are chastened of the Lord, that we should not be condemned with the world.*

We see several truths about chastening in this passage. First, Paul instructs believers to examine themselves before they partake of the Lord's Supper. Each Christian is to determine if he has any known sin in his life. Therefore, the responsibility first rests with the individual when it comes to God's discipline. If he finds sin in his life, he is to confess that sin and restore fellowship with the Lord (1 John 1:9). Remember that it is your own responsibility to examine yourself. Paul doesn't say, "Let every man examine his neighbor."

Then Paul says that those who do not deal with known sin in their lives are unworthy to partake of Communion. He says further that if they do take Communion, they have drunk damnation to themselves. This doesn't mean they have just sealed their fate in hell. The word *damnation* means a decision or a judgment. So those unworthy souls who partook of Communion are judged because of their deliberate actions. Paul states that there are many who are weak and sickly as a result of their deliberate disobedience. Some even sleep, which means they were taken home to heaven early. It is possible for the Christian to become so wicked that God needs to take him home.

The last part of this passage contains an additional truth. It says that we are chastened of the Lord as judgment so that we do not have to be condemned with the world. This should give us further assurance of our security in Christ. Once we have trusted Him, we are eternally secure in Him. No one can take us out of His hand. We will not be condemned with the world at the Great White Throne Judgment. But we will be disciplined when we deliberately go against the Lord's will. That is the nature of our great God, and here we see just one more aspect of the loving mercy of our God. He loves us too much to let us stray without correction. Remember, it is because He cares so much that He chastens us.

CHASTENING GETS OUR ATTENTION

A Puritan wrote, "I am mended by my sickness, enriched by my poverty and strengthened by my weakness . . . what fools are we, then, to frown upon our afflictions! These are our best friends. They are not intended for our pleasure; they are for our profit."[1]

If we never were chastened, we might be tempted to think that we can actually get away with our sin. We might think that God doesn't really care how we live, and we might not fear God. Author James G. Bilkey wrote, "You will never be the person you can be if pressure, tension, and discipline are taken out of your life."

Preacher D. Martyn Lloyd-Jones said, "How often do we hear about the discipline of the Christian life these days? There was a time in the Christian church when this was at the very center, and it is, I profoundly believe, because of our neglect of this discipline that the church is in her present position. Indeed, I see no hope whatsoever of any true revival and reawakening until we return to it."[2]

God works in our lives in different ways. When we are in sin, He will chasten us. When He desires to strengthen our character, He allows trials. When He wants us to learn to trust Him, He might delay an answer to prayer. The delay, of course, is only in our own minds. He has the perfect plan, and He knows the end from the beginning. He doesn't operate in the same time frame as you and I, and it is dangerous for us to think that He should. Instead, He wants us to trust Him and wait on Him.

A letter from John Newton describes the proper attitude we should have toward suffering:

> Had Israel enjoyed their former peace and prosperity in Egypt, when Moses came to invite them to Canaan, I think they would hardly have listened to him. But the Lord suffered them to be brought into great trouble and bondage, and then the news of deliverance was more welcome, yet still they were but half willing, and they carried a love for the flesh-pots of Egypt with them into the wilderness. We are like them: though we say this world is vain and sinful, we are too fond of it; and though we hope for true happiness only in heaven, we are often well content to stay longer here. But the Lord sends afflictions one after another to quicken our desires, and to convince us that this cannot be our rest. Sometimes if you drive a bird from one branch of a tree, he will hop to another a little higher, and from thence to a third;

but if you continue to disturb him, he will at last take wing, and fly quite away. Thus we, when forced from one creature-comfort, perch upon another, and so on; but the Lord mercifully follows us with trials and will not let us rest upon any; by degrees our desires take a nobler flight, and can be satisfied with nothing short of Himself; and we say: To depart and be with Jesus is best of all![3]

HIS FAR GREATER WAYS

When I was young, I remember building a go-cart with my dad. We worked on it for quite a while, and I remember the impatience of waiting for it to be finished as though it were yesterday. Have you ever had to wait? Maybe you continue to pray about the same request. Perhaps you are waiting for direction from God about a career change. It could be that there is a financial need in your life, and you are waiting for God to help you. Does this mean that God doesn't care? Are our problems unimportant to God?

What we often don't comprehend is that God's ways are greater than our ways. We simply don't possess the capacity to understand why He does the things He does (Isaiah 55:8-9). This doesn't mean He doesn't care. On the contrary, He does care, but He sees and understands everything about your life. He sees circumstances that you simply can't understand right at this moment. The big word is *trust*.

THE CARNAL CHRISTIAN

I've talked a little about carnal Christians before this chapter. The word *carnal* means fleshly. A carnal believer is more interested in satisfying physical appetites than he is in God's ways. Read 1 Corinthians 3:1-3: "And I, brethren, could not speak unto you as unto spiritual, but as unto carnal, even as unto babes in Christ. I have fed you with milk, and not with meat: for hitherto ye were not able to bear it, neither yet now are ye able. For ye are yet carnal: for whereas there is among you envying, and strife, and divisions, are ye not carnal, and walk as men?"

Carnality brings envying, strife, and divisions to the body of

Christ. Paul states that he wanted to speak to the Corinthians as spiritual believers, but instead he had to speak to them as carnal ones. These believers were spiritual babies, unable to bear the meat of the difficult things of the Word. Instead, they still needed milk, or the easy things of the Word.

This verse is not a criticism of young Christians who don't know a lot about the Lord. Just as there is nothing wrong with a baby being a baby, so there is nothing wrong with a new believer not understanding the more difficult doctrines of Scripture. The danger comes when the baby doesn't grow as he or she should. God understands that the new believer doesn't know much about the Bible. He just doesn't want the believer to stay that way. He wants the believer to follow the Bible and be an extreme hearer. Otherwise, he will be a carnal Christian.

Paul writes that he kept his flesh under subjection so that he would continue to be used of God. He didn't want God to "put him on a shelf" so that he couldn't be used. First Corinthians 9:27 says, "But I keep under my body, and bring it into subjection: lest that by any means, when I have preached to others, I myself should be a castaway." The word *castaway* is *adokimos* in the Greek, and it means "disapproved."

It is possible to be on your way to heaven and yet be of little use to God here on earth. You could come to a place where, though you have received the Lord Jesus Christ as Savior, you have never submitted to His authority. God will chasten you if you don't surrender to Him, for He desires you to produce.

Getting saved ten years ago does not automatically make you a spiritual person today. God gave you new life, but you must live out your new life. It's possible to be a spiritual victor yesterday and a pious disaster today. A carnal Christian is a stagnant Christian. Milk is fine for a baby to drink, but as the child grows, he or she needs solid food for nourishment. Carnal Christians still commit the same old sins in the same old way. They refuse to think biblically or to make decisions based on the Word. Paul says that the thing that marks carnal believers is their inability to eat spiritual food; they are not able to get into the deeper things of God.

STUCK IN A RUT

Are you struggling with your spiritual growth? Do you feel as though you are stuck in a rut, at the same place spiritually that you have been for some time, maybe even years? Growth only occurs with obedience—not half-hearted or partial obedience but a full surrender to God's will as revealed in His Word. Many people come to church to enjoy the "show," but they refuse to "grow" because they do not want to do what God has commanded. Blessing always follows obedience. God wants to bless you. Obedience is the key to growing up and experiencing the joys of being mature and complete in Christ.[4]

COULD I BE CARNAL?

These are the top five indicators of spiritual immaturity.

1. *A failure to grasp more than the basics of the faith.* "I have fed you with milk, and not with meat: for hitherto ye were not able to bear it, neither yet now are ye able" (1 Corinthians 3:2).

2. *An inability to articulate what you believe and why you believe it.* "But sanctify the Lord God in your hearts: and be ready always to give an answer to every man that asketh you a reason of the hope that is in you with meekness and fear" (1 Peter 3:15). "For when for the time ye ought to be teachers, ye have need that one teach you again which be the first principles of the oracles of God; and are become such as have need of milk, and not of strong meat" (Hebrews 5:12).

3. *Inability to put God's Word into practice.* You listen to the Word preached, but you do not apply the truths to your life.

4. *Neglect of a daily time of Bible reading and prayer.* "But be ye doers of the word, and not hearers only, deceiving your own selves" (James 1:22).

5. *Inability to make godly decisions.* "Woe unto them that are wise in their own eyes, and prudent in their own sight!" (Isaiah 5:21).

6. *Unwillingness to submit some area of one's life to God.*[5] "What? know ye not that your body is the temple of the Holy Ghost which is in you, which ye have of God, and ye are not your own?" (1 Corinthians 6:19).

Most Christians describe a spiritually mature person by pointing to things such as the length of time one prays or the eloquence of one's intercessions to God. Other people might say that those who have committed vast portions of the Bible to memory or who can teach or preach great truths are mature. Some people might speak of others who have an outward show of godliness. While a mature believer might have all these characteristics and more, all of these traits do not equal spiritual maturity. Mature believers apply the truth of Scripture to their lives. The fruit of the Spirit is evident. Mature believers have the ability to make wise and godly decisions. There is no part of their life that they haven't surrendered to the Lord. They are willing to do whatever the Lord wants them to do.

Spiritual immaturity guarantees that you'll never achieve your God-given potential, realize joy and a sense of fulfillment, and please God. Friend, I encourage you to put behind you any plans that do not include Christ and grow on to maturity with Him as your guide. Don't settle for a flimsy faith. Rather press on, grow on, and give it your all as you go forward in your spiritual quest.

PARABLE PRINCIPLE #28—Be faithful; God will bring the harvest.

"And he said, So is the kingdom of God, as if a man should cast seed into the ground; and should sleep, and rise night and day, and the seed should spring and grow up, he knoweth not how. For the earth bringeth forth fruit of herself; first the blade, then the ear, after that the full corn in the ear. But when the fruit is brought forth, immediately he putteth in the sickle, because the harvest is come" (Mark 4:26-29).

The harvest is the best part of the farmer's year, and so this parable principle is one of the best parts of the Christian life. As we continue to become extreme hearers, we start to see the harvest. This parable of the wheat's growth (the word translated in the Bible means "grain") shows us that God brings the harvest. When a farmer plants, he doesn't know how the actual growth occurs. But the farmer rejoices when the harvest comes. He knows that his hard work has paid off, and so it is with us. When we do the work of preparing our hearts to receive the Word and put ourselves in an optimal position to receive as much of that Word as possible, God blesses our faithfulness with a harvest.

Commentator John Burns wrote, "'The earth bringeth forth fruit of herself'—not of herself apart from God, but of herself apart from the man who sows the seed. He does his work, he sows the seed, and he goes on his way; and after he has done his part, he sleeps by night and rises by day, and the seed springs up and grows, he knows not how."[6]

There is a spiritual maturity process here as well. First we have the blade. The green shoot trembling in the breeze is the baby Christian, the believer who doesn't know much about the Word. Yet he knows that something wonderful has happened to him. He doesn't know how to explain to others what he believes, but he does it anyway. He might seem to be just a tiny shoot. However, if the believer continues to prepare the soil of his heart, he will go on to the next stage, that of the ear or the time when the shoot grows strong. Trials, chastening, disappointments, pressures—all these strengthen the growing plant, preparing it for the harvest. This is the time the believer should develop spiritual disciplines in his life. He should carve out a time each day to study the Bible. He needs to make prayer a priority. He should attend a Bible-believing and Bible-teaching church to become an extreme hearer. All of these things will strengthen the growing stalk, preparing it for a rewarding harvest.

STRENGTHENING THE STALK

One day Randy came to me with a question. "Dr. Scudder, I have a friend who just won't believe that Jesus is really who He said He was."

I knew Randy hadn't been saved for very long. It was important to fortify his faith so that he could in turn share the Gospel with others. I asked Randy if he had shown his friend the prophecies from the Old Testament that predicted Jesus' coming. He said that he didn't know about them. I showed him where some of the prophecies relating to Jesus Christ in the Old Testament are marked in my Bible with a highlighter. In the margin next to the highlighted text, I have the New Testament verse that is the fulfillment of that prophecy. Randy was so excited about this new witnessing tool that I thought I would share the list with you. Do what Randy did and mark these in your Bible. They are wonderful faith strengtheners. It is estimated that there are over 322 prophecies in the Old Testament that directly relate to some aspect of Jesus' life.[7] This is only a partial list, but if you look all of them up in both the Old and New Testaments, it will amaze you that they were fulfilled so accurately.

OLD TESTAMENT PREDICTIONS FULFILLED IN CHRIST

Christ's First Advent—Predicted Isaiah 9:6; Fulfilled Luke 2:11
Christ's Divinity—Predicted Psalm 2:7, 11; Fulfilled Matthew 3:17
His Forerunner—Predicted Isaiah 40:3; Fulfilled Mark 1:3
The Place of His Birth—Predicted Micah 5:2; Fulfilled Matthew 2:1
Adoration by Magi—Predicted Psalm 72:10, 15; Fulfilled Matthew 2:1
Descent into Egypt—Predicted Hosea 11:1; Fulfilled Matthew 2:13-15
Massacre of Innocents—Predicted Jeremiah 31:15; Fulfilled Matthew 2:15-16
Jesus' Ministry in Galilee—Predicted Isaiah 9:1-2; Fulfilled Matthew 4:12-17
His Miracles—Predicted Isaiah 35:5-6; Fulfilled Matthew 15:31
Purification of the Temple—Predicted Psalm 69:9; Fulfilled Matthew 21:12
Triumphal Entry into Jerusalem—Predicted Zechariah 9:9; Fulfilled Matthew 21:9
Betrayal by Friend—Predicted Psalm 41:9; Fulfilled Mark 14:10
Betrayal for Thirty Pieces of Silver—Predicted Zechariah 11:12; Fulfilled Matthew 26:15
Purchase of Potter's Field—Predicted Zechariah 11:13; Fulfilled Matthew 27:7-10
Silence Under Accusation—Predicted Isaiah 53:7; Fulfilled John 19:9
Crucifixion—Predicted Psalm 22:14, 17; Fulfilled Matthew 27:26
Offer of Gall and Vinegar—Predicted Psalm 69:21; Fulfilled Matthew 27:34

Death with Malefactors—Predicted Isaiah 53:9, 12; Fulfilled Mark 15:27

Casting Lots for Vesture—Predicted Psalm 22:18; Fulfilled John 19:24

Bones Not to Be Broken—Predicted Psalm 34:20; Fulfilled John 19:34-36

Vicarious Suffering—Predicted Isaiah 53:4-6, 12; Fulfilled Galatians 1:4

Burial with the Rich—Predicted Isaiah 53:9; Fulfilled Matthew 15:43-45

Jesus' Resurrection—Predicted Hosea 6:2; Fulfilled Matthew 28:6-7

These prophecies are just a small sample of the prophecies that Christ fulfilled in His coming, but they are a start. Taking the time to study them will help you in your own faith and in your witness for Christ to others.

PROOFS OF THE RESURRECTION OF JESUS CHRIST

I also shared with Randy some of the proofs of the Resurrection. This event more than any other gives us complete assurance that the Bible is true. When I go to Israel, I visit a lovely place called the Garden Tomb. It is believed that Jesus was buried there. The location fits the biblical description, and the Garden Tomb Society of England keeps the entire area beautiful. I know that on our trips to Israel, people really treasure their time in this picturesque place. On a door that opens to the tomb are the wondrous words, "He is not here, but He is risen as He said."

William Lyon Phelps, for more than forty years Yale's distinguished professor of English literature, author of some twenty volumes of literary studies, said:

In the whole story of Jesus Christ, the most important event is the resurrection. Christian faith depends on this. It is encouraging to know that it is explicitly given by all four evangelists, and told also by Paul. The names of those who saw Him after His triumph over death are recorded, and it may be said that the historical evidence of the resurrection is stronger than for any other miracle anywhere narrated; for as Paul said, "If Christ is not risen from the dead, then is our preaching in vain and your faith is also vain."[8]

Author and professor C. S. Lewis, in speaking of the importance of Christ's post-resurrection appearances, said: "The first fact in the history of Christendom is the number of people who say they have seen the Resurrection. If they had died without making anyone else believe this 'gospel,' no gospels would ever have been written."[9]

Professor J.N.D. Anderson writes of the testimony of the appearances:

The most drastic way of dismissing the evidence would be to say that these stories were mere fabrications, that they were pure lies. But, so far as I know, not a single critic today would take such an attitude. In fact, it would really be an impossible position. Think of the number of witnesses, over 500. Think of the character of the witnesses, men and women who gave the world the highest ethical teaching it has ever known, and who even on the testimony of their enemies lived it out in their lives. Think of the psychological absurdity of picturing a little band of defeated cowards cowering in an upper room one day and a few days later transformed into a company that no persecution could silence—and then attempting to attribute this dramatic change to nothing more convincing than a miserable fabrication they were trying to foist upon the world. That simply wouldn't make sense.[10]

Christ didn't appear to just one or two people after He rose from the dead. He appeared to as many as 500 at one time. One of the proofs of the Resurrection was the testimony of the many witnesses, all proclaiming the same event.

Look at the appearances of Christ after His resurrection:

To Mary Magdalene—John 20:14, Mark 16:9.

To women returning from the tomb—Matthew 28:9-10.

To Peter later in the day—Luke 24:34; 1 Corinthians 15:5.

To the disciples walking to Emmaus—Luke 24:13-33.

To the apostles, Thomas absent—Luke 24:36-43; John 20:19-24.

To the apostles, Thomas present—John 20:26-29.

To the seven by the Lake of Tiberius—John 21:1-23.

To over 500 believers on a Galilean mountain—1 Corinthians 15:6.

To James—1 Corinthians 15:7.

To the eleven—Matthew 28:16-20; Mark 16:14-20; Luke 24:33-52; Acts 1:3-12.

At the Ascension—Acts 1:3-12.

To Stephen—Acts 7:55.

To Paul—Acts 9:3-6; 1 Corinthians 15:8.

To Paul in the temple—Acts 22:17-21; 23:11.

To John on Patmos—Revelation 1:10-19.

THE EMPTY TOMB

The empty tomb is that silent testimony to the resurrection of Christ that has never been refuted. The Romans and Jews could not produce Jesus' body or explain where it was; nonetheless, they refused to believe.[11]

Professor E. H. Day writes: "In that empty tomb Christendom has always discerned an important witness to the reasonableness of belief. Christians have never doubted that as a matter of fact it was found empty on the third day; the Gospel narratives agree in emphasizing it; it [the burden of proof] . . . rests not upon those who hold the tradition, but upon those who either deny that the tomb was found empty, or explain the absence of the Lord's body by some rationalistic theory."[12]

Author G. B. Hardy wrote:

Here is the complete record:

Confucius' tomb	—	Occupied
Buddha's tomb	—	Occupied
Mohammed's Tomb	—	Occupied
Jesus' Tomb	—	Empty[13]

THE TRANSFORMED LIVES OF THE DISCIPLES

Author John R. W. Stott says, "Perhaps the transformation of the disciples of Jesus is the greatest evidence of all for the resurrection. . . ."

Apologist Paul Little asks, "Are these men, who helped transform the moral structure of society, consummate liars or deluded madmen? These alternatives are harder to believe than the fact of the Resurrection, and there is no shred of evidence to support them."

In my book *Beyond Failure*, I wrote about the incredible change in the apostle Peter after the Resurrection. Another author writes:

Notwithstanding the dismal failure to maintain his promised loyalty, Peter was completely different a few weeks later on the day of Pentecost. With amazing poise and courage, he openly accused the Jewish rulers of having crucified their Messiah, and affirmed that God has restored Him to life. His speech was not merely a rash burst of enthusiasm, for he consistently persevered in his conviction and was ready to suffer persecution. The only adequate explanation for Peter's sudden change was the new viewpoint that the resurrection afforded.

Similar transformations occurred in other disciples. The cynical unbelief of Jesus' brethren gave way before the convincing proof that Jesus had arisen, for James later became the leader of the church in Jerusalem. Thomas's sudden transition from skepticism to worship must have been produced by a powerful impulse, for it was contrary to the entire current of his previous mental habit. He did not even accept Jesus' invitation to touch the wounds and thus satisfy his desire for sensory evidence, but turned immediately from argument to adoration.

The most spectacular instance in the Biblical record occurred in the life of Saul of Tarsus. Like his fellow Pharisees, he believed in the principle of resurrection (Acts 23:6), but to him Jesus of Nazareth was an imposter who deserved the penalty of death. He undoubtedly had heard rumors that Jesus had risen, but did not credit them. Positive that Christianity was a pernicious heresy, he devoted himself to the task of exterminating it. His fanatical zeal took him to Damascus for the avowed purposes of bringing the believers to court for trial, but he never completed his errand. The manifestation of the risen Lord, whom he encountered on the road, changed him into a protagonist of the message he had endeavored to suppress. The reversal of his actions, attitudes, and theology was so drastic that his contemporaries could scarcely believe it (Acts 9:21) and accepted his new profession only with hesitancy. He remarked later about the altered values of his life. "What things were gain to me, these I counted loss for Christ" (Philippians 3:7).

The transformation of these personalities is indisputable, for they have left a permanent heritage of faith to the Christian church. There was nothing in their previous experience or attitudes to account for the change; in fact, without the resurrection, the disciples of Jesus would probably have disbanded, and the world might never have heard of Him through their agency. They had no analogy by which to create the illusion of a resurrection, nor had they the singleness of purpose and the cohesion to launch a crusade. The difference, however, was not due to a gradual recovery from disappointment, nor was it the result of shifting cultural influences. The renewed faith and enthusiasm which these persons exhibited can only be attributed to the truth that Christ had risen and had imparted to them new life.[14]

There are many more proofs of the Resurrection that I can't go into here. Among the many good books giving evidence in support of the Christian faith are *The New Evidence That Demands a Verdict* by Josh McDowell and *Know Why You Believe* by Paul Little.

YOUR HARVEST

As you strengthen your faith and absorb the seed of the Word, your life will produce a wonderful harvest. The full-grown corn will appear. At harvesttime we will think about doctrine, but we will also think about what is behind the teaching, our living God. Then our only goal will be to love and serve Christ. The petty things won't anger us as much anymore. The harvest comes when we look back at our trials and see that He has never left our side. It comes when we stop fighting every hardship and instead learn to lean upon His strength. It comes when we see the mercy that was shown to us when we passed through the dark valley. It comes when we view Christ as He ought to be viewed, as the central figure in our lives. As you faithfully work to receive the Word, consider the harvest to come. It is well worth every moment of preparation.

12

MUSTARD-SEED FAITH

God delights to increase the faith of His children. We ought, instead of wanting no trials before victory, no exercise for patience, to be willing to take them from God's hand as a means. Trials, obstacles, difficulties, and sometimes defeats are the very food of faith.
—GEORGE MUELLER

LANCE HATED ATTENDING SCHOOL, mainly because of Matt, an older boy who bullied him. Because Lance couldn't run very fast, he wasn't often picked to play baseball during recess. Matt enjoyed reminding Lance of this in front of the other students. One day the bully tormented Lance once too often. Lance reached into his pocket and took out a small pocketknife. He flipped open the blade and started chasing Matt around the schoolyard. A teacher noticed what was happening and raced over to Lance, ordering him to go the principal's office.

Lance remembers the long walk to Mr. Rodgers's office like it was yesterday. He stuck his pocketknife in the waistband of his pants so the principal wouldn't see it.

"I understand you were chasing Matt around with a pocketknife," Mr. Rodgers said sternly. Lance gave the principal a frightened look.

"Where is your pocketknife?" Mr. Rodgers asked.

"Uh . . . I don't know," Lance said. Then a pinging sound startled both of them. They looked down as Lance's pocketknife fell out of his pant leg. The principal leaned over and picked it up. Seeing Lance's terrified expression, he said, "Lance, you're a good boy. I know you are. Matt does torment you. I understand that. He badgers a lot of kids, but that doesn't excuse your running after him with a pocketknife."

Lance shifted nervously.

"I'm going to put this pocketknife in my drawer, and we're going to forget this ever happened. You have to promise me that you will never bring a pocketknife to school again."

Surprised that he wasn't going to be punished, Lance quickly promised. The teacher was more vigilant about the bully after that, but Lance never forgot the time he took the law into his own hands and went after the school bully with a pocketknife.

As believers, we are sometimes tempted to do the same thing. Perhaps we don't take such an aggressive approach, but we get impatient waiting for the harvest. We whip out our own solutions in order to hurry things up a bit, only to realize in the long run that God brings the harvest in His time, not ours.

PARABLE PRINCIPLE #29—God's way starts small and grows slowly.

"And he said, So is the kingdom of God, as if a man should cast seed into the ground; and should sleep, and rise night and day, and the seed should spring and grow up, he knoweth not how. For the earth bringeth forth fruit of herself; first the blade, then the ear, after that the full corn in the ear. But when the fruit is brought forth, immediately he putteth in the sickle, because the harvest is come" (Mark 4:26-29).

In our last parable principle, we saw that God will give the harvest when we are faithful. But we are now going to look at another aspect of this harvest. Many times we seem to think that God's way starts big and becomes gigantic. The truth is that God starts with small things. And His way isn't fast or slow. It is perfect.

The harvest depends first on our own faithfulness to the Lord, whether we are willing to put wholehearted effort into our spiritual walk. But then we have to understand that the harvest will not happen according to our schedule.

This realization brings another aspect of human nature to the surface—impatience. So many times we want to hurry God along and have Him fit into our plans. We pray, "Lord, I want Your will," but at the same time we chomp at the bit, anxiously wanting God to act and act fast.

God's laws of nature cannot be broken. There will always be a period of time between the planting of the seed and the harvesting of the crop. We've learned already how to make the field of our heart ready for the seed of the Word, and we've seen the habits and practices we can develop to optimize growth. Bible study, prayer, church attendance, and more strengthen and enrich the tiny shoot of faith. But what happens when you are doing all that you are supposed to, and the harvest doesn't seem to be anywhere near?

We all want results. As human beings, we are programmed that way. If we put an effort into something, we expect that it will yield a tangible reward. We expect a return for our labor. When Linda and I first came to Chicago to start the church, we expected instant results. But as time went on, and I didn't see the harvest, I tended to get discouraged. I felt like saying, "Lord, I've put so much time into witnessing to others. I'm preaching Your Word. I'm helping many people. What is wrong?"

Of course, I did have some results, but they seemed small, almost insignificant. Many had come to Christ, but not too many wanted to commit their lives to serve Him. It was then that I slowly began to understand a great truth. God had a bigger plan for my life than the one I could see. The results were in God's timing, not mine. God wanted me to prepare the soil of my heart. He wanted me to open myself up to as many opportunities to receive the Word as possible. He wanted me to become an extreme hearer who obeyed the Word. But He also desired me to learn to trust Him. When you are doing all the right things to prepare for your harvest, if you get impatient waiting for God's results, then you need to trust God.

GIVE ME PATIENCE

"Attention! Multitaskers," says an advertisement for a wireless telephone service. "Demo all these exciting features, E-mail, voice telephone, and pocket organizer, all in one." Even the microwave oven makes you feel that you have power over the passing of time.

Watching those seconds tick past on the digital display, you see that you have a minute and a half to make a quick phone call or run to the next room. If you just have a modem to connect to the Internet, you better get DSL. People use expressions such as "the fast track" and "the rat race" to describe the climate at their jobs. Even churches are joining the beat-the-clock game. One church in another state advertises its twenty-two-minute services where the sermons are only eight minutes long.

We are so used to having everything done and done right now that sometimes this concept of waiting for God to bring the harvest brings frustration. I'm not saying that I enjoy waiting for a website to open or for my coffee to heat up in the microwave, but we need to be careful that we don't transfer this "hurry up mania" to God. He works according to His timing and His plan, for He created time in the first place. Just as the farmer knows that the natural process of growth takes time, so we have to apply that principle to our spiritual lives. Read the following aspects of patience and see if you demonstrate these qualities.

1. *Patience is the ability to accept delays, disappointments, or detours graciously.*

How do you deal with delayed answers to your prayers? How about delays in general? Do you blame God? What about disappointment? Do you lash out at other people when you are upset? In the Christian life, you will face delays and disappointments. In a *Daily Bread* devotional, I read that detours on the road of life can be frustrating or time consuming. Yet in the spiritual life, God seems to allow us to be detoured. There are many people in the Bible who may have thought they were being detoured by God, but who later found they were on God's perfect road of blessing. Consider: Moses was detoured into submission. Those forty years in the wilderness tending sheep were not a waste but actually a training ground for tending Israel later on. The desert experience took confidence in the arm of flesh out of Moses (Exodus 3—4).

Paul was detoured into learning. "I went into Arabia . . . then after three years I went up to Jerusalem" (Galatians 1:17-18). Those years were good for Paul. He was able to learn of Christ and be trained for service.

Philip was detoured from crowd evangelism to personal evangelism. He went from winning multitudes to winning one man, the Ethiopian eunuch (Acts 8).

Enoch and Elijah were detoured into heaven (Genesis 5:24; 2 Kings 2:11). Is today the day we will experience such a detour? That would be the ultimate detour. When you are detoured on your spiritual journey, know this: When God has His hand on your life, the detour isn't really a detour at all. Rather, it is all a part of His wonderful, unfailing plan and purpose for you.

2. *Patience is the powerful attribute that enables a man or woman to remain steadfast under strain and continue faithfully serving the Lord.*

It could be that right now you are under terrific strain. The backbiting at work is getting to be more than you think you can handle. Perhaps your son or daughter isn't living the right kind of life. Perhaps you are caring for aging parents, or you have a loved one who is ill, and you are spending long hours in a hospital or nursing home. Remember, that is all part of strengthening your faith. Even though the experience might not be pleasant, God will work the circumstances out for good in your life. It is your job to be faithful.

3. *Patience is a calm endurance based on the certain knowledge that God is in control.*[1]

The story is told of an artist who went to visit an old friend. When he arrived, she was weeping. He asked why. She showed him a beautiful handkerchief that had great sentimental value, but it had been ruined by a spot of indelible ink.

The artist asked her to let him have the handkerchief, which he returned to her by mail a few days later. When she opened the package, she could hardly believe her eyes. The artist, using the inkblot as a base, had drawn on the handkerchief a design of great beauty. Now it was more beautiful and valuable than ever.

God works in this way. His plans will far exceed the plans you have for your own life. You can confidently place your trust in God no matter what circumstance you are facing. He will make of your life a masterpiece of design from the very inkblot of sorrow.

THE DARKROOM OF PATIENCE

It's not easy to develop patience. As I mentioned earlier, it goes against the grain in our instant society to advocate patience for anything. Developing endurance also goes against human nature. When a baby wakes up hungry in the middle of the night, she doesn't lie there and think, *Mom and Dad had a long day, and they are tired. I'll just wait until a more convenient time to let them know I want something to eat.*

The baby cries impatiently and continues to cry until she receives the attention she demands. I love my own grandkids, but they aren't very patient! If we are traveling in the car, they want to stop every few minutes.

A little boy was traveling with his mother and kept asking the classic, "Are we there yet?" over and over again. Finally the mother was so irritated that she said, "We still have ninety miles to go. Don't ask me again when we're going to get there."

The boy was silent for a long time. Then he timidly asked, "Mom, will I still be four when I get there?" To a child six hundred miles should only take a few minutes. My granddaughter Amy told me when she was about six that she thought it would only take us a month to build our 76,000-square-foot building.

PRIDE CHOKES OUT PATIENCE

The weeds of pride, selfishness, and anger can suffocate the fruit of endurance. Guard against these chokers. Otherwise your patience will become impatience. How do pride and selfishness choke out our patience? When we are proud, we are saying to God, "I have worked so hard for You. I have done so much for You. Why aren't You rewarding me as I deserve?" When we are selfish, we say to God, "Everyone else seems to be enjoying blessings. How come I don't have as many blessings as so-and-so?"

D. L. Moody once said, "My attention was recently called to the fact that in all the Psalms you cannot find any place where David refers to his victory over the giant Goliath. If it had been in the present day, there would have been a volume written about it at once; I don't know how many poems there would be telling of the great things that this man had done. He would have been in demand as a lecturer and would have added a title to his name: G.G.K.—Great Giant Killer."

Preacher Jonathan Edwards said, "Nothing sets a person so much out of the devil's reach as humility." Determine right now not to let the sins of pride and selfishness choke out your patience.

DEVELOPING PATIENCE

There is only one way to develop patience in your life, and that is to abide in Christ. John 15:5 says, "I am the vine, ye are the branches: He that abideth in me, and I in him, the same bringeth forth much fruit: for without me ye can do nothing." Here we see again that Christ has the power to bring the seed to fruition in our lives. He is our only source of nourishment. He is our only source of strength.

A French proverb says, "Laziness is often mistaken for patience." While it is important to develop biblical patience in our lives, don't confuse inactivity with patience. Does waiting on the Lord mean you are sitting back in your chair, twiddling your thumbs, and waiting for Him to fulfill your every desire? The biblical concept of waiting on the Lord is active, not passive. You are not just a bystander in your spiritual journey; God wants your life to change. He wants you to continue to faithfully do His work. He wants you to continue to break up the soil of your heart. He wants you to be steadfast and resolute in your pursuit of holiness. As you are doing all these things, you will face trials and hardships. Learning what God wants to teach you through those trials will make you a more loving person. When you've traveled a good way, you will look back and be surprised at how far you've come. You will say, "Lord, I still have a long way to go, but now I know what it means to trust. You are working all things out in my life for good even if I don't understand the 'whys.' It is enough to know that You are working through me." Then you will know that you are developing patience.

Are you a grumbler? Do you have a tendency to complain about your circumstances? I challenge you to determine to actively pursue God's way, to trust His every leading, to follow His every desire. Most surely you are then on the road to blessing.

GOD'S TIMING

"I'm tired of waiting," one woman said frankly. "I keep hanging on for God to send the right man into my life, but I don't think it's going to happen."

"My wife and I have faced a long adoption process," another man said, "and it doesn't seem that we will ever have the joy of raising our own child."

"My mother has been sick for a long time," a young wife said. "Sometimes I wonder if I can continue to bear up under the strain."

"My son has turned away from the Lord," some parents said. "We have prayed and prayed, but we don't know if he will ever come back to God."

There is real pain in these situations. Sometimes Christians feel almost helpless because it seems that there is no answer for their pain. However, instead of waiting for God's timing, they jump ahead of the Lord. They are tempted not to seek counsel when an important decision comes their way because they are tired of waiting. Maybe a Christian will marry the wrong person, even an unbeliever. Other people do not wait for God's timing for the right job or a suitable car, and now they are in an even deeper mess than they were before—all because they don't want to hear from either godly counsel or the Word of God: "Continue to wait on the Lord."

Look at the big picture of your life and the blessings God has sent your way even in the midst of pain. Perhaps you desire a Christian husband. That is a good desire, but instead of focusing on your desire, why don't you focus on what God has already given you? Perhaps you have a fulfilling job or a strong local church. Don't forget to thank Him for those blessings.

One elderly couple in our church just went through a difficult time. The wife, who suffers from diabetes, developed pneumonia and had to be hospitalized. Her husband supported her and helped her through this time, but her pain was great. One morning she said to her doctor, "I just want you to know that I'm going to heaven. I'm not afraid to die. I'm so glad I know that." She recovered, and her continued witness to the Lord's grace is a blessing to me.

In your pain God is there. He wants you to learn to be patient as you await His harvest. Poet Christina Rossetti said, "Obedience is the fruit of faith; patience is the bloom on the fruit."

Friend, how about you? Are you in a place of impatience? Are you ready to give in to the pressures around you instead of waiting for God's best? Are you tempted to complain and grumble about the trial you face? Why don't you take your burden to the Lord, realizing that He wants to help you to bear it? He wants to give you rest right now in the middle of your problems. Why don't you go to Him right now?

CLAIM YOUR REWARD

Two men in my church went smelt fishing. They shivered in the cold weather all day and only caught about one pound of smelt. From a financial standpoint, they would have been better off going to the store and buying cans of sardines! I roughly calculated the cost of their trip and realized that they paid $3 for each smelt, figuring in licenses, equipment, etc. Why did they do it? They believed the reward would be well worth the expense. As believers, we can look for our own reward with confident expectation. Remember, God operates on His timetable, not ours.

Focus on what God has done for you. He has sent His Son, given the Holy Spirit, made you coheirs of heavenly glory, and on top of all this, He promises to bring a harvest. Part of the harvest is here on earth. You will see the result of your labors here but not as fully as in heaven. When I speak of your reward, I don't mean how many vehicles you have parked in your driveway or how nice your home is. God's spiritual rewards are greater than any material blessings.

That's why as believers we need to say, "Nothing is too hard, and nothing is too much." What is your attitude toward Christ? Are you like the stingy believer who says, "Don't expect too much of me," or are you a spiritual person who says, "I'll do anything I can for Christ"? It is all in your focus, your attitude, and your perspective toward the Lord's service.

Christians should think that nothing is too hard and nothing is too much for them to do for God. The Christian life is light, love, hope, and action. Bind this all together with patience, and your harvest will be great.

PARABLE PRINCIPLE #30—God does a lot with mustard-seed faith.

"And he said, Whereunto shall we liken the kingdom of God? or with what comparison shall we compare it? It is like a grain of mustard seed, which, when it is sown in the earth, is less than all the seeds that be in the earth: But when it is sown, it groweth up, and becometh greater than all herbs, and shooteth out great branches; so that the fowls of the air may lodge under the shadow of it" (Mark 4:30-32).

My son-in-law Neal hoed a little patch of dirt outside their home. He planted strawberries and then watered each tiny plant with the correct dosage of Miracle-Gro. As he was working on another part of the yard, Julie came along and saw the new planting. Wanting the strawberries to grow too, she got the Miracle-Gro and liberally doused each one again. Neal came running when he saw what she was doing. "She fried the strawberries before they even had a chance to grow," Neal said later.

Sometimes we do the same thing when it comes to the harvest. We don't understand that it is God who will bring our mustard-seed faith to fruition.

Years ago we brought forty small trees from a camp we owned in Minnesota to plant around our current church property. We have several landscapers in our church now, and we know more about planting than we did then. At the time we didn't ball the roots. We just brought them back as fast as we could and planted them in the ground. Only one beautiful tree survived. When I look at that tree, I say, "Don't die!" That tree is an inspiration to me.

If you type in "mustard seed + faith" into a search engine on the

Internet, 392 Christian organizations are listed. They use the words "mustard seed" to describe their faith. It is an encouragement for the believer to say, "I have faith the size of a grain of mustard seed," when she is facing a particularly difficult situation. This is a good banner for the believer, for God does honor those who have faith in Him. Yet I believe that Jesus used this illustration so we could see the difference between the size of the seed and the size of the plant. Mustard seeds are one of the smallest seeds known in Israel. When Jesus gave this parable, the analogy couldn't have been clearer. Only God could bring that kind of growth. Only God could take the tiniest of seeds and bring forth a harvest of greatness. Only God has the awesome power to create the tiny seed in the first place.

The famed preacher Charles Spurgeon once said:

> Human teachings are barren. But within the Gospel, with all its triteness and simplicity, there is a divine life, and that life makes all the difference. The human can never rival the divine, for it lacks the life-fire. It is better to preach five words of God's Word than five million words of human wisdom. Human words may seem to be the wiser and the more attractive, but there is no heavenly life in them. Within God's Word, however simple it may be, there dwells an omnipotence like that of God from whose lips it came.

This divine life brings energy to our faith. It takes the smallest amount of faith and turns it into a strong, leafy tree.

PARABLE PRINCIPLE #31—Don't worry about how much faith you have. Look to the object of your faith, the Lord Jesus Christ.

A *Bible Hour* viewer wrote me this letter: "My dear husband died of cancer about three months ago. While he was dying, I had a friend say to me, 'If you had more faith, then God would cure your husband.' I tried to have more faith, but he still died. I'm wondering, is this my fault? My husband knew the Lord, and I know he is in heaven."

My heart feels so heavy for people who are in trying situations and are informed by sometimes well-meaning friends or relatives that if they had enough faith, their situation would turn around. However, the Bible is clear that it isn't the amount of faith you have. Rather it is where you place your faith. I think that is why Jesus used the tiny mustard seed to demonstrate faith.

Stephen was a man of faith and power (Acts 6:8), and yet he died a martyr. Would God have stopped the Jews from stoning him if he had just had more faith?

Paul healed a lame man (Acts 14:8-10), and yet when he asked the Lord three times to remove his own thorn in the flesh (perhaps a type of sickness, 1 Corinthians 12:7-9), the Lord said no. Does this mean that Paul had enough faith at one time but "lost" it?

We need to understand that it is the focus of our faith rather than how much faith we possess that is important. Jesus did speak of little faith (Matthew 14:30) because Peter looked away from the Lord in the storm. The real problem was that Peter had taken his eyes off the object of his faith, the Lord Jesus Christ, and as a result began to sink in the water. In Matthew 16:8 Jesus admonished the disciples for worrying that there was no bread to eat, saying that they had "little" faith. But He still provided food for them.

Jesus said that a centurion had great faith (Matthew 8:10) because he believed that the Lord could heal his servant without coming to his house. Jesus praised his faith and healed the servant. Yet Jesus still helped the disciples when they had "little" faith, and He kept Peter from drowning although he had "little" faith.

Faith delights God (Hebrews 11:6). But faith isn't a mystical potion that makes all of your problems go away. Faith is trust. It is dependence on the Lord. God is pleased when we trust Him. But we have to trust in Him regardless of the way circumstances turn out in our lives. It is wrong to say that someone's husband died as a result of a "lack of faith," for it isn't God's will to heal everyone. This doesn't mean that God can't heal. Rather it means that we trust God to work all things out for good in our lives.

During an especially trying time in the work of the China Inland Mission, Hudson Taylor wrote to his wife: "We have twenty-five cents—and all the promises of God!"[2] God's promises are true whether we have faith in them or not. But when we understand that

He will take care of us and we see His loving hand helping us, we will learn again to trust Him more. This trust pleases God. The object of our faith is strong whether we feel strong or not. He is our constant friend, watching out for us and caring for us with a far greater plan than we could ever have for ourselves.

FAITHFUL, NOT FAITHLESS

First Corinthians 4:2 says, "Moreover it is required in stewards, that a man be found faithful." More important than worrying about how much faith you have is to consider the extent of your own faithfulness to the Lord. It is essential that we are found faithful. If you apply the parable principles to your life, then you will be faithful. If you are reading the Word daily, praying, attending church regularly, showing love to others, witnessing, then be assured that you can look up and see a sign that says "Faithfulness Highway" because you are on it.

Author Joseph Exell writes, "Do not worry yourself about the growth of grace in others. Do not get frustrated looking for evidence of growth. Confine your care to the seed you sow and then leave the rest to God. Be not too anxious about the work of grace in your soul. Be patient with yourself. Plants that are meant to live long grow slowly. Consider the difference between the mushroom and the oak tree. If God has patience with you, have patience with yourself."[3]

One woman on crutches struggled to escape her office on the sixty-fourth floor of the World Trade Center's Tower Two A group of her fellow employees tried to carry her but made slow progress.

"They had me over their shoulder for five or ten flights and just couldn't do it," she recalled.

Finally a coworker she knew only as Louis hoisted the woman on his shoulder and carried her down the stifling stairway. When they reached the fifteenth or twentieth floor, a security guard told them they were out of danger and urged Louis to leave the woman and make his way down to the street. Louis refused.

"He carried me down all fifty-four flights and then out of the building," the woman said, " . . . and he stuck with me until . . . I could go in an ambulance."[4]

That woman had no choice but to lean on someone she barely

knew to help her down the stairs. Her rescuer proved worthy of her trust. As we travel down the stairway of this life, we can do no better than to rest fully on our Lord Jesus. Know for sure that He will carry you all the way home.

I encourage you to pray this prayer: "Lord, I want to be faithful in preparing the soil of my heart for growth. I want to be a faithful servant. I pray that I will trust You all the times regardless of what happens in my life. I pray I will not compare myself to others in this walk of grace. Rather, I will lean upon You and Your strength, knowing You will bring forth a harvest. In Jesus' name, amen."

Rev Up for Review

Parable Principle #22—It is a privilege to share the light of the Gospel with others.

Parable Principle #23—How you live affects your witness for Christ.

Parable Principle #24—You will be judged for deeds done for Christ.

Parable Principle #25—You will be judged by how much of the Word you use.

Parable Principle #26—The more you hear, the more you gain.

Parable Principle #27—God will correct you when you don't obey Him.

Parable Principle #28—Be faithful; God will bring the harvest.

Parable Principle #29—God's way starts small and grows slowly.

Parable Principle #30—God can do a lot with mustard-seed faith.

Parable Principle #31—Don't worry about how much faith you have. Look to the object of your faith, the Lord Jesus Christ.

Dear friend, we have looked together at the Thirty-one Parable Principles that will change your life. There is no comparison between the hopeless life I lived before I trusted Christ and the joyous life I live today. That doesn't mean that there are no problems on this road or trials and hardships. And yet look at what God has given us! Through the parable principles, we've seen how to study the Bible, how to find a Bible-believing and Bible-teaching church, how to make prayer a priority, how to be an extreme hearer, and how God will reward us for service, correct us when we're wrong, and then prepare us for a bountiful harvest.

Will you determine right now to remain faithful to the one who died for you? Will you take the help from the parable principles and use them to transform your life? It is before you—this wonderful life filled with the goodness of God. The Lord is waiting to help you take the first step. You don't have to worry. You don't have to fear. This journey will be the most precious you've ever taken.

STUDY SECTION

1—The Spiritual Life

PARABLE PRINCIPLE #1—Jesus taught in parables so that Christians could apply truth to their lives in practical ways.

PARABLE POWER POINTS

1. Read Mark 3:5. Why did Jesus radically alter His method of teaching?
2. How did Jesus' teaching differ from that of the Pharisees and Sadducees?
3. Why did Jesus' teaching both anger and scare the religious establishment?
4. Read Matthew 9:10-11. How did Jesus' teaching reveal the religious facade of the establishment?
5. Is there any connection between salvation and good works? For what reason should we serve God?

PARABLE PRACTICE

1. Jesus came to minister to the downtrodden, the ordinary, the weary, the common people. What does that fact tell you about the relevance of His teaching?
2. Jesus didn't exhort the crowds with ancient laws and little-known philosophy. He spoke in a way that enabled people to learn great truths for their lives. How does that make you feel about your ability to apply God's truth?
3. Jesus spoke in parables to make sure people understood what He was saying and to make such an impression on them that they never forgot His message. What does this teaching method say about the importance of His teaching?

4. The religious leaders were scared and angry when Jesus spoke. What does that tell you about the controversial nature of adhering to Christ's teaching?
5. The Lord's Supper gives us a wonderful illustration of Jesus' sacrifice for our sins on the cross. What does this sacrament reveal to you about the beauty of God's truth?

PARABLE PRAYER

Pray that God will help you cultivate a willing spirit, a spirit that isn't filled with pride like the Pharisees and Sadducees were. Ask the Lord to open your eyes to His truth (Matthew 13:16).

PARABLE PROJECT

Compare and contrast the teaching of the Sadducees and Pharisees with that of Jesus. Then explain why Christ's teaching gives you hope in your spiritual journey.

2—Enduring Support

PARABLE PRINCIPLE #2—Devote time every day to Bible reading.

PARABLE POWER POINTS

1. Why is it so important to take time to study Scripture systematically?
2. Read Jude 20-21. How do we build ourselves up in the faith?
3. Read Psalm 126:5-6. What role does Bible study have in a joyful life?
4. What does George Barna's research tell us about Bible ownership in the United States? Why don't all these Bibles have more of an impact on our society?
5. Read James 1:21. Why is the daily cleansing of our hearts so important?
6. Read Hebrews 2:1. Why is it crucial to heed the Word of God?

PARABLE PRACTICE

1. The Bible promises comfort, strength, hope, wisdom, knowledge, joy, power, and purpose. What does this provision tell us about the *priority* of studying God's Word?
2. Maybe the whole thought of reading the Bible each day overwhelms you. You may not think that you know enough about it to understand how to do it in an effective way. How does the Holy Spirit's role in your life *encourage* you to keep studying?
3. Sin in our lives blocks us from receiving the Word into our hearts. How important is the *cleansing* of our hearts before we study the Bible?
4. Psalm 119 describes Scripture as the following:
   A Direct Path
   Cleansing Water
   An Encouraging Song
   Solid Gold
   Wholesome Food
   Guiding Light
   An Amazing Heritage

What do these attributes say about the *blessing* of studying God's Word?

PARABLE PRAYER

Ask the Holy Spirit to guide you into the truths of the Bible. Confess your sin to God. Ask Him to prepare your heart to receive His Word. Seek the Lord's help in committing to a regular pattern of Bible reading.

PARABLE PROJECT

Thoroughly evaluate your Bible reading.

1. Study the secrets of famous Christians given in chapter 2. Choose one or two hints and use them in your study this week.
2. Evaluate your Bible study.
   a. Do you have a good Bible?
   b. Should you invest in a quality study Bible?

3. Which book of the Bible are you reading?
   a. Have you studied the basic books first? (See chapter 2.)
   b. Are you going to Scripture for specific situations? (See chapter 2.)
4. Check your technique.
   a. Are you confessing your sin first?
   b. Are you asking yourself questions as you read?
5. Are you consistent in your Bible study?
   a. Are you making the most of your time in the Word?
   b. Have you made a daily appointment for your Bible study?
   c. Are you memorizing Scripture?
6. Will any of the computer tools in chapter 2 make this process easier?

3—A Seed Called Preaching

PARABLE PRINCIPLE #3—Make it a habit to attend a Bible-believing, Bible-teaching church.

PARABLE POWER POINTS

1. How does the biblical idea of Christians needing each other contradict the self-sufficiency of our culture?
2. Read 1 Corinthians 12:25-26. Why is there a tremendous difference in spiritual growth between Christians who attend church and those who do not?
3. Read Ephesians 5:25-30. What does this image of a bride tell us about the church?
4. Read 1 Peter 5:2. Why is the role of a pastor so important?
5. Read 1 Thessalonians 5:12; 1 Timothy 5:17; Hebrews 13:17. Why are pastors to be treated with respect?

PARABLE PRACTICE

1. God knows that we need a place to meet in, a place to fellowship, a place to grow spiritually, a place to bring others, a place to learn about the Bible, a place to be used for the body of Christ. What does this tell you about the importance of attending church?

2. Christ lives in us, both individually and corporately, as the church. How does church attendance affect your relationship with Christ?
3. Celebrate God's presence. How does your church attendance affect your ability to worship?
4. Worship gives you an opportunity to talk with God. How does a church service focus your mind on spiritual matters?
5. Worship makes spiritual things real. How does attending church help the Bible become more real to you?
6. Volunteering at church makes your life more fruitful. What are some ministries in your church where your services could be used?
7. Church attendance keeps you accountable. Consider asking for counsel from the spiritual leadership for your upcoming major decisions.

PARABLE PRAYER

Ask for the Holy Spirit's leading in finding a ministry in your church where you may bear fruit. Be concerned for the needs of other members of your church. Pray that you might be a blessing to the body of Christ.

PARABLE PROJECT

Evaluate your involvement with your church.
1. Review the eight reasons to worship God in church. Commit yourself to worship God in the ways described.
2. Involve yourself in one of the three main outreaches of the church—evangelism, fellowship, or discipleship.
    a. Evangelism—Are there people in your world you can invite to church? Write down the names of friends or coworkers.
    b. Fellowship—Are there fellow believers in the church who need to be encouraged and strengthened in the faith? Write down their names and ask God to use you to help them.
    c. Discipleship—Write down the names of believers who would be willing to study the Bible with you.
3. Support your pastor.

a. Are you responding to his teaching in your daily life?
b. Are you supporting him in your conversations with other members of the church?
c. Are you seeking his counsel for some of your decisions?
d. Write an encouraging note to your pastor this month.

4. Prepare yourself each Saturday for the Sunday service.
a. Decide today to go to bed half an hour earlier on Saturday nights.
b. Plan what time you will get up Sunday morning.
c. Gather your Bible, notebook, and pen and put them by the door Saturday night.
d. Plan to participate in opening hymns.
e. Think about a way you will apply the sermon throughout the week.

4—Ready, Set, Prepare

PARABLE PRINCIPLE #4—Doctrine is essential to Christian growth.
PARABLE PRINCIPLE #5—Other people may not value your desire to grow in Christ.
PARABLE PRINCIPLE #6—Ready, set, prepare.
PARABLE PRINCIPLE #7—Give it time.
PARABLE PRINCIPLE #8—You will reap what you sow.

PARABLE POWER POINTS

1. Read Mark 4:2. Jesus taught doctrine. Why is doctrine so important to the Christian walk?
2. Read Romans 15:4. Why is it so important to understand the hard passages of the Bible?
3. Read Proverbs 2:3-5. How does sound doctrine solidify our faith?
4. Read Matthew 7:13-14. Why is the way leading to eternal life so narrow?
5. Read 2 Corinthians 4:4. Why should we be patient with those who do not know Christ?
6. Read Psalm 126:5-6. Why is it important to make good decisions?

7. Read 1 Corinthians 9:6. Why is the degree of our sacrifice important to our spiritual walk?
8. Read 1 Corinthians 3:6-7. What is more important—results or faithfulness?

PARABLE PRACTICE

1. The Holy Spirit will guide you in your study of doctrine if you let Him.
2. Properly prepared soil can transform a ho-hum Christian life. What are some areas of your soil that need to be better prepared to receive the Word of God?
3. Just as the child needs to wait for the plant to grow, so we need to wait for God's harvest. Is there an area of your life where it seems that God is not acting?
4. Often we cling to our old ways instead of trying God's way. We follow our own ideas instead of studying the Scripture to understand His ideas. How may impatience be hurting your spiritual growth?
5. You may think that the decisions you make every day aren't important, but really they are vital. Stop and think of some of the seeds you have sown this month.
6. What reassurance do you have that though you can't actually see God working in your life, He still is at work?

PARABLE PRAYER

Ask the Holy Spirit to help you understand the tough passages of Scripture. Pray daily for that person who is resistant to the Gospel. Ask the Lord to help you receive His Word and what it has to say. Pray for wisdom in making the small and large decisions in your life.

PARABLE PROJECT

Do something special for the person in your world who may be resistant to hearing the Gospel.

    a. A relative—Help him or her with a special project or chore.

    b. A coworker—Buy the person lunch.

    c. A neighbor—Volunteer to do some yardwork.

5—Spiritual Rx

PARABLE PRINCIPLE #9—When you hear the Word, obey it.

PARABLE PRINCIPLE #10—You engage in spiritual warfare when you share the Gospel with others.

PARABLE PRINCIPLE #11—Don't think you are "perfect too soon."

PARABLE PRINCIPLE #12—Sometimes you will be offended.

PARABLE PRINCIPLE #13—Guard your reaction toward trials.

PARABLE POWER POINTS

1. Read Mark 4:4. In what ways can our hearts become hardened to sin?
2. Read Mark 4:15. Why doesn't Satan want the seeds of the Word to take root?
3. Read 1 Thessalonians 2:18. In what way does Satan hinder the work of believers?
4. Read Mark 4:5 and Mark 4:16-17. How can a Christian who experiences a great spurt of growth in the beginning suddenly wither away?
5. How does pride halt spiritual development?
6. Read 1 Timothy 3:6. What prevents a Christian from losing his zeal?
7. Read Mark 4:17. What does our tolerance of offenses reveal about the depth of our spirituality?
8. Read 1 Corinthians 11:26 and Matthew 3:16. How do the two ordinances of the New Testament help us ensure deep roots for our faith?
9. Read Mark 4:17. How can a trial or circumstance derail spiritual growth?
10. Read Revelation 2:4. Why do Christians lose their enthusiasm for the Lord?

PARABLE PRACTICE

1. Consider the ways you've opened your heart to receive the Word in the last month.

2. The devil will try to wreak havoc in your witnessing opportunities. He wants to be in your way and in your face! What tools has God given you to fight the devil?
3. You engage in spiritual conflict when you witness to others. Has it seemed that the devil has gotten a victory in a recent witnessing encounter? How has that experience discouraged you from reaching out further?
4. Just as Jerry in chapter 5 missed the warning because of an approaching storm, it is easy to miss God's warnings. What warnings could you have missed?
5. Prepare for an offense that might come from someone you know. Ask the Lord for help now to deal with it.
6. The excitement when you first got saved was a testimony to everyone around you. How can you recapture that excitement?
7. The truth about trials is that the Bible promises them as a normal part of a believer's life. What hardships are you currently facing? How are you handling them?

PARABLE PRAYER

Pray for wisdom in your upcoming witnessing encounters. Ask the Lord to help you become grounded in Scripture. Pray that weeds of pride do not choke your spiritual development. Ask the Lord for humility of spirit in preparation for possible offenses to come. Ask the Lord for strength in the midst of your trial. Acknowledge your difficulty, but also acknowledge God's shaping and molding of your character.

PARABLE PROJECT

Take time to focus, reflect, and then apply the teaching of the Word to your life. Maybe you have succumbed to Wayside Hearers' Disorder. Go for the cure!
1. Focus Factor Multivitamin
    a. Do you see the Word as a way to learn more about Christ?
2. Reflective Supplement
    a. Do you meditate on the Word?

3. Application Nutritive Formula
    a. Are you a doer or a hearer?

6—Danger! The Big Three
Want to Choke You!

PARABLE PRINCIPLE #14—Your old nature hates holiness.
PARABLE PRINCIPLE #15—Your greatest spiritual help? The Holy
    Spirit.
PARABLE PRINCIPLE #16—Worry is a choker.
PARABLE PRINCIPLE #17—If you love the world, you do not love
    Christ.
PARABLE PRINCIPLE #18—Possess your possessions.

PARABLE POWER POINTS

1. Why are Jesus' warnings in Mark 4 critical in a world increasingly bent toward evil?
2. Read Romans 7:19-25. What does the apostle Paul's admission reveal about the intensity of the internal spiritual battle within a Christian?
3. How does gratifying the flesh weaken the Christian's effectiveness to serve?
4. Read 2 Corinthians 5:17. How is this verse often misinterpreted? How does Titus 3:5 clear up the misunderstanding?
5. What is the purpose of God's chastening?
6. Read Mark 4:18-19. How do the cares of the world choke our spiritual growth?
7. Read Isaiah 40:8. How does this verse help eliminate needless worry?
8. Read 2 Timothy 4:10. What does this verse reveal about Demas's true love?
9. Read Mark 4:19 again. What is the real definition of lust?
10. Read Romans 11:33. How can a realization of our spiritual riches help overcome unspiritual desires?

PARABLE PRACTICE

1. Jesus came to this earth to save sinners like you and me. How does this truth give us hope in the battle between our two natures?
2. There is a distinction between that which is born of flesh (your first birth) and that which is born of the Spirit (the second birth). How does this distinction affect your success in the Christian life?
3. Why haven't all your desires to sin faded away since you trusted Christ?
4. What happens when you don't live righteously? What actions does the heavenly Father take?
5. You serve Christ by grace just as you were saved by grace. You cannot live the Christian life on your own. What is the greatest God-given asset in building up your new spiritual nature?
6. You can easily let the cares of the world bog you down—not realizing that they are blocking your view of God. Explain why needless worry often halts your spiritual progress.
7. It is natural to worry. What is your greatest tool to combat anxiety?
8. The desire for worldly success clouds your desire to serve. Explain why a desire for more can create distance between you and Christ.

PARABLE PRAYER

Ask for the Holy Spirit's strength to live in your new godly nature and to avoid your old sinful nature. Ask the Lord to focus your eyes on the spiritual rather than the temporal. Thank the Lord for the physical and spiritual riches He has given you. Promise to use your earthly resources to further the kingdom of heaven.

PARABLE PROJECT

Are the Big Three choking your spiritual growth?
1. Is worry choking you?
   a. Write down your chief worry.
   b. Write down the very worst thing that can happen if your concern doesn't change and, in fact, gets worse.
2. Do you love the world, or do you love Christ?
   a. Have you fallen into the trap of wanting more?

b. Look at your budget and make sure that giving to the Lord is a priority.
3. Have you possessed your possessions?
   a. Compile a list of your earthly possessions, i.e., house, apartment, car, etc.
   b. Compile a list of your heavenly possessions, i.e., gold streets, mansions, the Holy Spirit.

7—The Good-Soil Christian

PARABLE PRINCIPLE #19—Don't compare your spiritual growth to that of other believers.
PARABLE PRINCIPLE #20—Fellowship with people who share your desire for spiritual growth.
PARABLE PRINCIPLE #21—Develop the habit of prayer.

PARABLE POWER POINTS

1. Read Hosea 10:12. Why is it so important to continually break up the soil of our spiritual lives?
2. Read Mark 4:8. Why do some Christians produce fruit while others do not?
3. Where do you find people of like mind who desire to grow spiritually?
4. What will happen to a believer's point of view if he or she continually fellowships with carnal Christians or with the unsaved?
5. How does fellowship help improve spiritual growth?
6. What does the Gallup poll reveal about the average American's priority regarding prayer?
7. Read James 4:2-3. How does the truth in these verses conflict with the popular idea of God as a grand genie?
8. What is the scriptural definition of prayer?
9. Read Romans 12:12; Psalm 42:8; Psalm 55:17; Acts 6:4; Colossians 4:2. How often should a believer go to the Lord in prayer?

PARABLE PRACTICE

1. The Good-Soil Christian has a plan when it comes to his or her spiritual growth. What is your plan, and how are you preparing for the next month?
2. Consider those Christians who have let worry, the world, and covetousness choke out their spiritual development. What should they do to see growth?
3. God is the ultimate judge. He knows that some Christians will produce more fruit than others. How does this reassure you about your own spiritual growth?
4. God is the only one we should please. How does that make you feel when you're tempted to compare your growth to that of others?
5. It is said that a bundle of logs burns much longer than a single log. Consider joining a small group in your church.
6. List some activities you could do with Christian friends that would help you draw closer to the Lord.
7. Prayer is our greatest weapon. It is the key that will unlock the door of God's blessing and power.
8. Prayer is not getting God to adjust His program to what we want. When we pray, it isn't God who changes; it is us! The purpose of prayer is to glorify God through His work here on earth. How will this truth affect the content of your prayer?
9. Earnestness in prayer is not indicated by its language, loudness, or length. Instead, prayer needs to be a discipline in your life. If you made prayer a discipline, how would this change the frequency of your prayers?

PARABLE PRAYER

Ask the Lord to reveal His perfect will. Pray that you will focus on God and what He thinks of you rather than on the spirituality of others. Ask for the Lord's help in setting aside a time each day to make prayer a priority in your life.

PARABLE PROJECT

Give your prayer life a thorough examination.

1. Check your church library or a Christian bookstore for a biography of a great Christian. As you read, pay special attention to the person's prayer life. How did it impact his or her life and ministry?
2. Have you given prayer a high priority?
   a. Decide on a time of day that can be regularly kept without interruption.
   b. Keep a journal of your requests.
   c. Log your goals for your prayer life over the next month. Do you want to increase your frequency, your faithfulness, or the length of time you spend in prayer?

8—Don't Be a Burned-out Bulb

PARABLE PRINCIPLE #22—It is a privilege to share the light of the Gospel with others.
PARABLE PRINCIPLE #23—How you live affects your witness for Christ.

PARABLE POWER POINTS

1. Read Mark 5:21. How does this verse and the ones that follow enforce the lessons from the Parable of the Sower?
2. Read 1 Thessalonians 2:2. Why is courage a crucial element of witnessing?
3. Read 1 Thessalonians 2:3. Why is sincerity important in witnessing?
4. Read 1 Thessalonians 2:6. How can a desire for glory become a stumbling block in leading someone to Christ?
5. Read 1 Thessalonians 2:11-12. What role does discipleship play in evangelism?
6. Read Titus 3:8. What impact does a surrendered life have on evangelism?

PARABLE PRACTICE

1. Paul's sincerity helped lead others to Christ. What does his example teach you about your method of witnessing?

2. Paul gave the Gospel, not expecting a tangible benefit in return. What is your motivation for witnessing?
3. Paul was gentle in his approach. What is your approach when witnessing?
4. Paul showed great love for the lost. What personal sacrifice do you make in witnessing?
5. What negative impact does selfishness have on your evangelism?
6. What negative impact does false humility have on your evangelism?
7. What negative impact does embarrassment have on your evangelism?

PARABLE PRAYER

Ask the Lord to give you a burden for souls. Pray that you would seize opportunities to witness, and ask for wisdom in sharing your faith. Ask the Lord to keep selfishness, false humility, and embarrassment from blocking your light as you witness for Christ.

PARABLE PROJECT

How effective are your witnessing skills?
1. Flip back to chapter 8 and review the steps in leading a person to Christ.
2. Memorize key salvation verses.
3. Find and use illustrations to drive home the message of the Gospel.
4. Seek out people who are open to hearing the Gospel.
5. Present the Gospel to one person in the next month.

9—Someday the Bugs Will Come Out

PARABLE PRINCIPLE #24—You will be judged for deeds done for Christ.

PARABLE POWER POINTS

1. How does human nature affect our view of God?
2. Compare and contrast a marathon with the Christian life.

3. Read Mark 4:22. How should the truth in this verse shape our attitude about the "secret things"?
4. What happens to Christians who clutter their spiritual lives with worldliness?
5. Reread 1 Corinthians 3:10-14. Why is it important that our foundation is built of the right materials?
6. What truths make the Bema Seat better than any human court?

PARABLE PRACTICE

1. God is recording the deeds of righteous believers for an exciting reason: He wants to reward our faithfulness. How does this fact help you endure in the spiritual life?
2. God isn't hoping we will live wrong. He is praying we will live right! The Bema Seat ought to excite us rather than deflate us. Christ's loving heart is actually cheering us on as we faithfully serve Him. How does this great truth motivate you to live for Christ?
3. We should serve the Lord out of gratitude, but He has also promised rewards to those who serve Him faithfully. How does this great truth give you joy as you live for Christ?
4. Currently we can't understand why everything happens the way it does in this life. But when we come face to face with Christ, we will know. How does this truth help you trust God during uncertain times?

PARABLE PRAYER

Offer thanks to the Lord not only for sustaining your spiritual life on earth, but also for giving you a heavenly reward system to motivate your service to Him.

PARABLE PROJECT

Conduct an in-depth study of the heavenly reward system.
1. Study the Bema Seat mentioned in 1 Corinthians 3:10-14.
   a. What happens to those who have cluttered their lives with worldliness?

b. How does the heavenly reward system differ from the world's reward system?
c. Contrast the Bema Seat judgment with the Great White Throne judgment in Revelation.
2. Write down the rewards you will receive at the Bema Seat.

10—The Extreme Hearer

PARABLE PRINCIPLE #25—You will be judged by how much of the Word you use.
PARABLE PRINCIPLE #26—The more you hear, the more you gain.

PARABLE POWER POINTS

1. How does contemporary advertising reflect our culture's "I deserve it" attitude?
2. How do the parable principles radically differ from the attitude displayed by our society?
3. What is the motive behind advertising?
4. Read 1 Samuel 3:9-10. What do you learn from young Samuel's response to God's call?
5. What are the warning signs that we are approaching spiritual emptiness?
6. What attitude is even worse than neglect?
7. What are the symptoms of indifference?
8. What are the results of indifference?
9. What is the key to preventing indifference?

PARABLE PRACTICE

1. Mark 4:24 focuses on the quality of the listener and not on the preacher. What does this verse tell you about becoming a good hearer?
2. How can the right focus change your attitude toward preaching?
3. We need a willingness, eagerness, and enthusiasm to hear God's words. The more we hear, the more we will gain. What does this parable principle say about becoming a willing hearer?

4. The more you open yourself up to the Word of God, the more you will produce. How would you assess your potential for spiritual growth?
5. There is no standing still in the Christian life. You are either going forward or backwards. In view of that fact, what are the dangers of stagnation in the Christian life?
6. Read James 1:2-4. What does this passage say about:
   a. The frequency of trials?
   b. The spontaneity of trials?
   c. Patience during trials?
   d. The purification process of trials?
   e. The perseverance produced in trials?

PARABLE PRAYER

Ask the Lord to help you develop your spiritual listening skills. Pray that God would enable you to prevent neglect and indifference from halting your spiritual growth. Ask the Lord for strength and resolve in the midst of trials.

11—Your Harvest Will Come

PARABLE PRINCIPLE #27—God will correct you when you don't obey Him.
PARABLE PRINCIPLE #28—Be faithful; God will bring the harvest.

PARABLE POWER POINTS

1. Read Matthew 18:12-13. What does this parable tell us about the Shepherd's love for His sheep?
2. How can a wrong view of God's chastening hand affect our relationship with God?
3. Read 1 Corinthians 11:27-32. What is the danger of harboring known sin?
4. What do these verses tell us about wrongly judging other people's trials?

5. How does obedience foster growth?
6. What is the mark of a true Christian?

PARABLE PRACTICE

1. God doesn't bring chastening for the fun of it or because He enjoys watching you suffer. Nothing God brings into your life is for your harm. What is the ultimate purpose in God's chastening?
2. We are not to despise God's chastening; instead we are to realize that chastening is an act of love. How does this truth keep you from despising God's discipline?
3. God disciplines us in order to bless us. So what should be the result of God's chastening?

PARABLE PRAYER

Ask the Lord to give you an obedient spirit. Thank Him for His protecting, chastening hand. Pray that your faith might be strengthened through the valleys of life.

PARABLE PROJECT

Increase your faith and knowledge of the Scriptures. Check your local Christian bookstore for the books *Know Why You Believe* by Paul Little and *The New Evidence That Demands a Verdict* by Josh McDowell.
1. Examine the proofs of the Resurrection
2. Examine the proofs for the Bible's authority.
3. Familiarize yourself with the Old Testament prophecies concerning Jesus Christ. Write a list of these in your Bible to use while you share your faith.

12—Mustard-Seed Faith

PARABLE PRINCIPLE #29—God's way starts small and grows slowly.
PARABLE PRINCIPLE #30—God does a lot with mustard-seed faith.
PARABLE PRINCIPLE #31—Don't worry about how much faith you have. Look to the object of your faith, the Lord Jesus Christ.

PARABLE POWER POINTS

1. Read Mark 4:26-29. Contrast our concept of growth and God's.
2. Read Exodus 3—4. How did the desert experience train Moses for leading Israel?
3. Read Galatians 1:17-18. How did the apostle Paul's detour into Arabia prepare him for ministry?
4. How does pride affect the development of patience?
5. Read John 15:5. What is the only way to develop patience?

PARABLE PRACTICE

1. God's way to grow isn't fast or slow. It's perfect. What implications does this fact have for your own "schedule"?
2. You've applied all the habits and practices to stimulate spiritual growth. You've made the field of your heart ready for the seed of the Word. What happens when you are doing all you are supposed to be doing, and the harvest doesn't seem to be anywhere close to coming?
3. Selfishness is a cause of impatience. What is our real motivation when we grow jealous at another's blessings?
4. Read Mark 4:30-32. What does this parable tell us about the power of God to bring growth?
5. What does this parable say about instant success?
6. We need to understand that it is the focus of our faith rather than how much faith we possess that is important to God. What hope does this fact give you about the amount of your faith?
7. God's promises are true, whether we have faith in them or not. What does this statement say about God's faithfulness in the season of harvest?

PARABLE PRAYER

Confess your impatience to the Lord. Submit to the Lord's timetable in your life. Ask the Lord to help keep your focus on Him, the object of your faith. Ask Him to take your small mustard seed of faith and yield a great harvest for His kingdom.

PARABLE PROJECT

Find a topical Bible and do a study of Scriptures on patience. Next carefully examine your own heart.

1. Do you accept delays, detours, and disappointments graciously?
2. Do you remain steadfast under strain and continue faithfully serving the Lord?
3. Do you possess a calm endurance based on the certain knowledge that God is in control?

NOTES

CHAPTER 1
THE SPIRITUAL LIFE

1. As quoted in *The New Encyclopedia of Christian Quotations*, Mark Water, ed. (Grand Rapids: Baker Books, 2000), p. 905.

2. "Saving Grace," Darryl Dash, DashHouse.com, July 22, 2001.

CHAPTER 2
ENDURING SUPPORT

1. Byron Rivers, "Gardening by the Foot," *The Massachusetts Eagle-Tribune*, July 26, 1999.

2. Barna Research Group, Ltd., 1993.

3. James Mooney, "How to Benefit from a Sermon," sermoncentral.com, May 1999.

4. As quoted in Mark Water, ed., *The New Encyclopedia of Christian Quotations* (Grand Rapids: Baker Books, 2001), p. 131.

5. Charles Spurgeon, "How to Read the Bible," The Spurgeon Archive, www.spurgeon.org.

6. George Mueller, *Autobiography* (New Kensington, Pa.: Whitaker House, 1984), p. 38.

7. Water, *The New Encyclopedia of Christian Quotations*, p. 139.

8. Travis Moore, "My Bible and Me," sermoncentral.com, January 2000.

9. Chuck Swindoll, *The Quest for Character* (Sisters, Ore.: Multnomah, 1993), p. 49.

10. Jim Butcher, "How to Discover What God Has for You in the Bible," sermoncentral.com

11. As quoted in Water, *New Encyclopedia of Christian Quotations*, p. 130.

CHAPTER 3
A SEED CALLED PREACHING

1. Timothy Peck, "What Christians Think About Church," sermoncentral.com, May 1999.

2. As quoted in *Bits and Pieces*, October 4, 2001, adapted from Marion Gaines, "Coat Check," *Guideposts*.

3. Woodrow Kroll, *7 Secrets to Spiritual Success* (Sisters, Ore.: Multnomah Publishers, 2000), p. 73.

4. As quoted in Mark Water, ed., *The New Encyclopedia of Christian Quotations* (Grand Rapids: Baker Books, 2000), p. 206.

5. Peck, "What Christians Think About Church," sermoncentral.com, May 1999.

6. Water, *The New Encyclopedia of Christian Quotations,* p. 209.

CHAPTER 4
READY, SET, PREPARE

1. John Henry Burns, *A Homiletic Commentary on the Gospel According to St. Mark* (New York: Funk and Wagnalls Co., n.d.), p. 127.

2. Rob Gilbert, *Bits & Pieces,* September 1994, pp. 7-8.

3. S. Stennett, as quoted in *The Biblical Illustrator, Mark* (Grand Rapids: Baker Book House), p. 125.

CHAPTER 5
SPIRITUAL RX

1. Joseph S. Exell, *The Biblical Illustrator, Mark* (Grand Rapids: Baker Book House, n.d.), p. 128.

2. John Henry Burns, *A Homiletic Commentary on the Gospel According to St. Mark* (New York: Funk and Wagnalls Co., n.d.), p. 132.

3. Ibid., p. 135.

4. John Reed, *1100 Illustrations from the Writings of D. L. Moody* (Grand Rapids: Baker Books, 1996), p. 257.

5. T. Adams, as quoted in *The Biblical Illustrator, Mark* (Grand Rapids: Baker Books), p. 130.

6. Ibid., p. 907.

7. Rob Gilbert, *Bits and Pieces,* June 1991, p. 7.

8. As quoted in Mark Water, ed., *The New Encyclopedia of Christian Quotations* (Grand Rapids: Baker Books, 2001), p. 937.

CHAPTER 6
DANGER! THE BIG THREE WANT TO CHOKE YOU!

1. Marco R. della Cava, "San Francisco Races to Halt Pedestrian Deaths," *USA Today,* October 4, 2000.

2. Donald Deffner, *Seasonal Illustrations* (Resource Publications, 1992), p. 130.

3. Charles Ryrie, *So Great Salvation* (Wheaton, Ill.: Victor Books, 1989), pp. 59-60.

4. "Today in the Word," Moody Radio Network, May 17, 1992.

5. R. A. Torrey, *The Holy Spirit* (New York: Fleming H. Revell Co., 1927), p. 101.

6. Vinita Hampton and Carol Plueddemann, *World Shapers* (Wheaton, Ill.: Harold Shaw Publishers, 1991), p. 105.

7. Alexander Maclaren, *Expositions of Holy Scripture, Mark Chapters I-VIII* (Grand Rapids: Baker Book House, reprinted 1982), p. 146.

8. Steve Farrar, *Family Survival in the American Jungle* (Sisters, Ore.: Multnomah, 1991), p. 68.

9. H. A. Ironside, *Illustrations of Bible Truth* (Lincoln, NE: Back to the Bible Publishers, 1945), p. 51.

CHAPTER 7
THE GOOD-SOIL CHRISTIAN

1. "Get into the Circle!" July 6, 2001, voicings.com

2. Joseph S. Exell, *The Biblical Illustrator, Mark* (Grand Rapids: Baker Books, n.d.), p. 137.

3. George Gallup, Jr., and Sarah Jones, *100 Questions and Answers: Religion in America* (Princeton, N.J.: Princeton Religion Research Center, 1989), p. 39.

4. Woodrow Kroll, 7 *Secrets to Spiritual Success* (Sisters, Ore.: Multnomah, 2000), p. 60.

5. Mike Hays, "Surprised by Prayer," sermoncentral.com, November 1998.

CHAPTER 8
DON'T BE A BURNED-OUT BULB

1. J. C. Ryle, *Expository Thoughts on Matthew and Mark* (Grand Rapids: Zondervan, n.d.), p. 68.

2. Ray Stanford, *Personal Evangelism* (self-published, 1991), p. 49.

3. Ibid., p. 224.

4. Gregory Dawson, "Labor Where You Are Planted; Witness Where You Walk," sermoncentral.com, October 14, 2001.

CHAPTER 9
SOMEDAY THE BUGS WILL COME OUT

1. Dr. Bruce Lockerbie, *Thinking and Acting Like a Christian* (Sisters, Ore.: Multnomah, 1989), p. 52.

2. Curt Suplee, "Lotto Baloney," *Harper's*, July 1983, p. 19.

3. Ibid., p. 15.

4. As quoted in Jim Kane, "God's Three Beacons," sermoncentral.com, December 1999.

5. Coy Wily, "God's Great Day of Rewards," sermoncentral.com, September 26, 1999.

6. Marion Gilbert, *Reader's Digest*, February 1994, p. 12.

7. Courtney Anderson, *To the Golden Shore: The Life of Adoniram Judson* (New York: Little Brown and Company, 1956), pp. 400-401.

8. John Henry Burns, *The Preacher's Complete Homiletic Commentary on the New Testament, St. Mark* (New York: Funk & Wagnalls Co., n.d.), p. 138.

9. Don Robinson, "Biblical Facts About Rewards," sermoncentral.com, October 16, 2001.

CHAPTER 10
THE EXTREME HEARER

1. "Council Worker Adds Cash When He Returns Lost Wallets," ananova.com, October 16, 2001.

2. Nancy Leigh DeMoss, *Lies Women Believe and the Truth That Sets Them Free* (Chicago: Moody Press, 2001), pp. 29-30.

3. Paul Ham, "Skydiver to Jump from 25 Miles Up," *The Sunday Times*, October 21, 2001.

4. Joseph Exell, *The Biblical Illustrator, Mark* (Grand Rapids: Baker Books, n.d.), p. 146.

5. Ibid.

6. As quoted in Vinita Hampton and Carol Plueddemann, *World Shapers* (Wheaton, Ill.: Harold Shaw Publishers, 1991), p. 96.

7. *Bits & Pieces*, June 24, 1993, pp. 20-21.

8. Lynn Buzzard, *Tell It to the Church* (Elgin, Ill.: David C. Cook, 1982), p. 23.

9. *Our Daily Bread*, as quoted in sermonillustrations.com, January 2002.

10. Ibid.

11. As quoted in Hampton and Plueddemann, *World Shapers*, p. 99.

12. "Today in the Word," Moody Radio Network, November 26, 1991.

CHAPTER 11
YOUR HARVEST WILL COME

1. As quoted in a sermon by Rev. Goettsche, "Vital Truths for a New Year," January 5, 1997. www.unionchurch.com.

2. As quoted in Mark Water, ed., *The New Encyclopedia of Christian Quotations* (Grand Rapids: Baker Books, 2001), p. 283.

3. Ibid., pp. 985-986.

4. Mark Hiehle, "Gotta Grow," sermoncentral.com, June 2001.

5. Mike Hayes, "Grow On" sermoncentral.com, October, 2001.

6. John Henry Burns, *The Preacher's Homilectic Commentary, St. Mark* (New York: Funk and Wagnalls Co., n.d.), p. 148.

7. Floyd Hamilton, *The Basis of Christian Faith: A Modern Defense of the Christian Religion* (New York: Harper and Row, 1964), p. 160.

8. Josh McDowell, *Evidence That Demands a Verdict*, Vol. 1 (Nashville: Thomas Nelson, 1999), p. 189.

9. Ibid., p. 224.
10. Ibid., p. 225.
11. Ibid., p. 226.
12. Ibid.
13. Ibid., p. 259.
14. C. Tenney, *The Reality of the Resurrection* (Chicago: Moody Press, 1963), p. 137.

CHAPTER 12
MUSTARD-SEED FAITH

1. Melvin Newland, "Patience—Fruit of the Spirit," sermoncentral.com, August 1997.
2. Warren Wiersbe, *Wycliffe Handbook of Preaching & Preachers* (Chicago: Moody Press, 1984), p. 242.
3. Joseph Exell, *The Biblical Illustrator, Mark* (Grand Rapids: Baker Books, n.d.), p. 157.
4. Rob Gilbert, *Bits and Pieces*, November 2001, pp. 4-5.